Studying Shakespeare Adaptation

RELATED TITLES

Essential Shakespeare: The Arden Guide to Text and Interpretation
Pamela Bickley and Jenny Stevens
ISBN 978-1-4081-5873-9

Shakespeare and Early Modern Drama: Text and Performance
Pamela Bickley and Jenny Stevens
ISBN 978-1-4725-7713-9

ShakesFear and How to Cure It: The Complete Handbook for Teaching Shakespeare
Ralph Alan Cohen
ISBN 978-1-4742-2871-8

The Arden Introduction to Reading Shakespeare: Close Reading and Analysis
Jeremy Lopez
ISBN 978-1-4725-8102-0

Studying Shakespeare Adaptation

From Restoration Theatre to YouTube

Pamela Bickley and Jenny Stevens

THE ARDEN SHAKESPEARE
LONDON • NEW YORK • OXFORD • NEW DELHI • SYDNEY

THE ARDEN SHAKESPEARE
Bloomsbury Publishing Plc
50 Bedford Square, London, WC1B 3DP, UK
1385 Broadway, New York, NY 10018, USA

BLOOMSBURY, THE ARDEN SHAKESPEARE and the Arden Shakespeare
logo are trademarks of Bloomsbury Publishing Plc

First published in Great Britain 2021

Cover design: Charlotte Daniels
Cover image © Oxygen / Getty Images

A catalogue record for this book is available from the British Library.

A catalog record for this book is available from the Library of Congress.

ISBN: HB: 978-1-3500-6863-6
        PB: 978-1-3500-6864-3
      ePDF: 978-1-3500-6866-7
     eBook: 978-1-3500-6865-0

Typeset by Integra Software Services Pvt. Ltd.
Printed and bound in Great Britain

To find out more about our authors and books visit www.bloomsbury.com
and sign up for our newsletters.

CONTENTS

ABOUT THIS BOOK

The purpose of this book is to show something of the range of Shakespeare adaptations across time and genre and to discuss current theorizing of adaptation itself. We have selected examples from the reverential to the iconoclastic and from the Restoration to the present day. We include brief reference to related works that might be of further interest (while being all too aware that there are innumerable examples we have not been able to consider). Individual case studies focus on key questions of the adaptive process, introducing readers to significant exponents of adaptation theory. At the same time, we show how the re-envisioning of Shakespeare's plays can cast new interpretive light on the original texts. Terminology in this field is 'highly labile', to use Julie Sanders's phrase, and, while acknowledging the contested nature of definitional terms, we have sought to make lexical choices appropriate to the contexts of the thirty-six individual areas under discussion. We tend to opt for 'adaptation' among the vast array of terms available, largely because of its plasticity.

As far as practicalities are concerned, we have referred to the most readily available editions; Restoration texts, for example, are all accessible in digital form as well as print, as are the visual images showcased. Wherever possible we have supplied URLs for theatre reviews and open-access journals. Each chapter can be read discretely, in the light of its Shakespearean source text; sections are organized chronologically. Equally, the book could be read thematically, across media or genre – contemporary fiction, for example, or Shakespeare without words. Films are discussed primarily through their directors, an angle that might be said to privilege the model of the 'auteur' but that is perhaps inevitable given the significant presence of Shakespeare from the earliest days of film. Digital technologies have, and will continue to have, an impact on the world of Shakespeare adaptation – in this book, discussion is proportionate to the historical range covered.

Introduction

Adaptation or appropriation?

Or afterlife, augmentation, amplification; or translation, transformation, transmutation; or reimagining, reinvention, revision, recontextualization, re-envisioning; or meme, mashup, offshoot, remix, remediation? These terms are just some of the many ways in which critical discussion has engaged with the cultural act of deriving inspiration or material from Shakespeare. The prefixes are telling: 're' implies a revisionist activity, revisiting and reinterpreting – taking an original source with the active intention of making it new, of recontextualizing it. 'Trans' suggests a crossing over, transmediating a text into a different medium or genre. Adaptation brings its own connotations of Darwinian survival; appropriation must always suggest a possessive and possibly aggressive act. Arguably, there is no neutral terminology. This is, in part, because of the critical theorizing of interpretation and reception: political and ethical issues enter the discussion. Marianne Novy's work highlights ways in which female writers have 're-visioned' Shakespeare; postcolonial writing has also appropriated and redefined it. Appropriative intentionality is at the forefront in these politicized interactions; it could be argued that the source text cannot remain unaffected or unchanged by the adaptive experience. Aesthetic considerations introduce intertextuality as a critical concept: if all literature is a mosaic of intertextual references, then what strategies can be brought to the analysis of individual adaptations of Shakespeare? In recent years, reception of the adapted text has certainly altered considerably, particularly the desire to make hierarchized comparative judgements. In general, the evaluative cry 'not as good as the original' is now fading. Some reviewers clearly remain affronted by the *lèse majesté* of refashioning Shakespeare, but it is surely missing the point to describe Jane Smiley's *A Thousand Acres* as 'shamelessly filched' from *King Lear*.

What can be stated is the extraordinary plurality and fluidity of the current situation. The texts themselves have been subject to 400 years of editorial modification; theatre performances are shaped by directorial interpretation and the conditions in which they are played. Nothing, it seems, is fixed or immutable. Beyond Shakespeare's text is the rich world of adaptation. The earliest appropriative act might be Fletcher's drama *The Tamer Tamed* (*c.* 1609–11) – the first instance of 'talking back' to Shakespeare. It is playful, comic, a female-led revenge for Petruchio's misogyny. From that point there is no period of Western cultural history that has not produced its characteristic Shakespearean interactions. Dominant genres – Victorian novel, Italian opera, Russian ballet, Hollywood and Bollywood – all engage creatively with Shakespeare. Appropriative activity has also long been transcultural, so the great auteurs of twentieth-century film – Kozintsev, Kurosawa, Welles – have also followed in this tradition. Why Shakespeare? Is it simply because of cultural capital or because the plays possess a certain 'palimpsestuous' quality that invites further exploration? It could be argued, as Linda Hutcheon does, that adaptation prolongs the life of the original: reinvention creates renewal. Shakespeare is never merely a historic figure: the adapted text offers an invitation to look anew and re-experience the original. In the words of American poet H. D., 'Remembering Shakespeare always, but remembering him differently'.

Shakespeare's adaptive art

A cursory glance at the eight volumes of Bullough's magisterial *Narrative and Dramatic Sources of Shakespeare* (1957–75) is sufficient to reveal something of the extraordinarily rich hinterland of tales, interludes, legends and histories feeding Shakespeare's imagination and shaping his theatrical practice. Equally, it is an instructive exercise to look at the text of Enobarbus' celebrated speech describing the beauty of Cleopatra ('The barge she sat in') alongside North's translation of Plutarch (1579) and observe the verbal similarities. Generations of readers have expressed surprise, even indignation, at the boldness of Shakespeare's apparent 'copying'. Western culture, in the present day, commends an ideal of 'originality' whereby individual artists inhabit their own unique imaginative world. Plagiarism is a pejorative term that designates an act of theft. In fact, the notion of the artist's distinctive inner life derives from the Romantic movement, postdating Shakespeare by some 200 years. Renaissance artists drew on classical models by way of homage: a practice of *imitatio* and *emulatio*. To acquire ideas or material from classical sources ensured all the authority of a noble and respected tradition. At the same time, pre-Christian stories, such as Ovid's, existed outside early modern morality, thereby offering an invitation to engage freely with salacious subject matter. A culture of literary borrowing does not imply slavish adherence, though; in Shakespeare, adaptive ingenuity can be found in the unexpected and unforeseeable results of dramatic reimagining.

Two examples from Ovid's *Metamorphoses* demonstrate Shakespeare's radical inventiveness. In *Titus Andronicus*, Shakespeare outdoes Ovid when Lavinia is raped by Chiron and Demetrius, silenced, like Philomela, by having her tongue cut out, then further mutilated by having her hands chopped off. But Lavinia knows her classical texts and reveals the truth by gesturing to Philomela's tale in her nephew's book. The ensuing revenge draws on Ovid, but Shakespeare intensifies the vicious cruelty of the original to unprecedented extremes – the more striking for being translated into performative art. Equally remarkable is Shakespeare's ability to reinvent a tragic tale: the pathetic story of Pyramus and Thisbe is transformed into hilarious farce as the interpolated entertainment in *A Midsummer Night's Dream*, while Bottom wearing an ass's head is an exuberantly comic reversal of the mighty Jove transmuting himself into animal form to ravish mortal maidens. *Metamorphoses* is both source material and metaphor for Shakespeare's appropriative methodology: his adaptive art operates on micro- and macrocosmic levels, subtly infusing the imagery of a text or shaping the structure of the drama. Shakespeare draws on a wide range of sources, creating wholly new dramatic effects through a creative fusion of literary models. *The Winter's Tale* is drawn from Greene's *Pandosto* but rejects the tragic conclusion of the original in favour of Ovid's story of Pygmalion. History can be reshaped: Holinshed's Duncan was far from the saintly figure murdered by Macbeth; Queen Margaret could not have appeared at the court of Richard III.

Shakespeare's dense web of adaptive allusiveness testifies to an attitude and practice of extraordinary artistic freedom; transformative reimagining is the guiding principle of his new and still-experimental theatre.

Adaptation and the word

Shakespeare's 'greatness' is commonly held to reside in the verbal uniqueness of his writing, and even the most seasoned actors report feeling a weight of responsibility when delivering the plays' best-known lines. The performance palimpsest of a Hamlet soliloquy, for example, places pressure on actors to breathe new life into the words at the same time as convincing an audience that full justice is being done to the hallowed verse. Shakespeare's language is praised for its poetic brilliance and affective power, and the playwright is lauded as a coiner of phrases that have become part of the idiomatic texture of modern English (though recent computational research suggests that Shakespeare was more an early adopter of neologisms than an 'inventor'). But Shakespeare's words have not always been so highly prized. In the Restoration period, his scripts were routinely cut, sanitized and modernized to make them 'fit' prevailing audience sensibilities, and it was not until the end of the eighteenth century that such practices began to be considered deviant, even sacrilegious.

Nowadays, the scholarly consensus is that there is no stable Shakespearean text to preserve, though this does not deter 'purists' from inveighing against cuts and modernizations. A case in point is the opprobrium former artistic director of the Globe, Emma Rice, received for what was viewed as her lack of reverence for the Shakespearean script – not to mention her admission that she sometimes found the language impenetrable. In fact, even the most conservative of directors, mindful of theatregoers needing to make the final train home, will efface some of the Shakespearean text: this is one reason why some theorists argue that *all* stage productions are, to varying degrees, adaptations. Indeed, of all the elements of Shakespeare's plays, scripted language is the most prone to alteration or removal in the adaptive operation. Reformatting a play for a different form, such as a comic strip or opera, will inevitably require some textual excisions; adapting one for children might require moderating its verbal bawdiness, and transmediating one into purely visual form will mean abandoning words altogether, raising some important ontological questions about what is actually meant by 'Shakespeare'.

In non-anglophone countries, Shakespeare's texts will usually be read and performed in translation, having undergone a process of interlingual, socio-cultural reworking, itself a type of adaptation. Given the various pitfalls of translating early modern drama (rhyme, metre, rhetorical patterning, puns and shifting pronominal forms, to name but a few), most translators opt for a 'domesticization' approach, which aims to make the text linguistically and culturally familiar to the target audience. Shakespeare's language tends, then, to reach non-anglophone audiences in modernized form, facilitating an ease of access that some argue should be extended to the significant number of native speakers who find Early Modern English indecipherable and estranging. While some argue fiercely that it is incumbent on readers and audiences to improve their fluency in Early Modern English, educational publishing testifies to the fact there is a growing demand for intralingual translations, doubtless driven by the high-stakes testing of Shakespeare in the school curriculum.

Shakespeare's language continues to feature large in adaptation studies. Whether evaluating the impact of digital technology, debating the siblings of 'adaptation' and 'appropriation', or examining the logocentricity of the 'fidelity' approach to rewritings, students cannot avoid engaging with the presence, absence and translation of the playwright's words in Shakespearean adaptation.

Adaptation and transmediality

In the initial stages of revisioning Shakespeare's plays, most adaptations were intramedial. From the Romantic era onwards, however, adapters have turned with ever-increasing frequency to other media to recreate Shakespeare for their own time, responding to shifting attitudes to dramatic literature and to the forms in which it might be represented. This ongoing experimentation with transmedial creativity has been energized by new media, film in the late nineteenth century and Web 2.0 social media platforms a century later being two highly significant instances.

Bringing the traits of two or more media into conversation with Shakespeare's plays can often uncover what might previously have gone unnoticed, unsettling critical dicta and pre-conditioned responses. The inter-artistic operations of transforming one signifying system into another (Shakespeare's dramatic imagery into a musical score, for example) can produce invigorating new perspectives, contributing to an ever-evolving process of reception and recreativity. As new media emerge, so hitherto unexplored artistic collaborations between the early modern and the present day are undertaken, shaped by a process which Jay David Bolter and Richard Grusin have termed 'remediation'. Resisting a teleological narrative whereby new media displace and abandon the old, the concept of remediation views new and established media as being in dialogue with each other, participating in a continuing practice of refashioning. The incoming YouTube platform, for example, reformats the Shakespeare film, just as television had done several decades earlier; this meeting of media can also entail 'retrograde remediation', whereby the traditional medium updates itself to incorporate the new, a case in point being stage productions that have followed Michael Almereyda's film adaptation of *Hamlet* in capturing the ghost of Old Hamlet on surveillance cameras.

Yet if adaptation theorists tend to welcome the infinite variety afforded by Shakespearean transmediality, regarding the transtextual relationship forged in the adaptive undertaking as being one of equals, there are others (scholars included) who hold fast to the playtext as the still centre of origin, the primary player, 'naturally' superior. Embedded within a complex net of social practices, no medium is neutral, ranked as it is in a hierarchy determined by factors such as the notions of 'high' and 'popular' culture and the conventional privileging of single-author works over co-created media. When conjoined with Shakespeare and the literary virtues associated with his work, transmedial negotiations grow even more complicated. Those looking to confine Shakespeare's plays to the sphere of high art may favour a wordless adaptive medium such as classical ballet over, say, a teen movie, despite the fact that the latter might employ a substantial proportion of the source text, whereas those who regard dramatic language as the plays' crowning achievement might be willing to accept the popular as the lesser of two evils.

To study transmedial Shakespeare, then, calls for engagement with the historical, social and aesthetic issues surrounding the perception of discrete media, along with knowledge and understanding of their semiotic systems and the academic domains in which they operate.

Adaptation and film

The most frequently adapted of any literary authors, Shakespeare has been a major source of filmic interest since the earliest days of cinema, when silent productions of his plays served to bring cultural kudos to a nascent art form. Film's relationship with Shakespeare has endured for well over a century, encompassing both the high-art world of the auteur and the commercial world of the Hollywood studios. All of Shakespeare's plays have been adapted for either television or the big screen (a sizeable number for both) and have been transcoded into an array of cinematic genres. The international scope of cinema and Shakespeare's status as a repository of 'soft power' have combined to produce a diverse corpus of non-anglophone adaptations. Whereas the global appeal of Shakespeare is commonly put down to the transhistorical, transtemporal nature of his drama, today's film scholars incline more towards a 'rhizomatic' model of adaptation, whereby localized reimaginings, with their own contextual specificities, spring up in no particular order, a paradigm that decentres the anglophone production.

In its fledgling stages, cinema tended to be compared to literature, then considered to be its closest artistic neighbour. As time went on, the relationship between the two media often proved restrictive, sometimes adversarial, especially when it came to adaptations of canonical literature. By the mid-twentieth century, leading auteurs such as François Truffaut were militating against what they saw as the hegemonic grip of literature on cinematic production and the critical assumption that the literary text was somehow intrinsically superior to the film text. In the same period, influential critics such as André Bazin were developing cinema's own theoretical frameworks and terminologies, insisting that screen adaptations should not attempt to replicate the form and style of the literary text but, instead, should apply film's own signifying codes to capture equivalences.

Although film managed to break free of theatre's sometimes oppressive influence, several canonical Shakespearean adaptations were nonetheless inspired by stage productions. Films such as Reinhardt and Dieterle's *A Midsummer Night's Dream*, Zeffirelli's *Romeo and Juliet* and Taymor's *Titus* are all examples of remediations, whereby a stage director has successfully transcoded the aesthetics of stage to screen. In the past decade or so, the theatre–film relationship has taken a new form in the hybrid genre of the filmed stage production. Sometimes termed 'Event Cinema', the broadcasting of live or pre-recorded theatre performance has developed rapidly, with Shakespeare gaining the most traction.

As the most familiar medium for adapting Shakespeare, film was an obvious starting point for adaptation studies and continues to dominate the field. Scholars working in the domain have attempted to establish typologies by which to categorize the diverse body of screen Shakespeare that has accrued, though these have required regular reconfiguration to accommodate new adaptive trends and experiments – and will doubtless continue to do so. Today, researchers or students of Shakespeare film adaptations will need to be prepared for the impact that recent digital technologies will have on their future production, distribution and reception, including the increasingly diverse participatory platforms and transmedial entertainment environments in which they might be encountered.

Global Shakespeare and adaptation

As an early modern playwright, Shakespeare was receptive to European influences, appropriating material from Cinthio's *Gli Hecatommithi* and the essays of Montaigne. Such cultural exchange was a two-way process. The story of a ship's crew performing *Hamlet* as early as 1607 may be open to question, but there is evidence that, in Shakespeare's lifetime, troupes of performing artists were travelling across northern Europe with playscripts that could be adapted to local festivals and performance spaces. The popularity of travelling players is evident from *Hamlet*, along with the players' willingness to adapt their scripts to suit the occasion. From those early beginnings in the late sixteenth century, Shakespeare as global export 'followed hard upon', irretrievably connected with trade and cultural colonialism. Performances of Shakespeare first appeared in India as a means of entertaining homesick colonialists; the first theatre was established in Kolkata in 1753 with the help of Garrick; thereafter, the Victorian colonial programme enshrined Shakespeare in the education system. At the same time, though, Shakespeare was being transformed and appropriated by translation into local languages – across Africa and East Asia as well as India – and excitingly 'un-English' adaptations proliferated. 'Global' Shakespeare has often meant local alterity and malleability rather than the replication of British theatrical traditions.

The dismantling of empire brought a concomitant interrogation of its symbols and its heroes, with Prospero the first Shakespearean ruler to be dethroned. *The Tempest* has been the subject of sustained postcolonial critique since the 1970s, as well as the point of departure for literary appropriations. French-Martiniquais writer Aimé Césaire's *Une Tempête* (1969) first introduced a new discourse of *négritude*, and Caliban's territorial rights, his rejection of Prospero's language and religion, and his own intense imaginative and sensory world have long informed critical discussion of the play. The global reach of Shakespeare inevitably means that the narrative of 'talking back' has become globalized too. *The Tempest* – in both performance and study – is irretrievably changed: as a global commodity it has become a revised, different product. Global influences mean that it cannot, now, allegorize a liberal humanist ideology: 'benign dictatorship' is a term that can only be oxymoronic. Postcolonial negotiation of cultural imperialism is complex, however; there is greater historic and geographic distance from the colonial hegemony. For Indian film auteur Vishal Bhardwaj, repurposing *Hamlet* provided valuable scaffolding for his filmic work on the political tragedy of Kashmir. Bhardwaj is no longer 'talking back' to the colonial centre but rather exploiting a presumed global authority to avoid local censorship.

Shakespeare is now more 'global' than he has ever been: the availability of filmed Shakespeare and the accessibility of digital media all ensure that versions of Shakespeare can travel from Aarhus to Zanzibar. Shakespeare's Globe Theatre (London) physically took Dromgoole's *Hamlet* to 197 countries and territories between 2014 and 2016. Individuals and groups travelled considerable distances to participate in the experience, bringing their own local perspectives. Global Shakespeare is not just a story of history and legacy but a vibrant world of inventive performances and afterlives.

1

Titus Andronicus

If part of the pleasure of adaptations comes from the disruption of the familiar, then *Titus Andronicus*, one of the least known of Shakespeare's plays, is a brave choice for adapters. Focusing primarily on the role of Aaron, this chapter considers how three artists, each working in a different century, have risen to this recreative challenge.

Edward Ravenscroft, *Titus Andronicus, or the Rape of Lavinia* (1678)

Ravenscroft's *Titus Andronicus* first appeared on the stage in 1678, contributing to an already well-established area of the Restoration theatre repertoire: the Shakespearean adaptation. In the 1660s, William Davenant had initiated the Shakespearean revival with *The Law Against Lovers* (1662), a mash-up of *Measure for Measure* and *Much Ado About Nothing*, followed by radically altered versions of *Macbeth* (1664) and *The Tempest, or the Enchanted Island* (1667), written with John Dryden. As theatrical conditions recovered from the dark days of the interregnum and confidence returned to the dramatist community, so playwrights began to turn their attention to some of Shakespeare's then (and still now) less popular plays, with Thomas Shadwell's *Timon of Athens, the Man-Hater* and Dryden's *Troilus and Cressida, or Truth Found Too Late* both appearing within a year or so of Ravenscroft's *Titus*. The paratexts of the first published edition of Ravenscroft's *Titus* (1687) provide valuable insights into the era's theatrical tastes and its approach to adaptation. The playwright's address to the reader has proven especially interesting to scholars:

> I have been told by some anciently conversant with the Stage, that it was not Originally his, but brought by a private Author to be Acted, and he only gave some Master-touches to one or two of the Principal Parts or Characters; this I am apt to believe, because 'tis the most incorrect and indigested piece in all his Workes; It seems rather a heap of Rubbish then [*sic*] a Structure.

Here, the blame for *Titus'* perceived infelicities is placed on an unspecified 'private Author', at once protecting the good name of Shakespeare and sparking off an authorship debate which continues still. As Barbara Murray observes, second-generation Restoration adapters refer to Shakespeare 'almost always with respect' (xxv), a tendency exhibited in a Prologue to Ravenscroft's *Titus* that the author claimed had been lost in the feverish days of the Popish Plot. First brought to light in Gerard Langbaine's survey *An Account of the English Dramatick Poets* (1691), the Prologue declares:

> To day the Poet does not fear your Rage,
> *Shakespear* by him reviv'd now treads the Stage:
> Under his sacred Lawrels he sits down
> Safe, from the blast of any Criticks Frown.
> Like other Poets, he'll not proudly scorn
> To own, that he but winnow'd *Shakespear*'s Corn;
> So far he was from robbing him of's Treasure,
> That he did add his own, to make full Measure.
>
> (Langbaine 465)

Although of uncertain provenance, the Prologue's depiction of the adapter as having merely 'winnow'd *Shakespear's* Corn' is in accord with Ravenscroft's relatively conservative treatment of the Shakespearean text, at least in the first half of the play.

One aspect of Ravenscroft's adaptation that is far from preservative, however, is its foregrounding of the role of Aaron (spelled Aron in the printed text). Where Shakespeare's Moor stands on stage as a mute prisoner for much of the first act, Ravenscroft's loses no time in winning the confidence of the emperor, enabling him and the queen to plot their vengeful strategies as court insiders. Nonetheless, Ravenscroft underscores how Aaron's Moorish identity renders him vulnerable to the white majority, his consciousness seemingly moulded by their racism:

> Hence abject thoughts that I am black and foul,
> And all the Taunts of Whites that call me Fiend,
> I still am Lovely in an Empress Eyes,

(2.1, p. 15)

Jonathan Bate reads these invented three lines as introducing 'the possibility that [Aaron's] villainy is a cry for attention, that [...] stems from a desire to be loved', drawing a parallel with the Bastard in Shakespeare's *King Lear* (Bate, *Titus* 50). While the parallel might hold true psychologically, the rhetorical force of Edmund's cry for attention, especially in his memorable first soliloquy, is nowhere matched by Ravenscroft's Aaron, not least because some of his most linguistically powerful lines in the pre-text have been omitted, stripping him of the eloquence associated with his biblical namesake. Aaron's periphrasis depicting the sun's movements is cut, along with his exuberant promise to 'be bright, and shine in pearl and gold' (*Tit* 1.1.518), an omission which denies him the glittering energy of his Shakespearean forerunner; instead, as if confined by his own physical nature, he becomes a 'black threatning Cloud' (2.1, p. 15). If, as Ayanna Thompson argues, Ravenscroft's attenuation of Aaron's verbal prowess is 'a type of linguistic and theatrical castration' (*Performing* 60), it is also a means of making Shakespeare's words 'fit' for a late-seventeenth-century audience. If Ravenscroft had no qualms about exposing Lavinia to the spectator's gaze with '*[l]oose hair, and Garments disorder'd as ravisht*' (3.1, p. 26), as promised in the play's titilating subtitle, he protects the perceived sensibilities of the Restoration ear through a selective phrasal fumigation, excising, for example, several of Aaron's obscene puns and metaphors; he makes no reference to 'steal[ing] a shive' from 'a cut loaf' (*Tit* 1.1.587) when planning the rape of Lavinia, nor to 'trimming' her body after it (*Tit* 5.1.94).

Close on a century separates Ravenscroft's *Titus* from Shakespeare's, years in which the transatlantic slave trade had become an established part of England's colonial ambitions. As Virginia Mason Vaughan explains, '[d]uring the 1670s the average Londoner was exposed frequently to people of color', a developing familiarity which brought with it fears of the 'biological pollution that accompanied overseas ventures' (*Performing* 141, 147). Certainly, Ravenscroft's drama throws a disturbing light on the consequences of miscegenation. Responses to the 'Babe of darkness' (5.1, p. 53) are noticeably more damning than in Shakespeare's script, with the infant repeatedly defined solely in terms of colour. But if the bi-racial figure of a 'black Imp' (5.1, p. 39) born to a white mother 'Tup'd by a Goat' (5.1, p. 51) disturbed and alarmed Ravenscroft's audiences, the brutal killings of child and father, enacted almost simultaneously, seem designed to put any such feelings to rest. Aaron is tortured on a rack and burnt to death on stage, a dramatic horror which exploited to the full the tastes and affordances of Restoration theatre. As Anthony Barthelemy remarks:

[t]echnical advances in stage properties as well as architectural changes in the theaters themselves made possible the staging of spectacles. Whether it was because of these technical advances or the love of spectacle [...] popular tastes in the 1670s and 1680s favored plays that depicted brutal tortures and grotesque murders. This accounts, in part, for Aaron's being racked and immolated.

(102)

Exactly how such a grim spectacle would have been mounted remains, and is likely to remain, a matter for conjecture (see B. Murray 469), though it is surely the apex of the adaptation's textual 'infidelity' and the chief reason why early-twentieth-century commentators, intent on upbraiding those who had dared to tamper with the works of the national poet, accused Ravenscroft of piling on 'extra horrors' (Odell, vol.1, 46), adding to 'the gruesomeness of a play already nauseously bloody' (Kilbourne 127).

The complex task of judging the relative bloodiness of *Titus* in the Renaissance and Restoration versions involves weighing up the extent to which audiences witness the mutilation of *sentient* bodies or the gruesome *insentient* aftermath. Such an evaluation reveals how, in Ravenscroft's adaptation, the live black body in pain is more the object of spectatorial gaze than any white counterpart: Titus' hand is severed off-stage, and while it is true that the audience sees '*the heads and hands of* Dem. *and* Chir. *hanging up against the wall*' (5.1, p. 54), it is shielded from the sight of their throats being cut while they are still very much alive ('*He cuts their throats*', *Tit* 5.2). And while in the printed Shakespearean texts Titus '*Unveils Lavinia*' (*Tit* 5.3) before killing her, the Restoration script directs that her veil be removed only *after* she has died, thereby concealing her death pangs. Furthermore, as Ayanna Thompson explains:

> Titus does not find it necessary to torture (either onstage or off) the two rapists, Chiron and Demetrius. [...] Titus reads their white skins as transparent. In other words, their whiteness, their ability to blush and reveal the 'close enacts and counsels of [their] hearts' (4.2.120), renders them translucent and easy to understand. The onstage torture of Aaron demonstrates the fear of the opacity of blackness[.]
>
> (*Performing* 63)

So if in the early stages of the play Saturninus raises the possibility that the black body is not essentially opaque ('Dark is the Case, but thro't a noble light / There Shines', 2.1, pp. 10–11), any such possibility has been firmly rejected by the drama's end.

If, as Thompson suggests, the racking of Aaron is a way to subject him to the 'white/right gaze' (*Performing* 64), it is also a means of testing and underlining his humanity. Ravenscroft follows Shakespeare in portraying Aaron's love for his child as affecting proof of his capacity for tender feeling, and nowhere is this more explicitly demonstrated than in the torture scene:

MARCUS
    Let any then forbear to move from's place
    'Till we have heard the *Moors* confession.
    Though he laughs upon the Wheel and mocks our torments,
    Yet I will try another Experiment.

[Marcus *holds the Child as if he wou'd Kill it.*]
Give me the Hellish infant: *Moor*, now speak
Or the young Kid goes after the Old Goat.
ARON
Save but the Child I'le tell thee wondrous things.
That highly may advantage you to hear.
TAMORA
Moor, speak not a word against my honour
To save the World.
ARON
Yes Empress to save that childe I will.

(5.1, p. 54)

Where the physical torments of the rack fail to force Aaron to confess his powerful secrets, the threat of harm to his son prompts him to offer them up unhesitatingly. Ultimately, though, the father fails to save his offspring. Strapped to the rack, he has no choice but to witness the murder of his son by its own mother – a violence in some ways as disturbing, if less remarked upon, as that inflicted upon the rack. If the killing of a baby on stage was by no means unprecedented (take, for example, the strangling of infants in John Webster's *The Duchess of Malfi*) and – as far as we know – enacted with a doll rather than a live figure, it was nonetheless a dramatic act guaranteed to provoke a strong reaction from spectators. How far Ravenscroft's audiences were surprised by the baby's violent end is questionable. Whereas Shakespeare's Tamora rejects her offspring, ordering Aaron, via the ill-fated Nurse, to 'christen it with thy dagger's point' (*Tit* 4.2.72), Ravenscroft elects that the child die at the mother's own hand. What makes the murder especially cruel is Tamora's feigning of maternal affection in order to inflict one final act of revenge:

I have now no other Son, and shou'd
Be kind to it in Death, let it approach me then,
That I may leave with it my parting Kiss. –

[*The Child is brought to the Empress, she Stabs it.*]
Dye thou off-spring of that Blab-tongu'd Moor.

(5.1, p. 55)

Aaron responds to his child's death in six blunt monosyllables: 'Give it me – I'le eat it' (5.1, p. 55), judged variously by critics as 'the most remarkable line in this play' (Friedman 12); 'bizarre' (Bate, *Titus* 52); 'sublimely evil, supremely funny' (Hughes 24); 'one of the most remarkable turnabouts in all literature' (Vaughan, *Performing* 140). How this outlandish line stands in relation to Aaron's fatherhood and, by association, his humanity is an intriguing matter for speculation. Does it play into contemporary audiences' stereotypes of African anthropophagy? Is it simply Aaron's futile attempt to compete with the woman who has 'out-done' him in his 'own Art' (5.1, p. 55)? Or is it more psychologically complex: a kind of reverse birth, whereby the father takes into his own body for safekeeping a child born from the flesh of a mother who subsequently treats him as a tool for vengeance? While the Restoration rewriting eliminates the uncertainty which surrounds the child's fate in Shakespeare's version, the diverse meanings that radiate from Aaron's outlandish response to its certain death linger at the play's close, suggesting that Ravenscroft did not want his villain to entirely disappear in the bonfire's punitive flames.

If nowadays Shakespeare's *Titus* holds an increasingly secure foothold in theatrical repertoires, the same could not be said for its Restoration predecessor. In *Woza Titus!*, an account of producing Shakespeare's *Titus* at the Market Theater, Johannesburg, Antony Sher recalls:

> Greg read somewhere that a version of *Titus* exists with a happy ending! God knows what this entails – they sew back the hands? Tamora is vegetarian? – but anyway it was written by the Restoration playwright Edward Ravenscroft, who said of the original Shakespeare play: 'More a piece of rubbish than a structure'.
>
> (Sher and Doran 116)

Given that the ending of the Restoration *Titus* is anything but 'happy', Greg Doran appears to be confusing it with Nahum Tate's cheerful revision of *King Lear* (1681). Such confusion suggests that while Ravenscroft's adaptation is now firmly within the purview of academic critics, it resides more within the realm of theatrical myth for theatre practitioners.

Ira Aldridge as Aaron on the Victorian stage

A browse through most modern scholarly editions of *Titus Andronicus* will quickly discover a portrait of the African American actor, Ira Aldridge, in role as Aaron (see, for example, Bate, *Titus* 56). Typically placed between the Peacham drawing and a photograph of Peter Brook's 1955 staging in introductory accounts of the play in performance, this 1850s engraving, developed from a daguerreotype, stands as one of relatively few iconic representations of Shakespeare's first tragedy. The image is a striking one: Aaron stands in what could be read as a defensive pose, seemingly alert to any dangers that might threaten the life of the tiny infant sleeping at his feet; costumed in earrings, turban and animal skins, performative of an exotic alterity, he wields a scimitar almost half the length of his body, thereby connecting the actor's stance directly with the textual quotation that stands at the foot of the engraving: 'He dies upon my scimetar's [*sic*] sharp point, / That touches this my first-born son and heir!' This suturing of image and playtext encourages the viewer to accept what they see as a moment in theatrical time, captured with the scientific accuracy of photography; to do so, however, would be to overestimate the technological capabilities of photography in the mid-nineteenth century. While the exposure period required for the daguerreotype reduced rapidly over time (it was estimated to be between fifteen and thirty minutes in 1839, the year of its invention), it remained an obstacle to capturing an image instantaneously; add to this the unwieldy, heavy equipment required for the process itself and it becomes obvious that the Aldridge picture does not depict a 'live' stage moment. As the theatre historian David Mayer points out:

> [m]any, indeed most, theatrical photographs before 1901 were made in a portrait photographer's studio. What we see in the portrait is, at best, a reenactment, not a performance. Actors, by and large, brought their own stage costumes to the studio, but hand properties, apparent stage furnishings, and painted backcloths, some of which may appear to us as if they are appropriate to the role in question, are from the photographer's studio and, especially before 1885, infrequently from the stage production in question.

(227)

Those readers leafing through current editions of *Titus Andronicus* need, then, to possess a knowledge of early photography if they are not to mistake a simulacrum for a snapshot of a live performance. Perhaps more significantly, they need to read the editor's commentary that accompanies the Aldridge portrait to realize that it showcases – albeit in simulated form – a radically reaccentuated version of Shakespeare's original.

As the first successful Shakespearean actor of colour to play on stages in Britain and on the Continent, Aldridge was already a celebrity figure by the time he performed his own unique version of Shakespeare's Aaron. He had gained plaudits for playing Othello, as well as major roles such as Shylock, Richard III and Macbeth, all performed in 'whiteface'. Unsurprisingly, given the socio-political climate of the time, such praise was more than matched by racialist slurs. Discountenanced by an African American having the temerity to embody the creations of the national Bard, some reviewers, most especially those based in London, deplored what they perceived as his ungainly appearance, ugly facial features and his inability to articulate Shakespeare's verse. More controversially, Aldridge was accused of manhandling the actress Ellen Tree, who played Desdemona to his Othello in an 1833 production at Covent Garden – his first and only experience of the patent-theatre stage. This charge (compellingly dramatized in Lolita Chakrabarti's 2012 play *Red Velvet*) played into a xenophobic stereotype of the savage, libidinous African, and Aldridge was no doubt acutely aware that to play Shakespeare's Aaron – a Moor who incites the rape of a white virgin and impregnates Rome's white empress – would be to risk perpetuating it. Instead, Aldridge commissioned his own version of *Titus*, one which would exploit the potential in Shakespeare's text for reading Aaron primarily as a loving, protective father, the courageous, humane saviour of the piece. Exactly how this transformation from villain to hero was managed can only ever be a matter for conjecture: there is no extant copy of the rewriting, and its adaptive strategies can only be surmised from performance reviews and from the letters that passed between Aldridge and Charles A. Somerset, an established writer of melodrama, commissioned to undertake the rewriting. Going by the commonalities across these numerous accounts, it can be established with reasonable certainty that this Victorian version expunged most of the brutish violence from the original and, with the exception of Saturninus, converted its sinners into near saints. Tamora becomes a chaste, though still feisty, Queen, whose sons are epitomes of filial obedience, refraining from laying a single finger on their adored Lavinia. Exceeding everyone in noble features, Aaron is chosen as King of the Goths and is Tamora's rightful husband; when their legitimate offspring is pitched into the Tiber on the order of the Emperor, the father, breaking free from the chains in which he has been bound, leaps into the river and saves him. Resisting too drastic a generic shift, Somerset ends his rescripting with a body count which, while falling short of that in Shakespeare's version, is nonetheless high enough to keep within the bounds of tragedy. Aaron and Tamora are both poisoned by Saturninus, though their orphaned child is saved by the (unharmed) Lavinia, who takes on the role of surrogate mother.

Aldridge played this freshly conceived Aaron to provincial audiences intermittently between 1849 and 1860 and to London audiences at Hoxton's Britannia Theatre in 1852 and 1857. What emerges clearly from the related reviews is that Somerset was responding to the sensibilities of his age in transcoding Shakespeare's bloody revenge tragedy into a thrilling melodrama, very much his theatrical *métier*. Somerset's adaptive approach, expressed privately in letters to Aldridge, was also announced publicly on playbills:

> The sanguinary incidents interwoven with the plot render it altogether repugnant to good taste and modern refinement; still it contains innumerable treasures – precious ore of the brightest lustre – Poetic gems of the most brilliant hue – richly worthy to be rescued from oblivion, and freed from the incumbrance of dross that entombs their beauty from the world. [...] It was therefore to rescue 'TITUS ANDRONICUS' from unmerited and perpetual oblivion (for it never could be acted as written, before a modern audience) that the present adaptation of this really wonderful play has been undertaken[.]
>
> (Playbill, cited in Lindfors 168)

It is interesting to note here the similarities between Somerset and his seventeenth-century predecessor, Ravenscroft: both adapters see themselves as excavators, uncovering the precious nuggets that lie beneath the 'dross' and performing a process of textual cleansing to render the work fit for public consumption. That the play was the ugly sister of the canon meant that the text to be excavated was relatively unfamiliar, a fact evidenced in a *Sunday Times* review of the 1852 Hoxton production, which includes misspellings of two of the main characters' names. Cuts, restructuring and language changes applied to *Titus* were, then, less likely to be identified, let alone regretted, than those applied to more popular plays of the time, such as *Hamlet* or *King John*.

That Aldridge could initiate, oversee and perform a drastically reconceptualized Shakespearean character in an era noted for its Bardolatry was undoubtedly made possible by the low esteem in which *Titus* was then held. Indeed, his portrait in the role of Aaron first made an appearance in the fourth volume of John Tallis's *Complete Works of Shakspeare* (1851–3), titled *Doubtful Plays*, a categorization that confirmed its marginal status, along with other plays such as *Pericles*, *Two Noble Kinsmen* and *King Edward the Third*. This four-volume edition was the first to illustrate the plays with engravings taken from daguerreotypes, the selection and number of actor portraits providing a visual guide to the relative popularity of Shakespeare's plays in the mid-Victorian period. While works such as *Othello*, *King John* and *Richard III* are amply illustrated with portraits of actors who had appeared in starring roles, Aldridge's Aaron portrait stands as the only performance illustration of the 'doubtful plays', perhaps testifying more to the actor's celebrity status than to any growing respect for Shakespeare's *Titus*. How far Aldridge was involved in the composition of the portrait (originally produced by Paine of Islington) is a matter for speculation; however, the choice of quotation that fills the cartouche at the foot of the image is one that captures the cross-over point of dramatic fidelity between the Aldridge and Shakespeare versions. The portrait encapsulates the character's paternal solicitude, his one redeeming feature and the basis for the noble Aaron that can be discerned in reviews of Aldridge's adaptation. It also plays into the Victorian penchant for the defenceless child, a figure much sentimentalized in the era's artistic imagination (see, for example, the popular artworks depicting the scene in Shakespeare's *King John* when Hubert threatens to burn out the child Arthur's eyes with hot irons). The baby at Aaron's foot in the Aldridge portrait is half naked and disproportionately tiny, his face and body suggestive of sleep, all features that emphasize his physical vulnerability. Yet for an observer coming to the portrait with no knowledge of the scene that it depicts, it is not immediately clear whether the armed man stands as assailant or protector; indeed, if viewers read only the first line of the accompanying text, they would assume it to be the former. By inviting the text-innocent spectator to presuppose the other as the barbaric killer, the portrait exposes and challenges those prejudices that kept people of colour socially and culturally marginalized.

In some respects, the very process of interpreting the actor portrait could stand in little for Aldridge's appropriative Shakespearean project. Judging by the reviews of the reimagined *Titus*, audiences expecting to see Shakespeare's Moor, guilty of doing 'a thousand dreadful things' (*Tit* 5.1.141), would have been presented instead with his antipode: a morally upright, self-sacrificing hero. There have been various suggestions made concerning the motivations behind this dramatic transformation. Aaron's moral makeover was doubtless a key factor in ensuring that Shakespeare's most notorious of tragedies did not threaten the *bonne moeurs* of the day, thus also ensuring commercial viability; it could also be seen to demonstrate Aldridge's desire to expand the repertoire of Shakespearean parts available to 'an actor of colour', as he frequently described himself. His first biographers, Herbert Marshall and Mildred Stock, suggest in addition that 'one really important point of departure was that the play was adapted from the point of view of the Negro' (171). More than half a century on, most scholars agree that Aldridge's recharacterizing of Aaron was, to some extent, driven by ideological impulses, though how far these were purposefully employed as a means of promoting the anti-abolition cause remains a matter for critical debate. In the absence of a scripted version of Somerset and Aldridge's collaborative recasting, it is impossible to evaluate just how overtly the Victorian *Titus* engaged with the slavery debate and how many of what Bate describes as Aaron's 'Black Power' speeches (Bate, *Titus* 54) were retained and exploited for the purposes of identity politics. Nevertheless, there is substantial evidence that Aldridge identified with the enslaved, not least in his adoption of the stage name 'African Roscius', a term alluding to Quintus Roscius Gallus, a great Roman actor born into slavery. When the phrase was employed sneeringly by a *Times* journalist reviewing one of Aldridge's early performances, the actor fought back by removing it from its original context, shrewdly repurposing it as a memorable trademark. Alan Dessen suggests that

> only with some strain can the Aldridge version be viewed as part of the stage history of Shakespeare's *Titus*. Rather, it represents the most extreme example of a long series of attempts (starting with Ravenscroft) to reshape this script so as to make it palatable or meaningful to later audiences who are deemed unlikely to accept essential features of the original.
>
> (*Shakespeare* 12)

Inevitably, perhaps, treating one of Shakespeare's bloodiest and most sexually violent plays with the bowdlerizing airbrush of the early nineteenth century would seem to have resulted in an 'extreme' outcome – one that Dessen regards as disqualifying it from a secure place in a timeline of *Titus* in performance. Yet omitting Somerset and Aldridge's adaptation from an account of the drama's evolution over time sits oddly with the prominence granted to it by the Aaron portrait, which has appeared, and still appears, in both single editions and collected works. As Dessen himself observes, the 'starting point for today's director is the received text, almost always a modern edition of the play' (*Rescripting* 3). As such, the prominence of Aldridge's picture in editorial paratexts goes some way towards ensuring that the adaptation it represents will remain a curious part of *Titus*' stage history.

The Hungry, dir. Bornila Chatterjee (2017)

The Hungry is a screen adaptation of *Titus Andronicus*, jointly funded by the Indian company Cinestaan and Film London. Its director, Bornila Chatterjee, a young independent filmmaker who has lived in both the United States and India, claims to have selected *Titus* because its relative obscurity afforded her greater adaptive freedom. Departing from the detail of the Shakespearean text was an important aspect of such freedom: Chatterjee recalled in interview how, with each successive draft of the screenplay, those working on the project 'gained the confidence to move away from the original plot and away from the idea of simply "recreating" the play as an Indian film' ('Bornila'). This distancing process resulted in just one line of the Shakespeare text being retained ('I'll find a day to massacre them all', *Tit* 1.1.455) and even this is recontextualized through a change of speaker and position in the storyline. In leaving Shakespeare's words behind, Chatterjee joins an ever-expanding list of filmmakers whose modernized screen adaptations, while dismissed by some Shakespeareans as mere 'pop cultural folly' (Welsh 152), have attracted sustained critical attention from those working in adaptation studies. One other liberating consequence of engaging with one of Shakespeare's less popular dramas was being spared the pressure of influence exerted by anterior film versions. Chatterjee is only the third director to take on a full-scale screen treatment of *Titus*, adding to an all-female body of directorial work: Jane Howell's small-screen BBC version (1985) and Julie Taymor's critically acclaimed film *Titus* (1999).

Chatterjee indigenizes Shakespeare's revenge tragedy, relocating the action from classical Rome to contemporary New Delhi and the world of Indian big business. Paring down Shakespeare's cast to six main roles, she retains the characters of Titus (Tathagat), Tamora (Tulsi) and Aaron (Arun), fuses Chiron and Demetrius into one son (Chirag), and reduces Titus' five surviving children to two: Sunny, who, as his name suggests, also has some connection with Shakespeare's Saturninus, and Loveleen (Lavinia). The timescale of the action is similarly contracted, with events taking place over three days of wedding festivities, mostly shot at the Mud Fort, Kuchesar. The marriage between Sunny and Tulsi, the widow of Tathagat's former business partner, looks set to knit the two families together into one commercial empire. However, any expectation that this union will be a happy one is soon undermined, as a series of chronological analepses reveal a vicious crime: the killing of Tulsi's favourite son, Ankur (Alarbus), on the orders of Tathagat. Although made to appear an act of suicide, Tulsi manages to uncover the true circumstances of her son's death, a discovery that instigates a revenge plot that will drive the film's narrative.

If Ira Aldridge undertook a moral transformation of Shakespeare's Aaron, so Chatterjee attempts a similar, if less drastic, reformation with Tamora. She recalled in interview wondering 'how different it might be if Tamora was [*sic*] the protagonist of her own story and not the nemesis in someone else's', a speculation that led to 'Shakespeare's arch villain [being] turned [...] into our heroine' ('Bornila'). This shift of emphasis is most apparent in Chatterjee's handling of one the most brutal and troubling events of Shakespeare's *Titus*: the rape and dismemberment of Lavinia. In contrast to the premeditated attack on Shakespeare's Lavinia, Chirag's assault on Loveleen is fuelled by alcohol and provoked by her calling Tulsi a 'fucking gold digger'. At the same time, Chatterjee's direction signals a more deeply rooted impulse behind the attack: a desire to subdue by force the liberated Indian woman. That Loveleen has been sexually assaulted is made clear when, injured and disfigured after the attack, she struggles to get under the shower (a screen cliché of the rape victim), still wearing the bikini top and harem pants which formed her costume for a Salome-style dance, staged as part of the extended wedding celebrations – and watched intently by Chirag. Female sexual display is, then, duly subdued and punished: a woman's body is not hers to control. Yet where Shakespeare's Tamora colludes with her sons in the rape of Lavinia, regarding their sexual aggression as a barometer of filial affection ('The worse to her, the better loved of me', *Tit* 2.2.167), Tulsi, fearing her carefully laid plans are being thrown off track, berates Chirag for his uncontrolled behaviour, calling him 'a fucking animal'. Later, she appears to exhibit genuine sympathy when she visits his tongueless victim, conveyed primarily through reaction shots as she faces the grotesque injuries her son has inflicted. In one of the film's several ironic twists, she helps the wounded woman light the 'dija' (an oil lamp used in Indian ritual), little suspecting that this is the mute Loveleen's way of signifying the identity of her assailant ('Chirag' is a transliteration of the Hindi word for 'lamp'). With this metonymic prop, Chatterjee references Shakespeare's text, finding a cultural equivalent to Lavinia's employment of Ovid. But for all her sympathetic gestures, Tulsi never strays from her role as the 'hungry' avenger. Taking the fabric which is staunching the bleeding from Loveleen's mouth to form a makeshift noose, she hangs her son's victim, guaranteeing her perpetual silence. Here, Chatterjee sets up a filmic parallel with the simulated suicide of Tulsi's own son, Ankur, drawing on the revenge tragedy tradition of violent repetition and creating a neat structural symmetry akin to those found in *Titus*. It is in scenes such as this that Chatterjee's avowed intention to create in Tulsi a character 'who is more real, therefore grey and bold' (IANS) might be discerned, though to claim that she is less 'black' than her Shakespearean counterpart is to overlook the fact that she initiates, and indeed carries out, several of the revenge killings in the film, whereas Tamora, for all her viciousness, never actually commits any acts of vengeance. The dynamics of revenge have proved especially amenable to adaptation over the centuries, and in its modernizing of motive and means, *The Hungry* proves no exception: revenge plots are contrived via smartphone, cocaine becomes a lethal weapon and guns join knives in the final killing spree. Less amenable to transposition, perhaps, is the concept of alterity, explored in *Titus* initially through the warring Goths and Romans but more significantly through the role of Aaron, the only person of colour. In Chatterjee's intercultural treatment, Aaron is very much 'incorporate' in Delhi, the indispensable right-hand man to the North Indian elite. If Taymor's Aaron has aspects of the 'supercool hipster' (McCandless 494) about him, Chatterjee's Arun is very much the 'geek'; bespectacled and always with clipboard in hand, he is the quiet observer, his otherness residing not in his ethnicity but in his servant status, which, like Shakespeare's Iago, he deeply resents. As the 'fixer' for both families, he facilitates Tathagat's corrupt business deals, supplies Tulsi with the impure cocaine intended to finish off her husband-to-be, wipes up the bloody remnants of Chirag's frenzied attack on Loveleen and, as revealed near the end of the film, carries out Ankur's assassination. Like Iago, Arun is the consummate double-dealer, arranging the flight of Chirag at the same time as helping Tathagat to capture him. This arrant duplicity is conveyed with powerful cinematic clarity in the film's final flashback: a long shot of Arun and his reflection captured in the mirror of the hotel room where he has just carried out Ankur's murder in cold blood. Arun's defining feature is, indeed, his cool, emotionless control, typified by his sipping water while watching those around him consuming immoderate amounts of alcohol and Class A drugs; his acceptance of Tathagat's offer of whiskey, just prior to the revelation of his machinations, signals his loss of control and his imminent demise. The carnivalesque moment of Tathagat working in the kitchen while his servant sips spirits is brought to an abrupt end as Arun is stabbed in the back by the household maid, Meena, the silently menacing chief-servant-in-waiting. Killed in the servants' quarters by a servant, the circumstances of Arun's death confirm the failure of his class ambitions. With no infant son to humanize him and with no alternative claim on the audience's sympathies, *The Hungry's* Arun is a much less compelling figure than his stage equivalent. Moreover, his death before the film's climactic banquet denies him the significance of his Shakespearean counterpart, who, like Iago, remains unsettlingly alive at the play's end.

Choosing not to follow Shakespeare in locating foreignness in one single character, Chatterjee focuses more broadly on the issue of Western influences in an increasingly globalized India. The outsider figures of *The Hungry* are the cosmopolitan sons of two rival dynasties. Sunny, a muddle-headed cocaine addict, is the puppet-heir of the Ahuja empire; Chirag, troubled and volatile, is the less-favoured son of Tathagat's former business partner. That the two sons are out of parental favour is underscored by their both having spent most of their lives abroad, Sunny in the United States and Chirag in Britain. Accordingly, both speak with accents that identify them as belonging elsewhere, in contrast to those who speak Indian English or who code-switch between what could be regarded as rival languages: Hindi and English. The older generation are the more frequent switchers, shifting between one tongue and another most noticeably in conversations involving conflict, emotional stress or deliberate deception. That Sunny and Chirag never code-switch at any point in the narrative is something that estranges them from everyday speech patterns in urban Indian society, marking them out as strangers in their own homeland, unable to navigate successfully between two cultures.

The Hungry's concluding scene is its most monocultural – visually, at least – as bride, groom and parents of the groom are brought together for the marriage feast, dressed in ornate Indian wedding finery. This is also the most recognizably Shakespearean scene in the film, not only because it preserves Titus' banquet, but also in its merging of wedding and funeral, an early modern trope played upon in tragedies such as *Romeo and Juliet* and *Hamlet*. Here, Nick Cooke's cinematography captures the lush, vibrant colours of an Indian festival, at the same time unsettling the viewer with extreme close-ups of cooked meat on the bone – an alimentary promise of the carnage to come. The cannibal horror of *Titus* comes in the form of Chirag's severed head, presented to the couple on a silver salver, slowly defrosting. As Sunny vomits up what he realizes is the cooked remains of his brother, he is stabbed through the throat by his father, a filicide that seems mainly motivated by the patriarch's desire to rid himself of an unsatisfactory heir. However, at this point, Tathagat declares that he and Tulsi are 'kindred spirits' before making a sexual move on her, a somewhat distracting, even gratuitous, addition that further obfuscates his motives for killing his own son. Tulsi's response to his advances is to shoot him three times before crumpling to a seated position on the floor. If Taymor chose to play up the black comedy of the banquet scene, Chatterjee leaves the viewer with an unmitigatedly morose vision: the broken Tulsi and her invalid mother-in-law stranded among the carnage of the banquet, the remnants of the feast now being consumed by marauding goats, formerly earmarked for slaughter. Still, if the director departs radically from Taymor's adaptation in tone, her closing focus on the extra-textual figure of Tathagat's helpless wife is indebted to its filmic vision. In framing much of the film's violent and corrupt deeds through the apparently innocent gaze of a woman who can neither breathe nor move independently, Chatterjee adapts Taymor's (and Howell's) framing device of Young Lucius, whose fresh, blameless eyes take in the fallen world of his elders. Yet while Taymor opens up the possibility that Young Lucius will show compassion towards Aaron's newborn son, thus breaking the cycle of revenge, Chatterjee offers comparatively cold comfort. An extreme close-up captures the invalid's face, partly obscured by a respiratory mask, with one solitary tear rolling down it, a shot which recalls an earlier image of Tulsi being prepared for her wedding, tears for her banished son destroying the make-up even as it is applied. Taken together, these two images would seem to represent the intergenerational suffering of women in an enduringly patriarchal society, contributing to Chatterjee's ultimately feminist revisioning of Shakespeare's first tragedy.

2

Richard III

This chapter examines political and theoretical appropriations of *Richard III*. For British playwright David Edgar, Shakespeare's text suggested analogies between Shakespeare's Machiavellian antihero and the corrupt politics of Richard Nixon, disgraced American president. In the field of disability studies, Shakespeare's Richard is seen as exemplary, first as the prototype early modern figure of disability and further as a 'dismodern' figure informing and shaping critical thinking about the stigmatized body. In contrast to David Edgar's comic lampooning, the BBC's *The Hollow Crown: The Wars of the Roses* is discussed as canonical BBC high art.

David Edgar, *Dick Deterred* (1974)

De Tragical History of de life and near-death of de biggest bugger of dem all – King Dick De Tird

Dick Deterred is a musical comedy, a repurposing of *Richard III* as a means of satirizing American President Richard Nixon and his fall from power following the scandal of Watergate (1972/3). In the early 1970s, British playwright David Edgar (b. 1948) was already associated with the New Left, the political counter-culturism that emerged from the Paris *événements* of May 1968. At Manchester

University, '[Edgar] chaired the socialist society; [he] marched against the Vietnam War; he campaigned against examinations' (Painter 13). In other words, he embraced wholeheartedly the revolutionary spirit of the times, using theatre as an expressive political medium and 'enlarg[ing] the thematic scope of political drama in a quite unprecedented way' (Bull 152). As Susan Painter establishes, it is David Edgar's 'equal commitment to politics and theatre that securely underpins his plays' (Painter 12). In common with Edward Bond (see Chapter 8), Edgar engages dynamically with Shakespeare, appropriating and recontextualizing with 'simultaneous admiration [...] and rejection' (Cohn 50). One of his earliest theatrical events, an adaptation of *Romeo and Juliet* entitled *Death Story* (1972, unpublished), set out to refute cherished ideas with a 'simple moral that love does not conquer all' (Barker and Trussler 10). *Death Story* was triggered in part by the aftermath of Northern Ireland's Bloody Sunday and a concurrent TV story of a Catholic–Protestant romance, together with Edgar's powerful response to Zeffirelli's film adaptation:

> I'd seen the Zeffirelli film of *Romeo and Juliet*, and walked out of the cinema shaking with fury, because I'd always been fascinated by the original play. So the first half of *Death Story* is me saying, I think the original is about this, and the second half of the play is me saying, I don't think the original is relevant.
>
> (Barker and Trussler 11)

He returned to *Romeo and Juliet* in burlesque form in the theatrical spectacular *The Life and Adventures of Nicholas Nickleby* (1982), where the Crummles's acting troupe stages a highly comic play-within-a-play, interweaving lines from the source text with Edgar's blank verse to achieve a surprising finale:

JULIET
   What's here? A cup, closed in my true love's hand?
   Poison, I see, hath been his timeless end.
   O churl! Drunk all and left no friendly drop
   To help me after?
   [...]
[JULIET *about to stab herself* [...] ROMEO *sits up*]

ROMEO
> Hold, hold! I live!

JULIET
> What, Romeo, not dead?

Paris, too, is 'not dead so much as stunned', and, in the final merry revelations, Benvolio becomes Benvolia, disguised in the style of Shakespeare's comic heroines, to pursue 'a love that fate denied' (Edgar, *Plays* 202–3, 204, 206). An iconoclastic desire to challenge the Shakespearean hegemony, united with an awareness of the dramatic potential of comic parody, came together in the writing of *Dick Deterred*.

Parody, as a genre, has ancient roots in classical authors and endures as a dynamic means of deriding and lampooning, whether subtly or savagely. As Linda Hutcheon contends, theorizing the difference between burlesque and parody is complex, involving questions of 'encoded or inferred intention' as well as evaluative considerations of travesty (Hutcheon, *Theory of Parody* 40). Where burlesque invariably caricatures a given hypotext stylistically, parody 'does not always lead to irony at the expense of the parodied work' (*Theory of Parody* 57). Rather, there is a 'critical distancing' between the appropriative parody and its source, whereby 'parodies today do not ridicule the backgrounded texts but use them as standards by which to place the contemporary under scrutiny' (*Theory of Parody* 57). This is a helpful distinction to bring to a consideration of *Dick Deterred*: the object of the satire is the disgraced Nixon; the ruthless scheming of Shakespeare's Richard III is the seemingly incongruous means. Jonathan Bate judges the parodist's art as 'aggressive' – ultimately 'a mean and limited thing when set beside the magnanimity and breadth of the plays themselves' ('Parodies' 89). With Edgar's play it is the parallelism itself that gives the political satire its acerbic bite. Where productions of *Richard III* have used twentieth-century dictators such as Hitler or Stalin to shed a modern light on Richard's tyranny, Edgar uses Richard 'to illuminate, if not impugn, Nixon' (Aune 38). The satire connects the world of power politics with murderously brutal ambition and suggests that Nixon as an individual is, like Shakespeare's Richard III, 'a consummate actor, a hypocrite, a clown, and an arch manipulator' (Saunders 109). As

Edgar himself recalls, London's Bush Theatre had commissioned a new work in the style of *Tedderella*, his comic send-up of Prime Minister Ted Heath as Cinderella. Catching sight of juxtaposed newspaper articles on the Ricardian Society of the White Boar and on Nixon, Edgar 'rang up the Bush [Theatre] and said, Watergate Richard the Third' (Barker and Trussler 12). In Edgar's mind, specific parallels came to mind effortlessly:

> Merrily, I set about transposing Hastings into Nixon's campaign manager John Mitchell, Buckingham into his Chief of Staff Bob Haldeman and the little princes into Democratic Presidential hopefuls George McGovern and Ed Muskie, all in referentially muscular blank verse.
>
> (Bradwell 54)

For the audience of 1974, Nixon was associated with comprehensive political ignominy: in 1972 Nixon's campaign managers commissioned a break-in to the offices of the Democratic Party's National Committee, in the Watergate complex in Washington, with the intention of stealing documents and bugging phones. Police apprehended the burglars; incriminating connections with White House staff emerged. Nixon gave a televised speech in which he denied all involvement and was re-elected in a landslide victory in November 1972. *Washington Post* reporters Woodward and Bernstein pursued the trail, uncovering direct links with the White House; at the same time some of the perpetrators confessed Nixon's complicity in order to protect their own reputations, revealing the existence of highly compromising tapes. This sealed Nixon's fate: White House lawyer John Dean testified that Nixon had taped every conversation in the Oval Office of the White House; the Supreme Court ordered the surrender of the tapes. Threatened with impeachment for abuse of power and obstructing the course of justice, Nixon resigned in August 1974. This was all played out against a political background of growing unrest over the war in Vietnam and extreme violence directed against student protesters. As early as February 1973, America's theatre world was making connections between Shakespeare's Richard and contemporary politics. Barbara Hodgdon, reviewing the Theatre Company of Boston's *Richard III*, saw parallels 'uncomfortably close to the age and body of our time, making our roles as spectators doubly significant' ('Richard' 375).

Dick Deterred referenced surveillance throughout by recording audiences on arrival, playing back the resulting videotapes during the interval while recording their responses and, finally, retaping the results and transmitting them to the departing audience. The play commences in 1968 with a Prologue spoken 'with a Texan drawl' by Edward IV Part Two (Lyndon B. Johnson) to establish the political context: 'some kinda schmucky war in some kinda short-ass Asian hell-hole [is] a kinda political disaster' (Edgar, *Dick Deterred* 13). The stylistic virtuosity of the opening soliloquy then sets the tone:

RICHARD

Now is the winter of our discontent
Made glorious summer by this Texan bum
And all the crowds that didn't duck the draft
Vacating are the bosoms of Saigon.
Our brows now bound with wreath of compromise,
Our bruised armies are demobilized,
Our napalm bombs are changed to Paris meetings,
Our My Lai massacres to diplomatic measures.
But I that am not shaped for aught but tricks [...]

(14)

This is followed by a rousing song that plays on the famous anti-Nixon poster from 1960 with its refrain, 'Would you buy / a used car / from me?' Thereafter, every scene has its source in *Richard III*, alternately 'invok[ing] the gravity of a canonical play and the levity of humor by exaggeration' (Aune 39). Parodic references are trenchantly topical: Clarence's 'fearful dreams' describe Chicago's Lincoln Park Peace protest, violently broken up by the Chicago police and the National Guard. Nixon's famous 'Checkers speech' – a sentimental televised appeal which cited his children's puppy – is sung to an 'oowahwah' vocal backing from Hastings and Buckingham (52–4), drawing attention to the inherent performativity of modern politics. The dramatic climax of Act 1 is the yoking of the murder of the two princes with the Watergate bugging, performed in pantomime style with comic song: 'If it moves, then bug it / If it leaks, then plug it / If it rings, then tap it / If you see it, insto-snap it' (61). The two young princes (George McGovern and Ed Muskie) are disturbed at night by Dighton and Forrest 'bristling with tape recorders, microphones, and wire' (59) – a scene reviewed as 'unbeatable theatre' (Monsell 86). The role of the women is greatly reduced: Richard seduces Anne, who appears as a drum majorette symbolizing the Republican Party, weeping over the 'poor key-cold figure of a holy king' (Eisenhower). Elizabeth is a lamenting Democrat, while Martha, Hastings' wife, appears as the analogue to Queen Margaret, malevolent prophetess of doom.

Act 2 dramatizes the post-Watergate fall-out: enter Catesby as Ron Ziegler, Nixon's Press Secretary: 'I must myself have knowledge of the truth / If I'm expected to deny it' (86). Richard appears between two nuns, 'two props of Christian virtue', singing of 'everlasting peace', but the stage is set for the inevitable final battle at Camp David, the presidential retreat, where Richard is discovered with the incriminating tape recorder. Richmond is Watergate Committee Chairman Sam Irwin, with Stanley as the Attorney General, Kleindienst. Richard is duly haunted by the ghosts of those accomplices who perjured themselves for his career and, in the final confrontation, is backed against a wall, throwing tapes at Richmond, who advances with drawn sword. As the victorious Richmond sings the final song, 'It's all over tricky Dicky' (111), the body of Richard is lowered into a coffin. But the climax is politically ambiguous:

> [A] hand appears out of the coffin. The cops turn back. Another hand. The cops return to stand at either side of the coffin, pointing their carbines into it. Richard rises to kneeling position. He reaches out for the crown and puts it slowly on his head.
> [...] in one beat, like lightning, the cops whip round to point their carbines at the audience.
>
> (112)

Unlike the slaughtered medieval monarch, 'Tricky Dicky' might rise again.

Edgar's 'muscular blank verse' includes satiric allusions to *Macbeth*, *The Merchant of Venice*, *Hamlet* and *Julius Caesar* as well as *Richard III*. To audiences recognizing the references, these intertextual citations intensify the parodic irony, seeming to emphasize the dichotomy between the Shakespearean source and the carnivalesque nature of Edgar's comedy. Or does the intertextuality imply a common currency whereby the machinations of ruthless ambition are equally sordid, whether in imperial Rome, feudal England or Washington, DC? In Act 1, Scene 4, Richard appears crowned, with the loyal Hastings and Buckingham. They are concerned at mid-term Republican losses and plan to run a smear campaign against their rivals. The scene winds up with the three plotters echoing the opening of *Macbeth*:

RICHARD
So – when shall we three meet again?
At San Clemente or Key Biscayne?
HASTINGS
When the hurley-burley's done
BUCKINGHAM
When the next election's won
HASTINGS
And we've all had lots of fun
[...]
ALL THREE
Fair is foul and foul is fair
There's no distinction anywhere.

(42)

The jaunty tetrameter is comic, as is the link with the three witches, but the politics is unscrupulous and their insouciance disturbing. A similar indifference to morality is seen in the murder of Clarence (Senator Eugene McCarthy), destroyed for his anti-Vietnam War platform; it suits Richard to decry the 'peaceniks':

Friends, Romans, Democrats, lend me your ears.
I come to bury Clarence, not to praise him.
The evil that men do lives after them;
The good is oft interred with their bones.
So let it be with Clarence.
[*Pause. He shrugs.*]
So let it be with Clarence.

(34)

Richard is all ambition – 'I gotta grab that tide in / The affairs of men' (24) – and perverts Portia's appeal for mercy in *The Merchant of Venice* when he brushes aside the dangers of the Watergate revelations:

> The quality of executive clemency's not strained
> It droppeth from within the Oval Office
> Upon the place beneath; and in this case
> It blesseth him that takes *and* him that gives.
>
> (74)

Beate Müller's discussion of parody, analysing Hamlet's 'To be' soliloquy with a parallel version based on tooth extraction, sheds light on Edgar's intertextual appropriation of *Hamlet*: 'parody is essentially a double-edged communication [...] a complex code demanding a reader who is capable of decoding two conflicting codes juxtaposed and layered in the parody' (153). In *Dick Deterred*, the famous soliloquy is channelled in the light of the central question – surveillance:

> RICHARD
> To bug or not to bug, that was the question.
> Whether 'twas nobler in the mind to suffer
> The slings and arrows of the *New York Times*
> Or, 'neath the veil of national security,
> By surveillance end them? To bug – to tap –
> No more! It's not my fault, I'm not to blame.
> It's Kissinger what did it.
>
> (49)

As Müller observes, the metaphysical complexity and profundity of Shakespeare's original, together with its distinctive metrical patterning, makes 'To be' a ripe target for parody. Here, it is the polarity between Hamlet's anguished meditation and the cynicism of Richard's opportunistic politics that creates the satiric effect.

The play was performed in London in 1972 and in New York in 1983 to critical acclaim, London reviewers clearly appreciating the Shakespearean parallels: to Victoria Radin, the plot 'fits so closely that it hurts' (38), while New York reviewer Richard Shepard found

the 'savage comedy [...] somewhat of an overkill for viewers who
have lived through the intervening ten years'. Academic Elizabeth
Swain, writing about the New York production, disagreed, arguing
the play's political relevance and quoting an alteration to the
original version, a short coda added by Edgar:

The Tyrant dies, the Tyranny's the same.
The King departs, the King-Makers remain.
[*A voice lists amounts of contributions to political campaigns
from individuals who hold high office in major industrial
corporations and banks, as the curtain goes down.*]

(123)

Edgar strongly identified with the idea of the writer as 'secretary
for the times' (Painter 2–3): in *Dick Deterred* he caricatures the
ruthlessness and paranoia that lies at the heart of power, using
Shakespeare as the means by which he can 'take our times by the
throat' (Page and Trussler 87).

Disability studies: Richard's deformed body

To what extent could twenty-first-century disability studies be seen
to have appropriated *Richard III*? Disability studies – a relative
newcomer to the field of literary theory – explores the representation
of the disabled body. As such it is an analytical discourse, concerned
with historic practices and attitudes; it is also a campaigning
discipline concerned with confronting existing prejudices and
demarginalizing the non-normative body. While it seems obvious
enough to analyse Shakespeare's depiction of Richard in terms of
early modern ideas of the disabled body, suggesting that disability
studies takes Shakespeare's *Richard III* as a starting point is
perhaps unexpected. But Richard's 'notorious identity' (Charnes)
is widely referenced, and from cultural perspectives it is not limited
to textual discussion. In a fascinating account of disability in the
postcommunist Czech Republic, Marcela Kostihová contends that
Richard's iconic status is an accepted fact: 'no one seems to come

to mind as prominently as Shakespeare's Richard III' (136), while for Tobin Siebers,

> Richard represents more than a character to be interpreted. He sets into motion an allegory of interpretation without which the existence of disability studies would be hard to imagine.
>
> (435)

Key scholars of disability studies Mitchell and Snyder also assert 'the repeated citation of [Richard] as central to disability characterization', notably in terms of 'a restrictive pattern [...] that usually sacrificed the humanity of protagonists'. Fundamental to their theorizing is 'literature's complicity in the historical devaluation of people with disabilities' (Mitchell and Snyder, *Narrative* 17). Hobgood and Houston Wood observe that 'Shakespeare's literary interest in staging disability begins early in his career, with numerous mutilated bodies in *Titus Andronicus* and the congenital deformity of Richard Gloucester in the first *Henriad*' (11); they suggest that early modern narratives of disability can reveal a new field of early modern scholarship together with a moral commitment to redressing contemporary injustices. Appropriating Shakespeare's disabled protagonist can, then, create a new ethical discussion.

There are specific reasons for appropriating Richard as '[f]oremost among the standard-bearers of disability studies' (Siebers 435), chief of which must be Shakespeare's vivid dramatization; Richard is 'famous for serving as Shakespeare's first "dense" character' (Houston Wood 142); the earliest example of 'a fully developed subjectivity' (Adelman 1). From the opening scenes of *Richard III*, Richard demonstrates his virtuosic ability to define and critique the terms of his disability as well as to anticipate and manipulate the stereotypically negative responses he encounters. Certainly, Richard's propensity to 'descant on mine own deformity' is intrinsic to his individuality, his sense of aspiration and agency:

> But I, that am not shaped for sportive tricks,
> Nor made to court an amorous looking glass;
> [...]
> I, that am curtailed of this fair proportion,
> Cheated of feature by dissembling Nature,

Deformed, unfinished, sent before my time
Into this breathing world, scarce half made up,
And that so lamely and unfashionable
That dogs bark at me as I halt by them –
Why, I [...] am determined to prove a villain
And hate the idle pleasure of these days.

                                    (*R3* 1.1.14–23, 30–1)

It could be argued that this soliloquy informs the first early modern definition of deformity and, conceivably, the first adaptive response to the play: as early as 1612, Bacon appears to have appropriated Richard as a prototype of the disabled psyche:

Deformed persons are commonly even with nature; for as nature hath done ill by them, so do they by nature [...] and so they have their revenge of nature. [It] is good to consider of deformity, not as a sign, which is more deceivable; but as a cause, which seldom faileth of the effect.

                                    (426)

Bacon's reference to the 'deceivable' sign seems particularly apposite – Richard himself refers to his 'dissembling looks' (*R3* 1.2.239). And Bacon further identifies both 'extreme bold[ness]' and 'great wit' as leading characteristics of deformity, the latter offering 'an advantage to rising' (426, 7). Here, too, Richard's darkly ironical humour comes to mind: when he challenges his brother Edward over the murder of Clarence, he suggests that 'some tardy cripple' (*R3* 2.1.90) has delivered Clarence's reprieve. Richard himself is the cripple, of course, but the reverse of tardy, pre-empting Edward in ordering Clarence's death. Where Bacon may arguably be drawing on Shakespeare to define deformity, Freud explicitly appropriates Richard to describe wounded narcissism, asserting that Shakespeare creates a 'secret background of sympathy' (315):

What the (opening) soliloquy thus means is: 'Nature has done me a grievous wrong in denying me the beauty of form which wins human love. Life owes me reparation for this, and I will see that I get it. I have a right to be an exception, to disregard the scruples by which others let themselves be held back. I may do

wrong myself, since wrong has been done to me.' [...] Richard
is an enormous magnification of something we find in ourselves
as well. We all think we have reason to reproach Nature and our
destiny [...] we all demand reparation for early wounds to our
narcissism, our self-love.

(314–15)

Freud's interpretation of the soliloquy draws attention to Richard's
own engagement with his image and sense of selfhood, a crucial
aspect of *3 Henry VI* as well as *Richard III*. In his first, lengthy,
soliloquy Richard makes an explicit connection between Nature's
treachery – as he sees it – and his murderous ambitions. Richard
defines himself as barred from the joys of romantic love from his
mother's womb, mocked by 'Deformity':

> Then, since this earth affords no joy to me
> But to command, to check, to o'erbear such
> As are of better person than myself,
> I'll make my heaven to dream upon the crown
> And whiles I live, t'account this world but hell
> Until my misshaped trunk that bears this head
> Be round impaled with a glorious crown.

(*3H6* 3.2.165–71)

There is a clear causal link between the privations and 'torment'
Richard suffers and the determination to 'hew my way out with a
bloody axe' (*3H6* 3.2.181). Shakespeare is introducing to disability
studies the earliest example of a self-defining individual forging
identity and motivation through his perception of alterity – a
'psychic myth of origins' (Adelman 2). To Richard, furthermore,
it is axiomatic that his sense of self is identical with a sense of
separateness: 'I have no brother; I am like no brother; / [...] I am
myself alone' (*3H6* 5.6.80, 83). In Bacon's terms, he sets himself
apart from religious and moral codes. In one of the earliest
discussions of literary depictions of disability, Leonard Kriegel
identifies Richard as typifying dramatic characterization 'at its
most gripping [...] and memorable'. He, too, finds in Richard 'a
pervasive sense of absence' causally related to a compulsive need
'to plot and scheme and burn with the need for revenge' (Kriegel

33, 34–5). Shakespeare's new and radical use of the soliloquy also means that Richard can engage the audience in his 'performance of the multiple and contradictory significations of a disabled body' (Mitchell and Snyder, *Body* 14).

Shakespeare's Richard is remarkable, also, for his ability to manipulate bodily difference: in *3 Henry VI* he takes delight in his Machiavellian ability to 'add colours to the chameleon, / Change shapes with Proteus for advantages' (*3H6* 3.2.191–2). The fact of his military supremacy might belie ideas of 'dis-ablement'; he is evidently physically powerful, an adept swordsman on horseback, commanding his troops. When he first appears as a soldier at the climax of *2 Henry VI* with his brother Edward, his father, York, refers to 'my two brave bears' (*2H6* 5.1.144). Shakespeare has bent time considerably in order to introduce Richard to the first battle of St Albans in 1455; historically he would have been three years old. Clearly the foregrounding of Richard as a warrior throughout the entire period of the Wars of the Roses is key to Shakespeare's invention of the character: he has been both perpetrator and victim of the violence of the times. Richard as York's true son is a crucial aspect of the central scenes of *Richard III*, Act 3, where disability disappears completely in Buckingham's speeches to the citizens: 'I did infer your lineaments, / Being the right idea of your father, / *Both in your form* and nobleness of mind' (*R3* 3.7.12–14, my italics). Yet Richard himself flaunts his arm – 'like a blasted sapling withered up' (*R3* 3.4.68) – as a means of ridding himself of Hastings. The bravura histrionics of the scene establish Richard's tyrannical control – by exploiting the superstitious unease associated with physical deformity. As Katherine Schaap Williams argues, Richard's rhetoric 'constructs his dramatic character' as well as 'forming a history to shape his own ends'; interpreting Richard as a 'dismodern' subject 'explores the possibility that bodily difference might actually be enabling'.

Society's fear, exclusion and rejection of disability is clearly highlighted in both *3 Henry VI* and *Richard III* and this, equally, is a major aspect of modern disability studies. The notion not simply of deformed otherness but monstrosity runs throughout *Richard III*, particularly through the curses of Queen Margaret, again historically out of place but a powerfully vengeful presence on stage. Margaret appears in the third scene of the play, ritually cursing the victorious Yorkists but reserving for Richard epithets that connect him with Satan – a degree of 'othering' beyond the physical taunts of 'bunch-backed toad' or 'bottled spider' (*R3* 1.3.245, 241):

> Hie thee to hell for shame, and leave this world,
> Thou cacodemon. There thy kingdom is.

(R3 1.3.142–3)

As a figure associated with Hell, Richard comprises both hound and serpent in Margaret's sibylline warnings:

> take heed of yonder dog.
> Look when he fawns he bites; and when he bites,
> His venom tooth will rankle to the death.
> Have not to do with him, beware of him;
> Sin, death, and hell have set their mark on him,
> And all their ministers do attend on him.

(R3 1.3.288–93)

In the 'lamentation scene' of Act 4, Margaret reappears to denounce Richard as 'hell's black intelligencer', prophesying, in apocalyptic language, his imminent end: '[e]arth gapes, hell burns, fiends roar, saints pray, / To have him suddenly conveyed from hence' (*R3* 4.4.71, 75–6). This scene – again, out of historical time – is dominated by the women: bewailing their murdered children, the former queens unite in their cursing of Richard. Here, too, the idea of the unnatural birth – first introduced by Richard himself in *3 Henry VI* – associates Richard with the satanic: 'From forth the kennel of thy womb hath crept / A hell-hound that doth hunt us all to death' (*R3* 4.4.47–8). The women, then, surround Richard with a typically medieval attitude where non-normativity is perceived figuratively as moral and spiritual aberration, a deterministic narrative of the body that has authorized the 'legacy of stigmatic correspondence between monstrous exteriority and immoral interiority' (Hobgood 26).

An extraordinary coda can now be appended to the story of Richard's much-disputed body. In September 2012, an archaeological team from the University of Leicester exhumed human remains from the long-buried ruins of the medieval

Church of the Grey Friars; poignant photographs of the skeleton emphasized trauma and vulnerability. DNA from a descendent of Richard's sister established the identity of the remains and osteo-archaeology revealed fatal injuries from the battle of Bosworth, as well as abuses inflicted after death by way of ritual desecration. The disabled body could be investigated in the light of modern medical knowledge: Richard was seen to have suffered idiopathic scoliosis with pronounced curvature of the spine, the right shoulder higher than the left and a characteristically shortened torso (*Discovery*). The historic Richard was finally reinterred in the sanctuary of Leicester's cathedral with full liturgical and ceremonial splendour. The archaeological project attracted wide interest and the funeral was attended by thousands of spectators. Richard's 'redelivery and reanimation from the earth' had an unparalleled result: 'a medieval king, always Shakespearean too, is our contemporary again' (G. Love 138).

The Hollow Crown: The Wars of the Roses, dir. Dominic Cooke (2016)

The Hollow Crown is a BBC TV miniseries, series 1 an adaptation of Shakespeare's second tetralogy, from *Richard II* to *Henry V* (2012), and series 2, *The Hollow Crown: The Wars of the Roses* (2016), based on the earlier tetralogy. BBC adaptations of Shakespeare – particularly on such an epic scale – are not culturally and politically neutral. If the BBC is guardian and arbiter of the nation's sense of cultural identity, then the combination of Shakespeare and medieval English history is a potent one. As Holderness has observed, '[the] radical potentialities of television Shakespeare [are] in practice systematically blocked, suppressed or marginalised by the conservatism of the dominant cultural institution' (*Visual Shakespeare* 22). This is particularly true of the 2012 *Hollow Crown*, which formed the cultural high point of the 2012 Cultural Olympiad alongside the Globe-to-Globe Festival – a 'new era of global Shakespearean appropriation' (Huang and Rivlin 1). The lavish spectacle and historical splendour of BBC costume drama 'reinforces the perception of an authoritative interpretation of Shakespeare's tetralog[ies] which risks normalizing the uncontroversial interpretive choices' (Leberg 30). Leberg's point is a valuable one: in terms of showcasing British theatre, *The Hollow Crown* offers impressive spectacle. But does the visual and aural magnificence create a highly conservative national narrative? The decision to cut the Jack Cade scenes (of *2 Henry VI*) means that explicit scenes of rebellion have been excised in favour of extended battle scenes. As Leberg argues, 'all adaptation choices are critically informed, deliberate, and expertly articulated' (28). An interesting comparison can be made with the earlier BBC Time-Life series (1978–85), which tended to see the history plays as conventional orthodox Tudor historiography, with the exception of Jane Howell, director of the Henry VI trilogy, for whom the plays possessed 'a peculiarly modern relevance and contemporary application' (Holderness, *Visual Shakespeare* 20). Howell chose to avoid the orthodox Tillyardian reading, seeing the plays not as a 'dramatisation of the Elizabethan World Picture but a sustained interrogation of residual and emergent ideologies in a changing society' (*Visual Shakespeare* 20).

The eight plays that are shaped into the seven episodes of *The Hollow Crown* are considerably cut, chronologically reordered and occasionally rewritten to simplify the complexities of genealogy and medieval aristocracy. Iconic landscapes and settings are used to reinforce the sense of historic time and national geography: the opening of the second series pans across the white cliffs of Dover with long shots connoting totemic scenes of English history from William the Conqueror in 1066 to the clichéd association with the Second World War. The Tower of London, and particularly the menacing entrance from the Thames through the 'Traitors' Gate', features effectively as the backdrop for scenes of murders and machinations. A sumptuous style of medieval costume and armour is consistent throughout the series. Prominent RSC and BBC actors are cast in the major roles (Judi Dench, Simon Russell Beale, Sophie Okonedo, Patrick Stewart and Tom Hiddleston, to name but a few). Benedict Cumberbatch, as Richard III, introduced areas of complex extra-textuality; lionized for his performance as Sherlock in the eponymous BBC series, Cumberbatch has an ardent fandom, for whom he epitomizes Sherlockian autistic genius. Casting Cumberbatch impacted further on the digital mediascape of *The Hollow Crown*: viewers accustomed to interacting with Sherlockian social media (@Sherlock221B,

#Sherlock) willingly contributed to #HollowCrownFans. As Romano Mullin observes, such participatory culture creates endless digital adaptation:

> @HollowCrownFans aims to [...] provide a platform for its followers' own Shakespeare-related creations, including GIFs, memes, mash-ups and links to Fan Fiction and YouTube videos.
>
> (212)

Two points about *The Hollow Crown*'s adaptation of the *Henry VI* plays should be emphasized before examining Richard's eponymous role in *Richard III*: first, the historical perspective, and second, the way in which the young Richard is portrayed. Intriguingly, Dominic Cooke, as director of the second cycle, appears to adopt a wholeheartedly Tillyardian approach: the opening shot of the first episode of the *Henry VI* plays pans across the iconic cliffs while a disembodied voice (Judi Dench) intones '[t]ake but degree away, untune that string / And hark what discord follows'. The quotation, from Ulysses' speech on hierarchy (*TC* 1.3.83–135), is at odds with the dynastic politics of the Wars of the Roses – although discord is certainly ubiquitous. The martial politics of the cycle focus overwhelmingly on ruthless ambition and opportunistic politicking, together with the brutal savagery of hand-to-hand warfare. The first film of the second series moves from war in France – with a horrifyingly graphic scene of the public burning of La Pucelle – to the beginnings of the Wars of the Roses with the first battle of St Albans. The physical violence is unsparing: gory deaths are followed by poignant scenes of father seeking son, son seeking father. Queen Margaret searching for her lover, Somerset, has his decapitated head delivered into her lap. The second film dramatizes the key battles of Towton, Barnet and Tewkesbury using montage and parallel sequencing to condense the realistic detail of the battle into the timeframe. Richard is present as the youth growing into adulthood throughout this turbulent time, and the film highlights his emotional response. The murder of the child Edmund (York's youngest son; in Shakespeare's text always 'Rutland') is seen entirely from Richard's view: as the Lancastrians storm the York family residence, Richard is ordered to hide his younger brother. The audience sees the avenging Clifford and the pleading, terrified child and hears the grotesque sounds of the murder as if from Richard's hiding place. The brutal revenge ethic of 'Thy father slew my father: therefore die' (*3H6* 1.3.47) is thus impressed on Richard, who is seen to be highly affected. The torture and murder of his father, York, is reported soon afterwards: it is not, then, only Richard who pursues revenge; it is endemic to aristocratic society. Equally, it is not only Richard who is capable of extreme violence; it defines both the campaigns in France and the civil war at home. Shakespeare is the first playwright to alter history by foregrounding Richard in events in which he was far too young to participate in order to create a Richard who is seen to emerge from his discordant times; director Dominic Cooke goes further by moving outside the text to highlight Richard's response to his brother's murder. Adaptation here goes beyond aesthetic or genre questions in order to suggest moral and psychological implications.

The standalone film of *Richard III* offers a bleak climax to the series. In interview, Dominic Cooke discussed his focus on the six battles that structure the entire cycle of *The Wars of the Roses*, drawing connections with the familiar tropes of war films:

> Richard's scenes are influenced by *Downfall* – a brilliant German film about the last days of Hitler in his bunker, and are monochromatic and austere.
>
> (BBC)

Antony Sher, researching and rehearsing Richard over several months for the 1984 RSC production, also chose to play Richard as psychopathic, spending considerable time reading accounts of Peter Sutcliffe, the infamous 'Yorkshire Ripper' of the 1980s, although his director, RSC's Bill Alexander, adopted a historical interpretation, seeing Richard as the product of his warring times (Sher, *Year* 84). Richard's disability is at the forefront of *The Hollow Crown*'s characterization from the beginning of the cycle: episode 1 concludes with the child Richard, his deformed shape, silhouetted darkly, centrally dominating the frame to climactic music; episode 2 features Richard throughout, his characteristic limp and conspicuous prosthesis always evident. At the opening of *Richard III*, his naked upper body reveals the extent of his scoliotic disability, and adaptations made by scriptwriter Ben Power, make explicit connections between Richard's disability and his ruthless amorality. The murder of Henry VI in the Tower of

London is powerfully filmed in terms of the menacing spaces of
the Tower at night and the quiet spirituality of Henry, who accepts
his death, prophesying the future suffering that Richard will cause
yet praying for mercy for Richard's dark soul. As the scene opens,
with Richard approaching the Tower by boat, an abridged version
of Richard's Act 3 soliloquy is spoken as an exculpatory preface to
the murder – arguably regicide – that is to follow. Richard's desire
for the crown as compensation for his diminished life emerges here
from his bitterness that 'Love forswore me in my mother's womb'
(*3H6* 3.2.153); Cumberbatch delivers the following lines quietly, as
profoundly internalized intelligence, up to the enumerating of his
disabilities, where 'like to a chaos' (161) is climactically forceful.
Characteristically, the full-face camera view invites the viewer's
understanding or even complicity. The speech is broken as Richard
arrives at the Tower, then concluded as he approaches Henry.
Similarly, Richard's later soliloquy, following the murder, is cut in
order to emphasize disability as motivation:

> Then, since the heavens have shaped my body so,
> Let hell make crook'd my mind to answer it.

> (*3H6* 5.6.78–9)

Ben Power's script also focuses on Richard's sense of separateness;
the scene concludes only with 'I am myself alone', omitting Richard's
plans for Clarence. The splicing of the two soliloquies cements the
notion that Richard's sense of otherness profoundly informs his
psychopathic commitment to violence. He is seen to attack Henry's
body with frenzied, egregious blows in a desperate rage.

The dark spaces of the Tower and Richard's haunted paranoia
structure the unfolding drama of *Richard III*: whispered plotting
in shadowy corners successfully effects his takeover after Edward's
death, but thereafter he is seen often alone in a cell-like space playing
chess, tapping neurotically on the side of the chess board. His
tyranny is shown here as terrifying and alienating: those who have
supported his rise, such as Buckingham, recoil from the suggestion
of the murder of the two princes; there is no ambiguity over the
death of his queen, Anne – she is seen to be hastily despatched in yet
another darkened room. Although Dominic Cooke retains some of
the black humour of Richard's asides to the audience, his focus is on
Richard's disquietude – there is no joy in the carefully plotted and

ruthlessly executed attaining of the crown. This is most apparent in the troubled nightmare preceding the final battle, Bosworth. In his haunted sleep Richard howls in anguish as he confronts his vengeful victims and utters the final summing up of his solitariness:

> I shall despair. There is no creature loves me,
> And if I die, no soul will pity me.

> (*R3* 5.3.200–1)

Dominic Cooke, in a highly effective addition to the text, reintroduces Queen Margaret to conjure the spectres that haunt Richard. She is seen reflecting the images towards him in a mirror, a gesture that recalls the witches in *Macbeth*. Certainly, Margaret possesses all the malevolence of a demonic spirit. *The Hollow Crown* makes effective use of the women; where Loncraine's 1995 film omits Queen Margaret, she is seen throughout *Richard III* as a wild and vengeful presence and, although the play is significantly cut, scenes featuring the women are added to the drama. Following the murder of the two princes, for example, Elizabeth, their mother, is taken by night to two graves in a wooded area. Together with the Duchess of York and Queen Margaret – their former enemy – the women join hands in declaiming their hatred of Richard. Margaret appears to exist also in a liminal sphere: in an entirely original addition, she appears at the very end of the play, surveying the bodies littering the battlefield. The final crane shots pan above the slaughter, moving outwards to reveal the extent of the carnage. In contrast with the somewhat tame speeches of Richmond or the union of Henry and Elizabeth, this final vision refuses to offer any Tudor glorification. History, at this point, has exacted a terrible toll.

3

A Midsummer Night's Dream

The fantastical world of *A Midsummer Night's Dream* has proved
an enduring stimulus for the creative and recreative imagination.
This chapter explores the interplay between the verbal and the
visual in three transmedial adaptations, all of which sought ways
to transcend the representational bounds of the stage and to
bring the *Dream* to a wide-ranging audience.

Henry Fuseli, *Robin Goodfellow-Puck* (1787–90)

On 23 April 2016, the Tate Britain in London commemorated the
400th anniversary of Shakespeare's death by staging scenes from
four of his best-loved plays, performed in front of four paintings
inspired by them. The pop-up event convincingly demonstrated the
bi-directional relationship between the visual arts and the dramatic
text: a play-reading or staging can be transmediated into the still
image, and the still image can be animated by the reader, actor or
stage director. At the same time, with the art exhibits ranging in
date from the 1790s to the 1840s, it highlighted the period during
which the vogue for presenting Shakespeare's plays on canvas was
at its height. The public appetite for pictorial Shakespeare is usually
thought to have begun with Nicholas Rowe's illustrated works of
Shakespeare (1709). A few decades later, the emergence of a British

art movement, a flourishing exhibition culture and the establishment of Shakespeare as the great national poet all came together to create the ideal socio-cultural climate for Shakespeare-inspired standalone paintings and prints. According to Stuart Sillars, a leading scholar of literature and the visual arts, such works would move artists' impressions of Shakespeare beyond the illustrated page to create a 'new order of aesthetic imagining that becomes a major vehicle for the mediation of the plays' (32). In the course of the eighteenth and nineteenth centuries, ways of imaging Shakespeare's plays included portraits of famous actors in role, individual scenes drawn from celebrated productions, and the concretization of events and actions merely reported in the text, the latter category often inspired by Shakespeare's own ekphrastic tendency. John Everett Millais' painting *Ophelia* (1851–2), for instance, depicts an off-stage moment vividly recounted by an on-stage character (Gertrude). One of the most enduring Shakespearean visualizations ever created, it is ubiquitously replicated on items ranging from mugs to jigsaws to yoga mats, and anyone coming new to *Hamlet*, via text or performance, might be forgiven for expecting the scene to feature in the tragedy's action. This section examines Fuseli's *Robin Goodfellow-Puck*, a picturing of Shakespeare's *Dream* that erases all sense of the stage, taking the viewer directly to the type of world that might be conjured in the mind's eye of the solitary play-reader.

One of the most significant events in the history of Shakespeare and the visual arts was the opening of John Boydell's Shakespeare Gallery in 1789. A purpose-built exhibition space in Pall Mall, the Gallery displayed specially commissioned works by emerging and established artists of the day. For all its avowed intention of supporting a national school of history painting through the lens of the national Bard, Boydell's Shakespeare project was very much a commercial enterprise (albeit ultimately an unsuccessful one), and the original exhibits were to reach customers far beyond the London venue in the form of reproductive engravings, some of which could also be viewed in a deluxe illustrated edition of the complete works, edited by George Steevens and published by Rivington. Considered by one recent scholar as marking 'the moment at which painting temporarily rivaled theater as the natural home of Shakespeare's art' (Pask 85), the Gallery drew great acclaim from visitors and press alike; *The Times* ('Shakespeare Gallery') saw it as 'the first stone of an English School of Painting', while the *Public Advertiser* ('Gallery of Shakespeare') felt that the exhibits amounted to 'a mirror of the poet'. Unsurprisingly, considering the sacrosanct nature of the subject matter, the Gallery also came in for some stinging criticism, both public and private. In a letter to the poet Samuel Rogers, Charles Lamb decried the very concept of the project, which he saw as an attempt to 'confine the illimitable' (*Letters* 3, 394). Famously opposed even to theatrical representations of the plays, Lamb considered their depiction in painting to be coercive, forcing a single vision of Shakespeare's work upon the individual, thereby closing down the subjective response central to the Romantic sensibility. Boydell, doubtless anticipating adverse responses to his intermedial project from similar-minded critics, included the following emollient statement in the exhibition catalogue's Preface: 'Though I believe it will be readily admitted, that no subjects seem so proper to form an English School of Historical Painting, as the scenes of the immortal Shakspeare; yet it must be always remembered, that he possessed powers which no pencil can reach' (vi).

A key contributor to the Boydell Gallery was Henry Fuseli, one of the most innovative artists of the Romantic movement and one who was commonly held to have come close to matching the 'immortal Shakespeare'. One of several eighteenth-century painters who 'turned away from theatrical sources to develop their own interpretations of Shakespeare's texts' (West 229), the painter was especially attracted to the playwright's supernaturalism. Fuseli's treatments of dramas such as *The Tempest*, *Hamlet*, *Macbeth* and *Dream* aligned him with the bizarre and the fantastic in the public imagination, tellingly demonstrated in one exhibition-goer's reported response to his pictures: 'La! What a frightful thing! I hate his fancies of fairies and spirits and nonsense. One can't understand them. [...] It's foolish to paint things which nobody ever saw, for how is one to know whether they're right?' (Wainewright 71). For Fuseli, painting 'things which nobody ever saw' was an exhilarating exercise for the artistic imagination, as was the opportunity to transform the words of Shakespeare, a writer he hailed as 'the supreme master of passions and the ruler of our hearts' (Fuseli 113), into purely visual form. The most extensive collection of Fuseli's Shakespearean paintings was produced for the Boydell Gallery, which hung nine of his canvases in all, three of which were based on *Dream*: two large paintings, *Titania and Bottom* and *Titania's Awakening*, depicting moments from 4.1, and one smaller canvas, *Robin Goodfellow-Puck*. If a modern artist planning to paint Shakespeare's *Dream* could turn to countless prior representations of its fairy characters in art, film and stage productions for inspiration, Fuseli had few iconographies on which to draw, not least because the play 'seldom reached the eighteenth-century stage' (Chaudhuri, *Midsummer* 11). His Boydell *Dream* paintings seem born out of his own startlingly original response to the text, shaped by a fascination with what he described in a Royal Academy lecture as 'diving into the invisible' (Fuseli 109). As one contemporary art historian observes, Fuseli's Boydell canvases 'advertised him as a Promethean figure, not the mere transcriber of his artistic and literary predecessors' (Dias 161), and these qualities are nowhere more evident than in the two paintings of Titania and her fairy kingdom, which offer up a phantasmagorical, erotic dreamscape, anticipatory of Jan Kott's ground-breaking view of the play as a discourse on transgressive, often brutal, sexual desire. And this vision is carried through into *Robin Goodfellow-Puck*, in which Fuseli pictures a Puck that seems to have none of the human qualities frequently identified in this traditional figure of folklore and myth.

In the Shakespeare Gallery catalogue, each exhibit is matched with an extract from the Shakespeare play depicted, a design that might invite the artwork to be read more as an illustration of the literary text rather than as a critical, creative interpretation in its own right. In the case of Fuseli's *Robin Goodfellow-Puck*, the playtext printed in the catalogue is Robin's speech to the Fairy (*MND* 2.1.42–58), describing some of the pranks that have helped secure his reputation as a 'knavish sprite' (*MND* 2.1.33). Fuseli's composition, though, goes beyond the anterior events recalled by the speaker: the starry streamer that trails from Robin's finger reminds the viewer of his promise to 'put a girdle round about the earth / In forty minutes' (*MND* 2.1.175–6) in order to fulfil Oberon's commands and, at the same time perhaps, his threat to whip Demetrius 'with a rod' (*MND* 3.2.410). The recurring elemental imagery of the play is also strikingly captured in the moonlight that illuminates Robin's figure from behind, combined with the splashing waters at his feet and the stars around his head. It is clear, then, that Fuseli's art, although fixed in time and space (in contradistinction to the temporal progression of a play performance or reading), is nonetheless able to conjure up multiple dramatic events, moods and images on one canvas.

Critics – though perhaps not so much stage directors – have tended to view the character of Robin as a fusion of near-human country homeliness and otherworldly devilishness, with the critical consensus coming down in favour of the former; Hugh Grady speaks for many in believing that '[w]e don't see Robin doing anything very harmful or frightening in this play [*Dream*]' (75). Fuseli's visual imagination, however, eliminates the benign, dwelling instead on the devilish, the cruel and the supernatural aspects of Shakespeare's creature. Robin presents himself to the Fairy as a 'merry' spirit, whose jests can make his master smile and whose mischievous escapades can cause 'the whole choir [to] hold their hips and laugh' (*MND* 2.1.55), but there is little trace of these ludic qualities in Fuseli's picture. Robin's facial expression appears more mocking than mischievous and it is hard to imagine such a creature pronouncing the lines 'Jack shall have Jill, / Nought shall go ill' (*MND* 3.2.461–2) with anything other than a sneer. And where the playtext emphasizes Robin's protean qualities as he shape-shifts through animal, vegetable and mineral states ('filly foal' to 'roasted crab' to 'three-foot stool'), Fuseli gives the figure an unnerving solidity. A muscular man-child of disturbingly strange proportions, Robin seems to fly towards the spectator with threatening velocity, the batwings which propel him seeming to belong more to the supernatural climate of *Macbeth* than the fairyland of *Dream*. Robin's trick of misleading 'night-wanderers' (*MND* 2.1.39) is given a nightmarish quality as the rider in the right-hand corner of the picture clings on to his horse for dear life, both man and beast appearing to be in a trance-like state, suggested by their closed eyes and open mouths, the symmetry of their facial features adding to the sinister impact of the composition as a whole. The rearing horse also brings a sense of violent movement to the piece, its flailing lack of control contrasting with the sturdiness of the central figure, toes splayed as if preparing for landing. And for all Robin might be sketched with only vestigial genitals, there is an erotic energy about him, emphasized by his signalling of the cuckold's horns with the fingers of his left hand and the goat-like beard that sprouts from his chin.

In the Preface to the Gallery catalogue, Boydell asserts the axiomatic primacy of the Shakespeare text, cautioning readers not to expect that 'the art of the Painter can ever equal the sublimity of our Poet' (vi), yet some would hail Fuseli's creations as coming close to equal with his literary inspiration, one reviewer declaring that 'if Shakespeare had been a painter [...] he would perhaps have given somewhat of a similar picture' ('Gallery of Shakespeare' 3) of the *Dream*. His portrait of Robin was almost unanimously preferred to that exhibited by Joshua Reynolds, likened by one critic to 'a portrait of a *foetus* taken from some anatomical preparation' (quoted in Sillars 208). Accounting for why Fuseli's art might be preferred to that of the President of the Royal Academy and the most celebrated artist of the day, one commentator wrote in the *Gazetteer and New Daily Advertiser*: 'It is the privilege of genius to be eccentric. Whoever leaves the beaten road has a chance of evading his competitors' ('Shakespeare Gallery'). Considered, along with William Blake, as having a seminal influence on the fairy-painting genre that proved so popular in the mid-Victorian era, Fuseli's *Dream* paintings marked both a departure from the 'beaten road' and an important opening to another.

A Midsummer Night's Dream, dir. Max Reinhardt and William Dieterle (1935)

I remember that day, the day *The Dream* began, as if it were yesterday. We all arrived in costume – we were a motley crew and no mistake. None of your soppy fairies with butterfly wings and floral wreaths. No, sir. As Peaseblossom and Mustardseed, our bras and knicks had leaves appliquéd at the stress points, there were little lights in our shaggy wigs, and when we saw how the rest had fared in the wardrobe, we thought we'd got off lightly, I must say, because some had antlers sprouting out of their foreheads and fur patches covering up the rude bits [...]. Dwarfs, giants, children, all mixed up together. Suddenly I had a sinking feeling; I knew it in my bones. This film is going to lose a fortune.

(Carter 129)

In this extract from Angela Carter's novel *Wise Children* (1992), a bit-part performer, Dora Chance, recalls her impressions of arriving on the set for a Hollywood adaptation of A *Midsummer Night's Dream*. It is but one of several thinly veiled references to the 1935 film directed by Max Reinhardt and William Dieterle and captures, albeit with a fair degree of fictional licence, some of the features that have come to characterize the movie: extravagance of scale, a fascination with the play's more threatening elements – and failure at the box office. Only the second full-length Shakespeare 'talkie' – the first was Sam Taylor's *The Taming of the Shrew* (1929) – the film was a determined move by Warner Bros., one of the 'Big Five' American studios, to adapt an iconic high-culture text in such a way as to make it appeal to popular taste. Keen to shake off its reputation as the 'gangster studio' and to accumulate some cultural capital, the studios hired Max Reinhardt, one of Europe's most highly regarded theatre directors, to co-direct the adaptation. But for all the high-mindedness of the enterprise, the 'defiantly anti-theatrical' (Cartmell, *Adaptations* 38) approach to casting suggests that the exigencies of commercial movie-making were paramount – hence the somewhat unlikely choice of James Cagney, a rising screen star best known for his gangster roles, to play Bottom.

Like many notable Shakespeare screen adaptations, Reinhardt and Dieterle's *Dream* was rooted in a theatre production: a hugely successful staging at the Hollywood Bowl (1934) featuring an adolescent Mickey Rooney playing Puck as a 'screeching primate' (Patricia 2), a role he would reprise in the film version. Despite being co-directed, it was Reinhardt's name that featured prominently in the publicity releases, Warner doubtless capitalizing on his reputation as a key figure of European Modernism. Although a seasoned director of classic drama (he directed over twenty Shakespeare plays in his lifetime), Reinhardt was a relative newcomer to the cinema, having been reluctant to embrace the medium in its silent days, deeming it a 'dangerous parasite of the theater, of painting, of music' (quoted in MacQueen 35). Initial reviews of the screen *Dream* focused on the process of remediation, several judging Reinhardt's move from stage to screen aesthetically unsuccessful. Graham Greene found much of the film 'poised [...] on the edge of absurdity because Herr Reinhardt cannot visualise how his ideas will work out on the screen' (606), while the drama scholar and early exponent of film Shakespeare Allardyce Nicoll complained that '[w]henever the theatrical intrudes, the spell [of film] is destroyed and the illusion vanishes' (94). Other reviewers turned their critical scrutiny on the actors' delivery of the dialogue, finding film a less than suitable medium for Shakespearean verse-speaking. One *Sunday Times* reviewer saw it as his 'obligation as a man of English descent on both sides for generations' to protest against a production in which '[o]nly one actor [...] has the slightest idea of proper Shakespearean diction' (Carroll 4), a criticism that tanged of the 'cultural ethnocentricism [*sic*]' (Willson 47) of the day; it also chimed with a general feeling that the new technology of the 'talkie' was wholly inappropriate for mediating the work of England's great Bard. As Cartmell observes:

> [s]ound afforded film a chance to adapt not just Shakespeare's stories, but to reproduce his words for the first time; and the manner in which the words were reproduced was met, on the whole, with disapproval, from both critics of Shakespeare and the movie-going public[.]
>
> (*Adaptations* 23)

Objections to sound Shakespeare were not confined to verse-speaking purists; cineastes were also ill at ease. A contemporary review, published in the then recently established film journal *Sight and Sound*, suggested somewhat counterintuitively that had Reinhardt 'dared to be revolutionary he would have had a shot at Shakespeare without words' (Williams 165). And it must be said that today's scholarly evaluations of the 1935 *Dream* tend to find more to admire in its visual, choreographic and musical achievements than in its spoken performances. Kenneth Rothwell extols the lighting as 'a miracle, wringing subtleties out of stark black-and-white' (35), R. S. White comments on its 'visual strangeness and magical realism' (25), and Orgel singles out its 'beautifully modulated' chiaroscuro as a 'notably imaginative cinematic interpretation of Shakespeare's poetic imagery' (91).

One of the major affordances of cinema is its ability to photographically capture 'real life', and Reinhardt takes advantage of this to actualize what is merely figurative in the text. Greene seizes mockingly on one such example: 'Herr Reinhardt is nothing if not literal, and when Helena declares, "No, no, I am as ugly as a bear; For beasts that meet me run away for fear," we see a big bear beating a hasty retreat into the blackberry bushes' (606). Such literalism might be seen to extend to the directorial decision to embody the changeling Indian boy on screen. Transforming a character only ever spoken about in Shakespeare's version is by no means unprecedented: he has been incarnated in numerous stage productions and paintings of the play, as well as in film adaptations. In Elijah Moshinsky's BBC version (1981), for instance, he is a beautiful, curly-haired black infant, small enough to nestle comfortably against the bosom of Titania (Helen Mirren) as she recounts the narrative of his gestation and birth, protecting him from the predatory Oberon. What *is* unusual about the 1935 *Dream* is the extent to which the Indian Prince (so named in the shooting script) is present on screen. Played by a five-year-old girl, Sheila Brown, the Rococo-styled Prince is an almost entirely passive presence. In the course of the film, he is placed, pulled, carried, garlanded, spun round and cast aside, a mere object of barter for his warring surrogate parents. And while the Prince's size and sturdy gait would place him securely in the telegraphic stage of language acquisition, he never utters a sound – a silence that further underscores his lack of agency.

Shakespeare's off-stage changeling has proven fertile critical territory, with different theoretical perspectives generating a diverse range of interpretations, many of which are informed by close readings of the speech in which Titania recalls her relationship with the boy's deceased mother, 'a votaress of [her] order' (*MND* 2.1.123). Notably, the film script of Reinhardt's adaptation omits all but the first two and last three lines of this speech, lines which provide a birth narrative for 'the loved boy' (*MND* 2.1.26) and thus a more distinct identity. The removal of this verse, with all its gynocentric power and energy, attenuates the play's evocation of strong matriarchal bonds and the concomitant threat that these pose to the patriarchal structures which prevail in both fairyland and Athens. Also lost is the lyrical summoning up of 'a feminine world rich with all the mysteries of fertility, conception, pregnancy, and birth' (Calderwood 416) and, consequently, the fairy queen's close association with the somatic world of maternality. Reinhardt's Titania (played by Anita Louise) is very much in keeping with these affective shifts: she might kiss, embrace and coo at the Indian Prince, but the sparkly brittleness of her costume, her high sing-songy voice and the awkward way in which she carries him (a marked contrast to Helen Mirren's earthy skin-to-skin embrace in Moshinsky's version) suggest that the child is more sentimentalized object than source of motherly joy. If Reinhardt's vision of the changeling boy is somewhat out of sync with gender-oriented or feminist readings of the play, it aligns more interestingly with postcolonial readings, such as that which identifies the 'discourse of mercantile colonialism' in Titania's account of his birth and, in the boy himself, 'a distilled essence of the East' (Raman 244). When in the film Titania's fairies leave him stranded at the water's edge as they fly off into the distance sniggering, he is framed as the marginalized other, flapping his hands in a futile attempt to become airborne. Starting life as property 'stolen, from an Indian king' (*MND* 2.1.22), he continues to serve primarily as a commodity in Titania and Oberon's economy of exchange, enslaved to their desires. As one critic points out, '[h]e might seem little better off than Theseus' turbaned Indian slaveboys who discreetly parallel him in the opening and play scenes' (Babington 267).

Of all the scholarly readings of the Indian boy, it is perhaps those which adopt a Freudian psychoanalytic framework that are most illuminatingly placed alongside Reinhardt's cinematic reimagining. Well-acquainted with the Oedipus myth, having produced an immensely successful staging of Sophocles' *Oedipus Rex* that boasted Sigmund Freud himself as an audience member, it is more than likely that Reinhardt brought nascent psychoanalytic ideas to bear on his portrayal of the boy's relationship with Titania. The Oedipal trajectory of the male infant, forced to relinquish the mother as his primary object of desire and to submit to the all-powerful law of the father, is emphatically played out in the film: the camera lingers for some time on the boy being lulled to sleep alongside Titania in her bower before tracking his inexorable expulsion from the maternal space. That Bottom transforms into both beast and the boy's successor as surrogate child is captured at the moment when Titania wakes to see the 'vile thing' (*MND* 2.2.38) Oberon has wished on her in his vengeful fury; fixing her gaze on her new 'gentle joy' (*MND* 4.1.4), she remains oblivious to the changeling's gesturing to be picked up, setting him aside with what appears to be an entirely emotionless, even automatic, movement. The transference of maternal care is further signalled when Titania removes the boy's chaplet of flowers and places it around an ass-ear of her new love, a symbolic exchange made all the crueller by the boy's initial expectation that she is merely about to adjust it. As Bottom takes up residence in what has now become a nuptial bower, the camera cuts to a wide shot of the Prince, sitting on the forest floor in the pitch black of night, the very image of abjection and vulnerability.

Whereas in the playscript Oberon's eventual possession of the boy is entirely peaceable ('I then did ask of her her changeling child, / Which straight she gave me', *MND* 4.1.58–9), the film presents it as an opportunistic kidnapping as Oberon, on horseback, swoops him up from the ground and places him in front of him. Now subjected to the '*nom du père*', he is obliged to forego the comforts of the female realm; the diaphanous ornament placed on the boy's turbaned head by Titania is replaced with a diminutive version of Oberon's headdress, antler-like branches fitting for a regal male spirit of the forest. The Prince's inscription into the male symbolic order is managed without any trace of lasting trauma. Seemingly undaunted by Oberon's 'Dracula-like malevolence' (Hindle 28), the boy smiles admiringly at his kidnapper–saviour, sharing his amusement at the 'sweet sight' of Titania sleeping next to a donkey. A confirmed member of the order wielding primary political and social power, he accompanies Oberon as he conjures up darkness, captured in the Mendelssohnian 'Nocturne' sequence, one of the film's most admired cinematic achievements. As the sequence culminates in the capture and conquest of the First Fairy by one of Oberon's batmen, memorably choreographed in an agonistic *pas de deux*, so the viewer is left in no doubt as to Oberon's superior dominion, of which the Prince is but a small, if somewhat fetishized, part. Once Titania's 'true' perception is restored and Oberon is reinstated as the source of 'all her joy' (*MND* 2.1.27), so the changeling disappears from the screen as though into the film's unconscious.

If the film's flying fairies, slow-dissolve transformations and camera-filter effects might appear quaint and dated to the modern eye, its cinematography was undeniably pioneering for its time. So too was its visualization of the play's more sinister elements, anticipating Kottian thinking of later decades. Moreover, its playful stylistic eclecticism has come to have considerable appeal for postmodern generations of viewers and critics, making it one of the most common points of departure in academic surveys of screen Shakespeare. As observed by one university lecturer writing at the time of the *Dream*'s distribution, '[t]his is not the kind of film which will be dismissed after one viewing' (Isaacs).

Appignanesi and Brown, *Manga Shakespeare: A Midsummer Night's Dream* (2008)

From the mid-twentieth century, Shakespeare's plays have featured in various graphic artforms, ranging from brief allusions in comic books and cartoons to full-length adaptations. It would, though, take until the end of that same century for such works to become a 'respectable and [...] serious subject for study by Shakespeareans' (Wetmore 171), a scholarly engagement in step with the increasing acceptance of graphic fiction as a literary genre. That this type of multimodal production was a relative latecomer to adaptation studies could be attributed to certain perceived binaries, one being that of high and popular culture, a notoriously problematic opposition to define or validate. Comics and cartoons tend to be regarded as undemanding: entertaining material for the child reader, far removed from the demands of an author commonly held to epitomize elite literary culture. One further binary that needs to be borne in mind is that of the visual image and the written word, the latter usually occupying the privileged position. In an influential essay, primarily concerned with film adaptation of the novel, Robert Stam examines what he terms '*iconophobia*, the culturally rooted prejudice [...] that visual arts are necessarily inferior to the verbal arts; and *logophilia*, the converse valorization, characteristic of the "religions of the book," of the "sacred word" of holy texts' (58). Bringing together the drawings of the graphic artist and the text of a revered world author, the collaborative, multimodal medium of comic-book Shakespeare might be considered a formal compromise between *logos* and icon. Yet, as this section aims to demonstrate, 'reading' a graphic version of a Shakespeare play involves more than simply following two discrete semiotic systems; rather, it demands multiliteracy, the ability to read simultaneously multiple sign systems, including language, visual symbolism and the aesthetic codes of sequential art.

Launched in 2007 by SelfMadeHero, an independent publishing house specializing in visual narratives, the *Manga Shakespeare* series transposes Shakespeare's plays into the hugely successful Japanese medium of the manga comic, with transcultural adjustments, such as 'flipping' the text to read from left to right, being made for the Western reader. Reflecting on the project, its chief driving force, Emma Hayley, explains that her 'primary aim with the *Manga Shakespeare* series was to introduce teenagers or first-time readers to the work of William Shakespeare via a medium they understood', positioning the titles in the publishing market 'as entertainment rather than as primarily educational' (Hayley 268–9). As it turned out, the first titles in the series to be published were received with equal enthusiasm as 'entertainment' and as a teaching resource, with reviews praising the production team's judicious editing and congratulating them on 'trying to do in book form what film director Baz Luhrmann did on screen' (Allman). The comparison with Luhrmann's *Romeo + Juliet* would doubtless have gratified the series' editor, who had initially looked to the film as 'a prime example' (Hayley 270); the connection between the two is also a telling instance of how Shakespeare adaptations are often influenced by significant predecessors, in this case one from an entirely different medium. Yet if the *Manga Shakespeare* series follows Luhrmann's adaptive approach in keeping 'true to the original Shakespearean language' and using 'visual imagery to refashion the story for a contemporary audience' (Hayley 270), it is debatable how far it adopts what is generally seen as his postmodernist aesthetic. While reformatting Shakespearean text in comic form could be considered inherently postmodern, the declared aims of the series' pioneers veer more toward the traditionalist. In interview, the then script adapter, Richard Appignanesi, spoke of maintaining 'the spirit of the original' (Hayley 275), an ambition regarded by most Shakespeareans today as outdated in its essentialism and in its assumption of a stable 'original' text. That said, the main customer base for the series, the school student, is one that depends on a 'true-to-the-text' approach. It was surely no accident that the series was conceived during a period when, for the first time, studying a Shakespeare play was compulsory for the Key Stage 3 Standard Attainment Tests (SATs), taken by all fourteen-year-olds educated in UK-maintained schools, as well as for GCSE English: a potential market of hundreds of thousands.

A Midsummer Night's Dream was published in 2008, one of the second tranche of plays to be given the manga treatment. As with all books in the series, the first nine pages are in full colour – a divergence from the Japanese all-black-and-white manga – and serve as a kind of cast list, introducing each main character through a full- or half-length illustration labelled with a brief noun phrase defining them either by societal role ('*Egeus, a nobleman of Athens*') or amatory inclination ('*Helena, in love with Demetrius*'). Characters are further individuated by one-line quotations placed next to them on the page; taken from across the first four acts of the drama, these serve to prepare readers for the multiple strands of the plot to come: the impending marriage of Theseus and Hippolyta; Egeus' insistence that Hermia marry Demetrius; Helena's unrequited love; the discord between Oberon and Titania; Puck as 'merry wanderer'; and preparations for the workmen's play. These largely panel-free pages are spaciously laid out and appealing to the eye, a design strategy which adapts to the needs of readers likely to be coming to the play for the first time and for whom readerly pleasure will necessarily derive from the adaptation's immediate appeal and not, as is the case with other works featured in this book, from a knowing *intertextual* appreciation.

In common with film or stage directors, those collaborating on each manga Shakespeare must engage with the transcultural negotiations involved in adapting an early modern text for the here-and-now. Past, present and future time settings are all represented in the *Manga Shakespeare* series, though in the case of the *Dream*, the approach is somewhat more eclectic. Described by Hayley as being set in 'an alternate modern-day Athens' (275), the courtly characters are costumed in a mix of ancient Greek and modern Western clothing, thus eschewing the Elizabethan dress which, according to Richard Burt, is the default choice of numerous comic-book Shakespeares, one that renders them 'among the most conservative in any medium' (Burt, vol. 1, 10). Although the toga-like features of the costumes serve to keep the original historical setting in focus, it is the modern that carries the greater weight of signification. If some markers of the contemporary world (popcorn, post-it notes, trainers) are included solely to promote a sense of familiarity, others are crucial to the adaptation's overall design and interpretation. The motif of the screen, for example, threads together the three classes of the play. The court's imposing television monitors (which double as panels in the graphic representation of Egeus' 'complaint') seem to function as a means of surveillance, of keeping a watchful eye on the rebellious young courtiers. And the artisans' rather more modest wall-mounted screen, albeit hampered by less-than-perfect reception, keeps them up to date with the progress of their drama 'pitch'. Yet it is the fairy creatures that have the ultimate overview: in a wordless panel at the foot of page 138, Robin and Oberon are sketched sitting in front of a cinema screen, the former insouciantly throwing popcorn into his mouth, savouring the 'fond pageant' of earth-bound mortals (*MND* 3.2.114), while the latter puts his head in his hand, a gesture of exasperation at his servant's bungling. This is just one of many instances where the manga *Dream*'s illustrator, Kate Brown, evokes the relationship between the human and fairy worlds in a way that takes full advantage of the comic-book medium. Elsewhere, the reader is encouraged to 'see' the supernatural through the eyes of both sceptic and believer: Cupid is depicted both as a stone classical icon on an Athenian fountain (Appignanesi and Brown 37) and as a live, animate creature 'all armed' (62); Titania and Oberon are pictured as two sculpted figures on a musical box (199), as if trapped and controlled by the human world, and, three pages later, in a lifelike embrace, with the three pairs of earthly lovers pictured entwined, perhaps even captured, in Titania's typically manga tresses.

In what might be viewed as hankering after a fidelity to a more established form of adaptation, the *Manga Shakespeare* series is commonly praised for its proximation to experiencing the plays on stage or screen. Graphic adaptations of drama are often viewed as more capable of evoking the experience of live performance than a word-by-word reading of the playtext: the reader has the characters inked out in front of them, and their actions, words, emotions and relationships can be expressed through techniques unique to the comic book, such as panelling, speech balloons and noise words. In the manga *Dream*, the emotional excesses and torturous wrangling of both human and fairy lovers are visually evoked through the relative shapes, sizes and positioning of the panels. One instance is the three panels which occupy the lower section of page 19. With Hermia depicted in the centre, the two rival lovers on either side of her, the narrowness of the panels conveys a sense of the patriarchal boundaries recently reinforced by Egeus and the Duke, while the lack of lined borders anticipates the dreamlike experiences that await the lovers when they leave the societal restrictions of the city to venture into the wild domain of the wood. Likewise, the shape, outline and size of the speech balloons help to convey tone, feeling and volume, with jagged edges often employed to indicate extreme emotions such as anger or despair. When, in the play's first scene, Hermia is called upon to defend her choice of lover, the angular oblongs containing the speeches of Theseus and Egeus, both male authority figures, are in visual contrast to the softer curved balloons that hold the pleading of the disempowered female (see pages 20–1, for example). The manga convention of 'emanata' further promotes a sense of characters in action: the polysemic symbol of the droplet can represent at once Demetrius' sweat as he beats a hasty retreat from Helena (70), Helena's tears of frustration when she fears she is being mocked by Lysander and Demetrius (130) and Bottom's excitement at hearing that his company's play is 'preferred' (176). The comic medium also has recourse to techniques commonly associated with film: figural positioning within panels resembles the composition of camera shots, and the graphic artist can manipulate perspectives in a manner akin to the cinematographer. In the manga *Dream*, Oberon and Titania's disputatiousness is pictured in a similar manner to reverse-shot filming (59), while the rivalry between Lysander and Demetrius is established in panels framing the two of them side by side, the comic-book equivalent of a medium two-shot (24).

Perhaps the biggest challenge for the mangaka tasked with transcoding Shakespearean drama is how to present lengthy monologues and soliloquies. Dividing the speeches into appropriately sized snippets and the sequencing of moment-to-moment transitions between panels must be carefully managed if the reader's attention is to be held. In the case of the soliloquy which ends the *Dream*'s first scene (*MND* 1.1.226–51), the illustrator and editor of the manga version succeed in conveying the main import and mood of Helena's first solo speech in just two graphic pages (Appignanesi and Brown 37–8). The speech is cut by more than half: the final six lines, crucial for the action to come, are retained almost word for word, while lines expressing the transformative power of love, one of the most complex themes of the play (and perhaps the most intractable to graphic representation), are removed. Helena's downcast state is tellingly presented in a half-page drawing of her seated on the base of a water fountain, head bowed in desolation, with the bouquet of flowers that has formed part of her costuming up to this point lying discarded beside her, a visual metaphor for Demetrius' refusal to acknowledge her beauty. Underneath this image of Helena in the immediate present is a triptych of narrow panels, two of which take us back to the time when Demetrius 'hailed down oaths' of love for her, a past relationship captured in the image of a locket on a chain (presumably a love token from Demetrius). Divided and broken by the gutter between two panels, the locket itself lies open and empty in the right-hand panel, a symbol of lost love. This temporal shift is further indicated by Helena's recollections of past times being placed in speech bubbles within the panels, while the interiority of her present soliloquizing is conveyed through lines presented directly on the page.

All Shakespeare adaptations are to a lesser or greater extent shaped by the limitations of the medium in which they are created. In the case of the manga *Dream*, it is perhaps something of an irony that the limitations of the comic-book form are more evident in its treatment of the play's comedy than in its depiction of the emotional turmoil of the lovers, with noise words such as 'thwak', 'shuff', 'thud' and 'yoink' doing little to generate the kind of hilarity easily produced on stage. Yet to judge the comic-book version by the same criteria as the theatre is to neglect what Will Eisner, the inventor of the graphic novel and an influential theorist of his own work, regards as the 'unique aesthetics of sequential art'. The manga adaptation allows the reader's eye to roam freely over the individual page, as well as back and forth across the text, taking in the story solely through pictures or through a combination of word and image, a readerly freedom that makes for a stimulating cognitive and imaginative encounter with Shakespeare.

4

Romeo and Juliet

Of all Shakespeare's plays, *Romeo and Juliet* is probably the most firmly embedded in the popular consciousness, its familiarity stemming from a complex interaction of educational, cultural and commercial forces. This chapter explores the diverse ways in which the tragedy's recognizability has been exploited to create adaptations ranging from drama commissioned by the Royal Shakespeare Company to children's animation to user-generated productions on YouTube.

Shakespeare: The Animated Tales (1992–4)

Altering literary texts to suit the needs of children is a little-trodden area of adaptation studies, with critical attention being largely fixed on adaptations of notable historical significance. Such neglect could be put down to the overt purposiveness of the reworking being perceived as precluding any real subtlety of process or outcome, making it undeserving of scholarly attention. Yet, as this section seeks to demonstrate, analysing Shakespeare for young people involves engaging with some of the key concerns of adaptation theory along with the complex web of political, educational and cultural conditions in which rewritings for children are produced. Deborah Cartmell asserts that '[w]hen it comes to adaptations of children's literature, the battle between film and literature seems to be at its most ferocious'

('Adapting' 168), a disputatiousness that might be attributed to anxieties over literacy standards and the substitution of what is often seen as less challenging, and thus inferior, versions of the 'original' works. With Shakespeare currently the only compulsory author on the UK school curriculum, as well as in many other jurisdictions, film versions of his plays are more than usually prone to sparking controversy; *Shakespeare: The Animated Tales* is one such example. Broadcast in two six-part series in 1992 and 1994, the *Tales* were co-produced by the Welsh television network S4C and the Soyuzmultfilm Studios in Moscow, with animators working with three main techniques: cel animation, oil on glass and puppetry. Leon Garfield, whose first volume of *Shakespeare Stories* (1985) had proved a mainstay of children's canonical reading, was tasked with scripting the *Tales* so that each film conformed to a running time of just under thirty minutes. This transmedial project, which included illustrated play scripts, was overseen by an advisory panel, including the esteemed Shakespearean scholar Stanley Wells and the academic Rex Gibson, whose 'Shakespeare in Schools' project had revitalized the way Shakespeare's plays were studied in secondary classrooms.

If and when children should encounter Shakespeare's plays are long-debated questions. Nowadays, it tends to be assumed that knowing about Shakespeare confers 'cultural capital', a term introduced in the 1970s by the French sociologist Pierre Bourdieu (1930–2002) and which appears with increasing frequency in twenty-first-century mainstream educational discourse (albeit in a manner that fails to acknowledge its Marxist influences). A case in point can be found in the introduction to a recent collection of essays about primary-level teaching, which states that knowing Shakespeare is 'seen as one of the key markers of a good education by influential people' and 'can help you to feel part of the culture of the powerful' (Winston and Tandy 5). The idea of Shakespeare as a socio-cultural gatekeeper was very much in the political consciousness when the *Tales* were under development in the early 1990s. The introduction of a National Curriculum by the then Conservative government, and with it the compulsory study and assessment of Shakespeare at the ages of fourteen and sixteen, saw head-on clashes between cultural materialist academics and those who sought to preserve and disseminate the 'literary heritage'. As one scholar reflected: 'While the academics were advocating letting Shakespeare rest in peace, the Conservatives had long been trying to enlist him into their party' (King 205). That the patron of the *Tales* project was none other than the Prince of Wales might have positioned it firmly on the traditionalist side of the argument; however, the project's choice of animation as the adaptive medium – a form commonly placed at the 'popular' end of the cultural spectrum – lent it a more radical edge. Reviewing the series for a leading children's books journal, Peter Thomas, a secondary English teacher implacably opposed to the government's 'enshrining of Shakespeare', hailed the *Tales* as 'a ray of light', judging them 'performances with their own artistic integrity' (Garfield and Thomas 37), well-suited to a video-oriented generation.

But if the project's choice of adaptive art form embraced the rapidly developing audio-visual technologies of the late twentieth century, its unquestioning commitment to the 'timeless' qualities of the plays looked back to the liberal humanist tradition that literary theorists of the 1980s had sought to dismantle. Similarly belated was its assumption that any reworking of Shakespeare would be subordinate to the 'real thing'. Marketed as a kind of milk-teeth Shakespeare, the *Tales* seemed to reinforce the traditional evaluation of a work of adaptation as 'secondary and inferior' (Hutcheon, *Theory of Adaptation* xiv). Some people involved in the project were keen to stress the inadequacy of their own artistic efforts when compared with Shakespeare's 'genius'. Garfield, for example, chose the metaphor of physical dismemberment to describe the damage done to the pre-text in the editing process: 'every cut was to the play's detriment; all I could possibly hope to do was staunch the flow of blood from the wounds, and leave a little life in the lacerated remains' (Garfield and Thomas 36). Nonetheless, the blurb for the 2005 DVD box-set praised Garfield's scripts as 'masterly abridged renditions [...] fully faithful to [Shakespeare's] narrative and language', confirming that the end product justified the scriptwriter's avowed editorial brutality and underlining textual fidelity as the desideratum of the adaptive enterprise. And, indeed, while some scholars endeavour to 'jettison fidelity as a main criterion to evaluate adaptations [for children]' (A. Müller 1), a good proportion of the academic writing on the series has turned ineluctably to gauging how much of Shakespeare's text remains intact.

Romeo and Juliet, dir. Efim Gambourg (1992)

Romeo and Juliet, one of four tragedies included in the *Tales*, was doubtless chosen for its dateless appeal for the young – not to mention its curricular ubiquity. Described by one critic as 'a very pretty cartoon' (Osborne 110), Efim Gambourg's cel animation is perhaps the safest, most Disney-like of the twelve and one in which the curbs and checks, put in place with the child spectator in mind, are especially evident. First among these is the limited running time, managed by extensive cutting and the filmic staple of the voiceover to transport the viewer from one event or place to another: the audio-visual equivalent of the narrator employed in the seminal *Tales from Shakespeare* (1807), prose versions of the plays written by Charles and Mary Lamb. It must also be said that the Lambs' characterizing of Shakespeare's collected works as a 'manly book' seems to have persisted into the late twentieth century. Only three of the twelve *Animated Tales* are steered by female narrators and, of these three, *Romeo and Juliet* is the only tragedy, a gender distribution not unlike that found in the Shakespearean textual editing culture of the early 1990s. That a woman is allowed the authority divested in the narrator in this instance is perhaps on account of *Romeo and Juliet* being outside A. C. Bradley's 'four principal tragedies' and the only one devoted primarily to the 'unmanly' theme of romantic love. In effect, the non-diegetic narrative voice tends to detract from the immediacy of the moving images, not helped by Garfield's oddly minimal use of the present historic tense – potentially a useful grammatical strategy for injecting a sense of the moment. That the 'telling' mode so frequently asserts itself over the 'showing' mode has attracted some critical unease, not least because the *Tales*' privileging of story over language or character, on account of its being the most accessible and engaging element for children, sits uncomfortably with the fact that it is also the least unique to Shakespeare. As one academic commentator explains, 'there is major irony in this sort of construction […] for the obvious reason that very few of the stories told by Shakespeare are actually Shakespeare's stories' (Semenza, 'Teens' 63). In this respect, then, the *Tales* might be considered unintentional reappropriations of pre-Shakespearean literatures.

Like the Lambs before him, Garfield was committed to preserving as much Shakespearean language as feasible within the constraints of scripting for young audiences. With children generally presumed to have shorter attention spans and lower boredom thresholds than adults, the *Tales* needed to compel and retain the interest of the young viewer, hence the excision of soliloquies and monologues such as Mercutio's Queen Mab speech. The roles of both the Nurse and the Friar are significantly reduced in ways that make them less morally questionable. The former is retained largely for comic effect, with anything that might be construed as self-serving pragmatism, such as her recommendation that Juliet enter a bigamous relationship with Paris, being erased. Likewise, the voiceover's repeated references to the 'good Friar' preclude any wondering about the disinterestedness of his motives or whether he is not being rather cowardly in leaving Juliet alone with her dead husband in the Capulet tomb. Also edited out is much of the play's distinctive verbal imagery, though some is evoked instead through the visual semiotics of animation. As Abigail Rokison observes of the series generally, '[t]he mood, tone and themes of the plays are enhanced not only by the mode and style of animation but also by the dense visual imagery which augments and sometimes replaces the imagery of the texts' (136). In the case of Gambourg's *Romeo and Juliet*, the image of the moon, ominously clouding over once the lovers dedicate themselves to each other, stands in for some of the premonitory speeches; Juliet's picking up and then placing on her own face the mask that Romeo drops when retreating from the Capulet ball signals succinctly both their union and its enforced secrecy; and the red rose Romeo holds in his hand as he tries, and subsequently fails, to stem the violence that erupts between Mercutio and Tybalt is visually suggestive of the hero's fear that Juliet's beauty has made him 'effeminate' (*RJ* 3.1.116).

A major imperative of adapting Shakespeare for school-age audiences is the removal of overtly sexual content. Fumigating the Shakespearean text to make it age-appropriate is a well-established practice, initiated as far back as the early nineteenth century. In the same years that that the Lambs were cleaning up Shakespeare for their model reader, so another brother–sister partnership, Henrietta and Thomas Bowdler, was preparing *Family Shakespeare*: deodorized versions of the plays deemed fit for women and children. Two centuries later, Garfield's sanitizing of *Romeo and Juliet* involved stripping out bawdy innuendo, such as that bandied back and forth by Samson and Gregory; however, given the linguistic knottiness of so much early modern sexual word-play, this particular editorial strategy may well have been driven as much by the exigencies of comprehensibility as by a safeguarding censorship. Nonetheless, the strain of male sexual aggression found in instances such as Samson's threat to 'thrust [...] maids to the wall' (*RJ* 1.1.16–17) and Mercutio's envisioning of Mab teaching virgins how to 'bear' (*RJ* 1.4.93) a man's weight during sex has become increasingly inimical to modern sensibilities, so that teachers presenting Shakespeare through the *Tales* might well be grateful for its absence.

If this international animation project came close to being derailed by an attempted coup against Gorbachev, it was also momentarily disrupted by a clash of artistic vision regarding how the lovers' wedding night should be handled. According to the *Sunday Times*, the Russian director 'alarmed his British co-producers with his insistence that the eventual consummation of the star-crossed lovers' passion should be seen in all its naked intensity' (Dickson 61). The final cut suggests that a compromise was reached: it *does* show the two unclothed, except that only Romeo appears to have nipples, and the transcendent sexual ecstasy of the moment is chastely suggested by superimposed floating images of the lovers, shown at one point in the company of Cupid. Of course, there is no direct representation of sexual consummation in the early modern version, and it is noteworthy that, in the picture-book edition of the abridged scripts, Garfield follows the established Shakespearean text closely in having the lovers appear '*aloft at the window*' (*RJ* 3.5) – and fully clothed. In fact, here, as in several other instances (Mercutio's playful teasing of the Nurse; the physical appearance of the young male characters; Juliet's mane of hair covering her nakedness in the marital bed), Gambourg's visuals seem as much influenced by Zeffirelli's film adaptation as by the Shakespearean script. That said, the animated film is less inclined to linger on the lovers' physical passion than is its 1960s filmic predecessor; their embraces are captured in distancing long or medium shots, and whereas in Zeffirelli's version the dying Juliet falls (with unfeasible elegance) on the body of her husband, the animated tale pictures them lying separately side by side.

If, as the *Tales'* director, Dave Edwards, claimed, animating Shakespeare was intended to 'attract 11–15 year-olds' (quoted in Bottoms 6), its main success has been in reaching pre-teens, whose palimpsestic memory is more readily in tune with the chosen medium. As far as the Shakespeare classroom is concerned, Baz Luhrmann's exuberantly postmodern film adaptation, released just two years after the second *Animated Tales* series, has long occupied the top spot – though with director Spike Lee's hip-hop film version of *Romeo and Juliet* on the horizon, it remains to be seen how long it will remain there.

Ben Power, *A Tender Thing* (2009)

In an influential psychoanalytic reading of *Romeo and Juliet*, Julia Kristeva poses the question: 'What if [the lovers] had escaped their persecutors, and once the clans' hatred had been appeased, they experienced the normal existence of married couples?' (75). As a postscript that imagines Juliet and Romeo staying alive and married into old age, *A Tender Thing* might stand as a dramatized response to Kristeva's 'what if?' Power's script is composed almost entirely of lines taken from *Romeo and Juliet*, lines that the author rearranges, reassigns and occasionally rewrites to create an elegiac theatrical depiction of an ageing couple as they move towards a euthanasic *Liebestod*. First performed by the RSC at Northern Stage, Newcastle (2009), and then at the Swan Theatre, Stratford-upon-Avon, as part of the World Shakespeare Festival (2012), Power's transformation of what is conceivably the most famous story of youthful passion into one of mature married love might be credited with setting an adaptive trend. In *Juliet and Her Romeo* (2010), a stage adaptation by Sean O'Connor and Tom Morris, the co-adapters take a similar approach to Power in rearranging Shakespeare's lines and recontextualizing the love story to focus on the elderly. Set in a Verona care home, the play reframes and reverses the power dynamic of the pre-text so that it is the daughter, the Goneril-like Ms Capulet, who, fearing for her inheritance, objects to her mother marrying Romeo, a patient on the ward designated for impoverished geriatrics. And in 2014, *The Last of Romeo and Juliet*, written and directed by Mitchell Cushman, premiered in Toronto. As with *Juliet and Her Romeo*, Cushman's adaptation reorders Shakespeare's lines to fit the context of a retirement home, where the objections of the residents' uncaring, money-grabbing children stand in the way of late-life romance. Describing himself as a 'text doctor in the old-fashioned John Barton way' (Edwardes), Power, for all his relative youth (he was in his late twenties when *A Tender Thing* premiered), is already an adept at remoulding literary 'greats' into new, sometimes radical, shapes, reworking for the stage texts as diverse as Milton's *Paradise Lost* and Wilde's *Salome*, and writing screenplays for two series of the BBC's *The Hollow Crown*. Yet of all the canonical works he has treated, *Romeo and Juliet* arguably brought the heaviest weight of expectation and, concomitantly, the opportunity to defamiliarize the play in new and exciting ways. Scanning theatre reviews of *A Tender Thing* reveals how far what Power describes as his 'remix' of the play (Royal Shakespeare Company) can disorientate spectators. Lyn Gardner, for instance, likened seeing the play to 'walking into a room you thought you knew well, only to discover that the walls have been painted a different colour and the furniture moved around'. This dislocating effect is primarily achieved through what is sometimes labelled 'collage', an adaptive technique most readily associated with the iconoclastic Charles Marowitz, whose irreverent rearrangements of Shakespeare's plays sparked outrage in some quarters of the British theatre establishment. Writing in the 1970s, Marowitz claimed that the 're-structuring of a work, the characters and situations of which are widely known, is an indirect way of making contact with that work's essence' (12). Marowitz's notion of a play's 'essence', while in some ways adrift from modern-day critical approaches, is also discernible in Power's claim that his twenty-first-century Shakespearean collage retains the 'pulse' (Royal Shakespeare Company) running through the prior version. Certainly, *A Tender Thing* matches the speedy pace of *Romeo and Juliet*, albeit that the hectic travel from love at first sight to teenage suicide is replaced by the rapid deterioration of an ageing Juliet, afflicted by an unspecified degenerative illness and, consequently, desperate to end her life with the dignity afforded by euthanasia. Also preserved is the circular structure and teleological drive of the early modern tragedy. Power retains both prologue and epilogue, joining the two together through staging: both scenes feature '*a large bed*', the dancing couple and the movement of the sea, evoked by means of video back-projections in recent productions.

That *A Tender Thing* is composed using lines from *Romeo and Juliet* – mixed occasionally with lines from a handful of the *Sonnets* and a song from *Twelfth Night* – also keeps a Shakespearean 'pulse' beating. Yet it is precisely the presence of this familiar metrical beat that proves disorienting. Akin to watching moving images with two soundtracks playing simultaneously, encountering the play onstage is at once a disorienting and exhilarating experience – and more so for anyone highly familiar with the language of Shakespeare's version. Indeed, the extent of the spectator's textual memory will substantially shape how it is received as an adaptation, as individuals are pulled between watching the play as 'completely its own thing' (Royal Shakespeare Company) and attempting to hold onto well-known lines, now resituated, reassigned and occasionally supplemented by the adapter. Anchoring the dialogue of Power's play in its Shakespearean foundation proved a perilous business for some theatre journalists. *The Guardian*'s reviewer was not alone in the erroneous belief that 'the words are all Shakespeare's' (Hickling), with one critic assuming Juliet's plea to Romeo to help her 'end this unnatural decay' to be Shakespearean when it is, in fact, one of several lines composed by the modernizer (see Tripney). This critical 'mishearing' challenges any notion that Shakespearean language possesses some unique quality or 'essence' intuitable by an expert ear; it also underlines how seeing Power's drama unfold in a playing-time of around half that of its early modern predecessor is a very different experience from a reading of the playscript, especially one with a copy of *Romeo and Juliet* to hand.

Close attention to a portion of *A Tender Thing* uncovers the various compositional strategies by which Power transforms *Romeo and Juliet* to evoke how the elderly commonly experience a simultaneity of youth and age in mind, if not in body. Take, for example, the slightly abridged passage below:

JULIET
Many a morning have I seen you here,
With tears augmenting the fresh morning dew.
[...]
Tell me, what sadness lengthens Romeo's hours?

ROMEO
What, shall I groan and tell thee?

JULIET
Your looks are pale and wild, and do import
Some misadventure.

ROMEO
'Tis nothing, love, but that my mind misgives
Some consequence yet hanging in the stars.
I dreamed a dream tonight ...

JULIET
Be ruled by me, forget to think on it.

ROMEO
O, teach me how I should forget to think!

JULIET
By giving liberty unto thy soul.
Come, gentle Romeo, we must have you dance!

ROMEO
Not I, believe me. You have dancing shoes
With nimble soles, I have a soul of lead
So stakes me to the ground I cannot move.
I am past my dancing days.

JULIET [*trying to lift him up to dance*]
You are a lover; borrow Cupid's wings,
And soar with them above a common bound.

ROMEO
I am too sore inflicted with these thoughts,
These dreams and visions of unnatural death,
To soar with his light feathers, and so bound,
I cannot bound a pitch above dull woe:
Under death's heavy burden do I sink.

(Power 16–18)

Taken from near the beginning of Scene 2, this dialogue comes a little over one-third of the way through the play, by which point Juliet is beginning to show distinct signs of physical deterioration. Here, a conversation about Romeo's gloomy anxiety, brought on by his wife's failing health, is formed for the most part from lines transposed from early scenes of *Romeo and Juliet*, when the hero is still pining for Rosaline. This creative collision of exuberant youthful feeling and the graver, deeper emotion of old age is one of many examples whereby 'the play invites its audience to recall and rewrite *Romeo and Juliet*, playing tricks with collective memory by destabilizing the familiar and substituting new memories through the distorted life history of Power's characters' (Kirwan 250). So, then, the audience must realign the self-dramatizing Petrarchan 'groan' of the teenage courtly lover, with its erotic connotations, to fit the world-weary senescent husband's fear of the 'consequence yet hanging in the stars': his wife's as-yet-undiagnosed terminal illness. To ease this realignment, Power makes one of many textual interventions, exchanging Shakespeare's 'love's heavy burden' (*RJ* 1.4.22) for 'death's heavy burden'; if love and death meet with untimely haste in *Romeo and Juliet*, their meeting in *A Tender Thing* follows a more prolonged, less dramatic trajectory.

One of the defining recreative strategies of Power's two-hander is his reassigning to the hero and heroine lines from almost every character in *Romeo and Juliet*. In some instances, the lovers deliver words allocated to their partner in the Shakespearean text, a two-way exchange that suggests the linguistic convergence that can develop over the course of a long marriage; in others, the lovers deliver speeches formerly assigned to personages of a different sex, age or social class. In this extract alone, Juliet delivers lines from the parts of Montague, Benvolio, Mercutio and Balthazar, with the majority being drawn from Mercutio, one of the Shakespearean characters most frequently re-embodied in the heroine. This particular textual transfer was singled out as gratuitous by some theatre critics: the *Telegraph*'s Dominic Cavendish quipped that assigning Juliet the Queen Mab speech (placed a few lines after the extract printed here) was 'a stroke that feels barely less sacrilegious than handing Macbeth's "All our yesterdays" speech to the Porter'. Leaving aside Cavendish's odd choice of textual equivalence, his mention of sacrilege reveals why this literary transposition proved so jarring. Detaching one of the most regularly anthologized speeches in the Shakespearean canon from its sixteenth-century context is clearly a more noticeable, some might say audacious, distortion of the hypotext than would be the case with a more obscure passage. And yet, as the given extract illustrates, Mercutio's words seem to rest easily in Juliet's mouth, both in terms of Power's portrayal of her as a mercurial, free-spirited woman and in the dramatic context of a wife trying every means she can think of to revive her husband's flagging spirits.

Moving beyond the printed passage, another of the play's remarked-upon reallocations is Juliet's mourning for the 'prettiest babe that e'er was seen' (Power 20), an emotional burden carried by the Nurse in Shakespeare's version. This redistribution of past suffering adds an extra dimension to the couple's enduring union; far from having lived 'blissfully through adulthood together', as one literary critic sees it (Bennett 698), this is a couple that has weathered one of the most testing life experiences imaginable: the death of a child. It is a trauma that threatens to divide husband and wife, as they each deal with the loss in very different ways. In Power's dramatic reassembling, Juliet speaks the Nurse's recollection of her daughter's birth, toddlerhood and death in Scene 3 and once again in Scene 4, a repetition that drives home the impossibility of putting such a memory to rest. Romeo, on the other hand, obdurately refuses to engage with it. In the final stage of her illness, Juliet pulls away from him, demanding, in the words of Shakespeare's Lady Capulet, '[W]here's my daughter?' (Power 30) before recounting once more the deceased child's babyhood; unwilling or unable to witness such raw maternal grief, Romeo tells her abruptly 'hold thy peace' and 'stint thou' (31). As one academic observes, '[b]y aligning Lady Capulet, the Nurse and the two Juliets in this moment, Power turns Shakespeare's brief mention of a lost child into an emotional polyvocal cry' (Kirwan 251), perhaps achieving here his declared intention of finding 'the moments in the text where what was being talked about was universal' (Royal Shakespeare Company).

In *Romeo and Juliet*, the impetuous energy of youth is set against the physical deterioration that comes with increasing age. Capulet's wife mocks her older husband's call for his 'long sword' (*RJ* 1.1.73), insisting that a man of his years would be better off calling for a crutch, while her daughter, impatient to hear how the Nurse has fared in arranging her marriage, characterizes the elderly as '[u]nwieldy, slow, heavy and pale as lead' (*RJ* 2.5.17). Power's collage, though, resists any simple youth–age binary, portraying a senior couple who, despite increasing infirmity, retain a youthful spirit, manifested in their staged dance movements. In the extract printed here, the elderly Romeo speaks Capulet's line 'I am past my dancing days', a verbal reassignment that takes on a sharp edge of foreboding in Power's recontextualization: Juliet's illness will soon bring an abrupt halt to the couple's playful choreography as the physical intimacy of dancing is replaced by that of the sick bed. Only at the close of the Epilogue, when the drama circles back to present the lovers as flirtatious young strangers once more, does their dancing recommence. The final stage direction, *'She takes his hand and they begin to dance. The sea engulfs them'* (Power 39), leaves the play open to multiple readings. Is this the commencement of a blissful afterlife? A moment of obliteration? A dramatic rendering of the theory of eternal recurrence?

As a theatrical collage, *A Tender Thing* is a striking example of what Julie Sanders describes as '[t]he purposeful reassembly of fragments to form a new whole' (*Adaptation* 6). An illuminating and dramatically compelling dialogue between old and new, Power's reutilizing of Shakespeare's lines creates a fresh, contemporary vantage point: elderly marital relationships lived out at a time when increasing life expectancy poses dilemmas barely thought of in Shakespeare's day.

Romeo and Juliet on YouTube

The technological development of social media platforms has substantially altered how Shakespeare is promoted, viewed and interpreted. Since the first shaky video was uploaded in April 2005, YouTube has grown into the major video-sharing platform, currently estimated as being visited by 1.9 billion logged-in users per month. In the words of Barbara Hodgdon, YouTube is at once 'a library and laboratory for playing with Shakespeare' ('(You)Tube' 327), giving free access to a wealth of Shakespearean screen and stage performances, as well as to creative responses to the plays and poems. With algorithms in charge of promoting and demoting what is offered up to the viewer, a basic search for a Shakespeare play returns a heterogenous mass of productions, with established theatre companies such as the RSC and the Globe rubbing frames with high-school projects and irreverent mashups. As such, the site appears to be a democratic space where the usual boundaries of 'high' and 'popular' culture are broken down – or at least made porous.

The profound impact that YouTube has had on Shakespeare studies has not gone uncharted by academics, with Stephen O'Neill's *Shakespeare and YouTube* (2014) providing the first full-length study of the platform. In this important contribution to the field of digital humanities, O'Neill explores the tensions between YouTube's apparent openness to user-created material and the commercial drivers of the company; he also underscores the difficulties of researching and writing about a site which is, by its very nature, always in flux. Restrictions around areas such as the default length of video uploads or copyright legislation substantially curb the practices of the creative YouTuber, while the impermanent nature of the archive renders problematic scholarly conventions such as referencing and footnoting. Most academics who have published studies of YouTube Shakespeare are, by virtue of their research engagement, predisposed to recognizing its significance for the academy and its value as a teaching and learning tool. Christy Desmet believes that YouTube's infrastructure 'encourages sharp comparisons and pointed revisions with each successive video that is uploaded' (65), and Ayanna Thompson finds value in 'the opportunity for dialogue and debate across the borders of nation, race, ethnicity, sexuality, age, class, physical ability, and education' ('Unmooring' 356). But even the most avid exponents of YouTube acknowledge that its mantra of 'Broadcast Yourself' can result in a morass of mediocre material, some of which is execrably bad. Luke McKernan, whose BardBox blog was the first systematic attempt to gather noteworthy Shakespeare-related videos, although convinced that YouTube is 'the natural home for the Bard', also acknowledges that it is overrun with 'truly lame Shakespeare raps, *Star Wars* parodies, hopeless audition pieces and overwrought recitations'.

At the time of writing, a 'relevance' search for 'Shakespeare *Romeo and Juliet*' reveals a preponderance of student-oriented uploads, especially summaries of the entire play or of individual scenes. Performance videos include a full-length version of the critically panned 2013 film adaptation, directed by Carlo Carlei, and, somewhat surprisingly, the 2010 Globe production of *Romeo and Juliet*, filmed for Globe on Screen, a subscription-only site; there are also snippets from RSC productions and an abridgement of the entire play, as performed by the Reduced Shakespeare Company. Fan remixes of Baz Luhrmann's 1996 film adaptation are in abundance, as are remediations of Franco Zeffirelli's 1968 version, several of which make explicit the homoeroticism that academic critics have tended to read as merely subtextual. Two such examples are *Benvolio/Mercutio: I would have loved You all my life*, published on 3 January 2014 by McFif (6,669 views), and *Benvolio X Mercutio; too cold*, published on 23 April 2017 by yoonmini (3,564 views). Both remixers queer the relationship between Benvolio and Mercutio, disrupting the film's chronology and alternating Zeffirelli's sumptuous vibrant colours with their own black and white, a type of reverse-colourization process. Yet for all their commonalities, the versions differ distinctly in atmosphere thanks to the popular music tracks selected by the videographers. Set to the plaintive strains of Ryan Star's 'Losing Your Memory', McFif's film represents the gay relationship as 'one that dare not speak its name'; conversely, yoonmini's selection of The Neighbourhood's upbeat alt-rock track 'Sweater Weather' – although jarringly incongruous with the film shots of violent male deaths – has the effect of making Zeffirelli's beautiful young men appear as if from the Pride era. The song lyrics from these user-selected tracks are the only words in evidence (heard on the soundtrack and read in snippets on the screen), any link with Shakespeare relying solely on the viewer's familiarity with Zeffirelli's film adaptation. The remainder of this section fixes attention on two further user-created adaptations, which also engage the spectator with *Romeo and Juliet* without recourse to any of its words.

Romeo and Juliet: A Silent Film Finished Version

Early screen Shakespeare is currently a subject of considerable scholarly interest, albeit confined to the relatively few surviving films of the era. YouTube stores several authentic silent films but none of *Romeo and Juliet* (the researcher would need to seek out more specialist film sites to access those still watchable). As if in response to this absence, some YouTubers have produced their own ersatz silent *Romeo and Juliet*s, reworking Shakespeare's text for a transmedial genre of a bygone era in a way that is fitting for contemporary YouTube culture: a creative process involving multiple adaptive considerations.

Romeo and Juliet: A Silent Film Finished Version, published on 24 April 2016 by Frankie Thompson (1,163 views), is an eight-minute video that imitates some of the more obvious conventions of the silent movie. Set to the music score of Charlie Chaplin's *The Kid* – a silent cinema classic – it is filmed in black and white, punctuated by intertitles, employs frequent iris shots and is performed with much extravagant gesture and mumming. At the same time, it draws on contemporary YouTube Shakespeares, such as The Geeky Blonde's popular *Condensed Shakespeare* series. Thompson follows The Geeky Blonde (Rhiannon McGavin) in acting all the key roles herself, distinguishing between characters by means of hats, coats and scarves, only departing from alternating one-shots for Romeo's death scene, when she fakes a two-shot through synecdoche: Romeo gazes at a Juliet represented by an absurdly curly wig lying on the sofa-cum-tomb. And just as The Geeky Blonde uses her own home as performance space, so Thompson films in what appears to be her own living quarters; a bedroom mural (a Rousseauesque forest scene) serves as backdrop for the Capulet orchard and a reproduction of Edvard Munch's *The Scream*, hanging on the wall outside Juliet's bedroom, foreshadows the Nurse's screams on discovering the apparently dead bride-to-be. Also comparable with The Geeky Blonde productions is Thompson's use of anachronism for parodic effect, though the absence of spoken dialogue means that this is necessarily done through screen props and intertitles. A bottle of child-friendly Piriton (an over-the-counter syrup administered to relieve hay fever symptoms) stands as both the Friar's drug and Romeo's poison, its tempered potency played on for comic effect when, in the final scene, Juliet struggles not with the fact that Romeo has drunk all the draught and left 'no friendly drop' (*RJ* 5.3.163), but with the 'Bloody child-proof bottle[s]' (quoted from intertitle). Similarly bathetic is Romeo's refusal to accept Juliet's invitation to join her on the balcony on account of his 'bad back' (quoted from intertitle). Yet where The Geeky Blonde intersperses action with frequent, sometimes sustained, Shakespearean quotation, Thompson employs only the first two words and concluding couplet of the play to bookend her comic appropriation. Intertitles are in modern English, functioning as narrative links or as a means of characterization; we are told that Juliet is 'innocent' and the

Friar is 'cunning' – perhaps the closest the piece gets to critical interpretation. Even when Thompson mouths words to the camera, they are in the demotic, so Romeo's response to having murdered Tybalt is not 'O, I am fortune's fool' (*RJ* 3.1.138) but 'Shit, shit'. Like most Tuber-creatives, Thompson is working under the technological constraints of a video-sharing platform, including time limitations akin to those of early silent filmmakers (a 'one-reeler' lasted around ten minutes). Yet where producers of the first Shakespeare films went about compressing a whole play into a narrow timeframe with pioneering zeal, Thompson does so with postmodern cynicism. There is nothing of the fan in this treatment; rather, there is a distinctly irreverent take on both the romantic idealism that has built up around the play's doomed lovers and the iconic status of their creator. As one intertitle states, as if in exasperation at the convoluted nature of the tragic action, 'Will this play never end?'

Romeo & Juliet Short Animation

There is no shortage of animated Shakespeare on YouTube, from stop frame animation using Lego or clay figures to clips from commercially marketed series such as *Shakespeare: The Animated Tales*. *Romeo & Juliet Short Animation* (559,659 views), titled in Hungarian as *Rómeó és Júlia* on the video itself, was published on 14 July 2009 and represents a more unusual specimen of this ubiquitous YouTube medium. According to its creator, Balázs Simon, it was produced using a 'custom light box and peg bars' to represent the play's iconic balcony scene. This gently quivering animation opens with Juliet – dressed for no obvious reason in a long strapless gown and elbow-length evening gloves, more fitting for the opera than a nuptial bedroom – opening the curtains of a large domed window to reveal an image of a juddering, sparking sun. After performing what appears to be an oblation to the element, Juliet's uplifted arms transform into wings and, once her avian metamorphosis is complete, she flies first around the sun and then beyond the frame of the window. A split second later, two birds come into long-shot view, performing a swift airborne choreography of love before flying once again out of shot. Returning then in mid-shot, the two birds metamorphose into Romeo and Juliet, situated on either side of the window; as they stretch out their arms to touch one another, a red heart appears above their clasped hands, a figuration of their union. But as the screen darkens, turning the figures into mere silhouettes, the spectator becomes increasingly aware that the image forming in front of her is that of a skull: the lovers' heads are now eye sockets, their extended arms a toothless jaw bone, the crowning heart a nasal bone structure.

Despite not employing one word of the hypotext (it is devoid of any subtitular or intertitular text), this fleeting animation visualizes several of its dominant tropes: the light–dark binary; the iterative imagery of the sun; the multiple references to birds. Captured, too, through the uniting of the lovers in the image of a skull, is the drama's characteristic fusing of love and death. Several of the 500-plus comments posted in reply to the animation, although admiring of its translation of the verbal into the visual, insist on bringing the linguistic mode back into focus, resisting what Douglas Lanier has termed 'post-textual Shakespeare'. Displaying various degrees of Shakespearean literacy, respondents engage with the text by quoting directly from it or by raising broader questions concerning the skull's relation to Shakespearean tragedy and whether it can be defined as an 'ironic symbol'. Here, then, one of YouTube's paratexts enables viewers to recall, interpret and argue about the 'missing' written text. Additionally, the comments thread exemplifies how the platform's participatory culture encourages responsive adaptive initiatives. The piano piece that originally accompanied the animation, named by the uploader as 'Akatsuki no Kuruma from Gundam Seed', was later muted due to copyright infringement. While this audio-disabling generated some discontent at the damage inflicted on the animation's aesthetic integrity, a few viewers posted their own suggestions for suitable audio material. One such was 'A Martyr For My Love For You' by The White Stripes, music so dissimilar to the wordless, anime-inspired piano piece chosen by the animator as to bring an entirely new tone to the adaptation, not least because of the extra semiotic layer provided by the song lyrics.

As Stephen O'Neill observes, '[w]e are only beginning to explore the uses of the YouTube Shakespeare world' (144) and, with its user numbers increasing steadily year on year, any such exploration looks set to grow ever more involved, specialized and labour-intensive. As far as adaptation is concerned, it remains to be seen how far the platform will prove an enduringly democratic arena for propagating new and imaginative responses to Shakespeare or more a repository for fanfiction remixes and homework assignments, primarily shaped by examination assessment criteria and the questionable authority underpinning them.

5

The Merchant of Venice

The Merchant of Venice is arguably the most difficult and controversial play of the Shakespearean canon. Adaptive appropriation affords opportunities for engaging with questions of antisemitism: Mark Leiren-Young confronts the contested question of performance and Trevor Nunn locates the play in a proto-fascist context. In Howard Jacobson's novel, Shylock's story is recontextualized in twenty-first-century England.

Mark Leiren-Young, *Shylock: A Play* (1996)

Mark Leiren Young's one-act monologue, *Shylock*, is a polemical and confrontational appropriation of Shakespeare, drawing on *The Merchant of Venice* to address two highly controversial issues: first, in this post-Holocaust age, should *The Merchant of Venice* be censored, possibly banned from the stage altogether? The second question relates to performativity: should Shylock be portrayed only and inevitably as the play's tragic victim? The *donnée* of the monologue is that the actor, Jon Davies, has made the artistic and ethical decision to play Shylock as a villain. Leiren-Young, then, challenges performance ethics in present-day theatre and satirizes the modern predilection for seeing enlightened egalitarianism or 'relatability' in Shakespeare's writing. The play had already won a prestigious Canadian award before its first production at Vancouver's Bard on the Beach Shakespeare Festival in 1996, where it was directed by John Juliani, and it has since been staged across Canada and North America. Critical and popular reception to the piece has been overwhelmingly positive, reviews praising the play's 'direct engagement with the controversy around antisemitism' (quoted in Buntin).

In Leiren-Young's drama, the actor who has been playing Shylock addresses his audience at the post-play talk-back session following the final performance of *The Merchant of Venice*: the play has been axed because of noisy public controversy. In particular, an aggrieved academic, Professor Marcia T. Berman, has publicly attacked the production, calling (successfully) for a boycott. Her argument is that '[the] history of *Merchant* is the history of anti-Semitism' (Leiren-Young 31); she abhors Davies's interpretation of the role and questions further, '[why] should anyone perform this play in this day and age? Why should anyone see this play?' (12). Davies appears at the beginning of the talk-back in full costume and make-up, complete with false nose, gradually removing all these external props as he speaks, 'a kind of dismantling that signals a journey towards some kind of truth' (Levenson 249). His monologue is interspersed with Shylock's speeches, which he declaims in 'full character'; indeed, the play opens with Shylock's Act 3 speech in its entirety (*MV* 3.1.48–66), played 'for maximum villainous value' (Leiren-Young 1). Davies's talk-back session is, in part, a defence: Berman has accused him personally of racism, raising questions about how far actors can be held individually responsible for the text they speak or directorial decisions about the interpretation of a given role. Further, when he reveals to Marcia Berman that he is, himself, Jewish, she accuses him of being a traitor and 'a self-hating Jew' (10). On one level Leiren-Young's play contributes to the wider discussion about the ethics of performing *Merchant* – a debate which has gained urgency in the latter part of the twentieth century. But Leiren-Young goes further than the basic question of whether the play should now be abandoned: he intensifies and problematizes by exploring the trope of a deeply unsympathetic, vengeful Shylock. Jon Davies and his director have considered the implications of this controversial interpretation and Davies defends his judgement as historically valid. He believes himself to be playing the role as Shakespeare's audience would have received it, dramatizing, quite deliberately, the antisemitism of the Elizabethan age. As he explains, as a seasoned actor he has interpreted the role in various ways in the past:

> [The] first time I played Shylock I played him as a clown, a fool, an 'ethnic' fool. That's what I wanted, it's what the director wanted. It worked but the play didn't. It's wrong. Comic relief. A few years later I had another shot at the role [...] The director decided Shylock was motivated by hurt, by his pain at being abused by the Christians. This was a sympathetic Shylock – a wounded Jew, a victim of antisemitism who was crying out for acceptance.
>
> (14)

Theatre academic Errol Durbach observes that 'Mark Leiren-Young's image of Shylock as a "layered" creation is vital. It suggests the archaeology of the role, the intertextual Shylocks who lurk beneath the surface and wait for the appropriate time and place to select their layered selves' (quoted in Leiren-Young xiii). Davies is acutely aware that his audience want to see an abused, suffering Shylock; he quotes from 'Hath not a Jew eyes?' more than once, sensitively and 'beautifully' (16), provoking his listeners with the challenge that the 'safe, "correct" response' (15) is to transform Shylock into the demonized victim of the play. As well as shielding audiences from the spectacle of an evil Shylock, the sympathetic portrayal functions equally as a defence of Shakespeare himself. Jon Davies rejects as '[a]bsolute bullshit' any attempt to homogenize Shakespeare's mindset with modern liberal values:

> Was Shakespeare an anti-Semite?
> Of course he was.
> That was the fashion of the day [...] It would be lovely to pretend Shakespeare wasn't a bigot. That he was trying to point out Shylock's wounded inner child [...] But somehow I doubt it.
>
> (16, 17)

The monologue opposes two rival value-systems: Professor Berman represents historical ethics – the position that *Merchant* is an antisemitic play, uniquely offensive to Jews. Davies speaks for the values of ethical aesthetics – the position that 'Art is about truth' and that theatre, if not simply entertainment, should also be 'about truth', however uncomfortable (21). To Jon Davies, this might be 'forcing the Christians in this play, and the Christians watching this play to confront the way Jews have been mistreated' (21–2). Leiren-Young's underlying premise is that interpreting Shylock as a murderous revenger is now inadmissible; his question is whether theatre must always gratify present-day feeling, avoiding the offensive even where historically a given text might have expressed the views of its time. The challenge is a radical one: 'Does every production of every play have to be "comfortable" for everyone in the audience?' (34). To what extent can – or should – theatre be troubling and controversial?

This stylized caricature of Shylock as the alien moneylender is, then, the occasion for the ensuing controversy: to Professor Berman the production is a 'wretched piece of neo-Nazi propaganda' and Jon Davies 'a Sturmer cartoon come to life' (12). Berman has sent a lengthy letter to the local newspaper – read in full by Davies – in which she condemns the production as 'a cruel attack against the Jewish people of this community' (12). Crucial to the argument dramatized here is that the actor is not defending *Merchant* as a play enshrining present-day notions of tolerance; rather, he argues that the uncomfortable in literature must be faced with intellectual honesty. The monologue includes a brief account of Henrietta Bowdler – 'the patron saint of self-righteous censorship' (23) – and the published text appends a postscript of 'Shakespearean Censorship' which rattles through a brief history of bowdlerization, from Elizabeth I's excising of Richard II's deposition to recent stories of queasiness over Juliet's age, cross-dressing in *Twelfth Night* and supernaturalism in *Macbeth* and *Hamlet*. Antisemitism can be found in Orwell, Fitzgerald, H. G. Wells, T. S. Eliot and 'half the icons of English literature' (24). In other words, the 'sensitivity police' would be forced to remove cherished works such as Dickens's *Christmas Carol* – because surely Scrooge is a Jew? – from the literary canon. Davies is incredulous over Berman's protest, partly from reasons of proportionality: '[in] a world where talk show guests can claim the Holocaust never happened [and] the ambassador of the United Nations turns out to be a former Nazi, there are two dozen people spending their evening in the theatre protesting a production of *Merchant*' (26). Professor Berman and her university offer an open invitation to the company to defend their production and Davies rises to the challenge: 'fighting for Shakespeare. Fighting for art. [It] was a holy war and I was on the side of the angels' (30). Quite soon, though, the inevitable connection with Nazism arises:

> Then she tells me: 'You know that Hitler loved your play.'
> Now it was 'my' play. And I was on the side of Hitler.

(33)

Jewish identity and Jewish reactions to Shakespeare's *Merchant* underlie this troubled debate. Writer John O'Connor charts the history of Shylock performances, consulting London's Rabbi Julia Neuberger to explore contemporary responses to the play. Neuberger – a 'well known and respected liberal Jew' (O'Connor 144) – finds the play 'unpleasant' rather than 'dangerous', while David Nathan, drama critic for the *Jewish Chronicle*, considers the question about antisemitism less appropriate than 'Is it offensive?' where the answer is 'an unequivocal "Yes"' (quoted in O'Connor 144). In Leiren-Young's text, the campaigning Professor Berman is characterized in hyperbolic terms; spitting at the actor is a profoundly ironic gesture in the context of *The Merchant of Venice*. At the same time, Jon Davies brings to the role his own Jewish history. When Berman first accuses him of bigotry and antisemitism, she assumes that his surname is non-Jewish. Davies explains that his grandmother had been advised to change her surname from Davidovitch when she arrived in North America. There is a parallel in Leiren-Davies himself: his mother's name, Carol Young, was similarly altered – from Yankovich to Young – for purposes of assimilation. As Davies addresses his audience, he is acutely aware of his cultural connections with Shylock: 'I've studied my history. I know the reason so many Jews used to loan money was because it was one of the few jobs they were allowed to do. Because they – we – were considered infidels, we were consigned to the jobs our Christian brethren considered unworthy' (Leiren-Young 18). His anger over the encounter with Berman and her students arises from their accusations of racism and his inherited pain over the Russian history of his family – his *zaida* (grandfather) taken away, presumably killed; his father as a young child violently threatened. Leiren-Young offers no resolution, no middle ground between Berman and Davies and their clashing Jewish perspectives. There is an interesting connection with Howard Jacobson in this context; discussing his own reimagining of Shylock, he argues forcefully against censoring *The Merchant of Venice*: 'I don't approve of censoring anything. I think "anything" has to be out there and we have to deal with it' (Jacobson and Poole 24).

Leiren-Young's appropriation, then, foregrounds issues of performativity: why should the portrayal of Shylock be qualitatively different from, say, Macbeth or Iago, where villainy is unarguable? The answer to the latter, disingenuous, question is of course that Shylock is not simply an individual: he is 'the Jew'. As playwright Arnold Wesker observes in the prefatory comments to his own *Shylock*, '[the] portrayal of Shylock offends for being a lie about the Jewish character [...] No matter with what heavy tragedy the actor plays the role, no matter in what setting [...] the image comes through inescapably: the Jew is mercenary and revengeful, sadistic, without pity' (178). In his own reimagining of *The Merchant of Venice*, Wesker reinvents Shylock completely and he is transformed into an elderly bibliophile who enjoys cataloguing his rare manuscripts in the company of his great friend, Antonio. As Wesker contends, '[the] real Shylock would not have torn his hair out and raged against not being allowed to cut his pound of flesh, but would have said, "Thank God!"' (181). For Julia Pascal, *Merchant* is always 'the hardest Shakespearean drama for any Jew to watch' (11); her adaptation embeds Shakespeare's text within a frame-tale set in the Venetian Ghetto. Sarah, a survivor of the 1942 Warsaw Ghetto, is a tourist in Venice: in the first performances of the play, the role was played by Ruth Posner, a Holocaust survivor. Trapped by rising water from the Venetian canal, Sarah is temporarily forced to remain within the confines of the Ghetto as a theatre company rehearses *The Merchant of Venice*. Pascal's audience thereby sees Shakespeare's text on Sarah's terms; she hates the play, intervenes to address Jessica directly and becomes a witness at Shylock's trial. To appropriate the source play as a play-within-a-play for an audience consisting of an elderly traumatized Holocaust survivor compels a re-evaluation on Pascal's terms. To Pascal, the process of creative adaptation proves cathartic:

> I've always found the play very difficult and I've ignored it. Then I felt I was running away from the problem of being an English Jew. So by writing it, re-visiting, re-visioning it, I made myself confront it. And it proved a very tough and unpleasant journey, but I felt I had to do it.
>
> (Etienne 207)

Similarly, Leiren-Young invites his audience to consider antisemitism and *The Merchant of Venice* from the perspective of a Jewish actor, bringing his own theatrical experience and integrity to the role. Davies's final gesture is one of defiance: he concludes, as he has begun, with Shylock's words: 'What judgement shall I dread, doing no wrong?' (*MV* 4.1.88); like Shylock, he challenges his listeners, 'I stand for judgement; answer, shall I have it? He takes a bow, smiles, salutes and exits – proudly' (Leiren-Young 37). As Jill Levenson thoughtfully suggests, 'he leaves the impression of an artist who has faced and resisted, at personal cost, the limits at times imposed by his craft' (249). Leiren-Young writes in the same tradition as Jacobson, Wesker and Pascal – Jewish writers for whom the hindsight of history is inescapable. James Shapiro offers valuable insight: he concludes his magisterial work *Shakespeare and the Jews* with the observation that the wiser course must be to confront the problems raised by the play rather than shutting down debate: '[to] avert our gaze from what the play reveals about the relationship between cultural myths and peoples' identities will not make irrational and exclusionary attitudes disappear. This is why censoring the play is *always* more dangerous than staging it' (228). Jon Davies has been condemned, even vilified, but ultimately retains his defiant belief in the power of theatre:

> Maybe it is all dangerous. Galileo was dangerous, Moses was dangerous. Maybe Shakespeare is dangerous. Maybe that's a chance we've got to take. Maybe that's what art is. And maybe you don't just do the play because it's art. Just maybe you do it because it makes you talk about issues like this.
>
> (Leiren-Young 36)

The Merchant of Venice, dir. Trevor Nunn, Chris Hunt (2001)

Shylock would not have held the stage for four hundred years if he were a mere stereotype. His greatness is to be himself, to transcend the roles of representative Jew and conventional usurer. He is Shylock, with his own private history, his own vivid individuality.

(Gross 63)

Productions of *The Merchant of Venice* arguably bear the weight of history more than any other Shakespearean play and in two ways: the legacy of twentieth-century antisemitism and the Nazi Holocaust and, concomitantly, the history of Shylock on stage. As the discussion of Mark Leiren-Young's *Shylock* demonstrates, staged performance can be fraught with controversy. Yet the play remains popular, with landmark productions in the UK for Shakespeare's Globe Theatre, the RSC and the National Theatre. J. C. Bulman, in his account of the performance history of the play, suggests that adaptability itself is the reason for its survival:

For better or worse, it has entered our historical consciousness as no other Shakespearian comedy has, converging with the pressures of history to yield meanings Shakespeare could never have imagined.

(153)

John O'Connor, similarly, exploring the many Shylocks of stage history, suggests that as well as cultural or socio-political reasons for engaging with *The Merchant of Venice*, Shylock himself compels our attention because 'he is ambiguous, protean and constantly re-interpretable' (106). Trevor Nunn tackles the problem of history head-on by setting the play between the wars in an uneasy atmosphere of febrile dissipation among the young bloods who parade their willingness to exclude and scapegoat the outsider. The film opens with a montage of daguerreotype snapshots of a vanished world: cocktail gaiety and colourful cafés on the one hand, the serious demeanour of elderly Jewish men in narrow cobbled streets on the other hand – kaleidoscopic images that are both ominous and elegiac. The opening *mise-en-scène* elaborates on this extra-textual montage, taking the viewer directly into the decadent nightclub world; later, the jazz music, cocktails and dance routines are all redolent of Christopher Isherwood's Berlin and its offshoot, *Cabaret*, with a similar hysteria underlying the merriment. Gratiano, predictably loutish, staggers around with his trousers around his ankles; Antonio is the self-appointed melancholy loner, his northern accent, fussy demeanour and sentimental attachment to Bassanio all establishing him as the pathetic older man who pays the bills for his profligate companions (while they cruelly mimic his accent and mannerisms). When Shylock first enters this moneyed world, he appears as fellow businessman; his public persona is genial, perhaps ingratiatingly so, but he is economically their equal, a well-to-do, immaculately attired gentleman. The animosity between Antonio and Shylock is certainly emphasized at the outset through Antonio's almost visceral dislike and Shylock's hostile asides. Antonio is reluctant to sit beside Shylock and shrinks from the offered handshake that seals their bargain. The 'ancient grudge' is marked on both sides, an enmity not adequately explained by theological squabbles over interest rates.

The domestic Shylock is perhaps the triumph of this production; again, extra-textual material creates highly charged emotions between Shylock and his daughter. Within the supposed safety of his home, Shylock's cultural and spiritual orthodoxy can be expressed: reviewer Michael Billington identified 'a world of Hebraic faith' set against the 'Christian hedonism' (Billington, 'Money'). The casting of Jewish actor Henry Goodman adds conviction: in interview Goodman stressed his understanding of Shylock's daily sense of alienation; he desired to bring to the domestic scenes 'a real sense of a culture and a life off-stage ... I wanted to get the sense of a man who reads Hebrew all day long, who speaks Yiddish at home, for whom English is a second language' (O'Connor 141). Before the verbal exchanges between father and daughter, Shylock is seen lighting his lanterns; two ritual candles are placed beside a framed photograph of Leah – in Goodman's opinion, the bereavement is recent (O'Connor 114). Certainly, the interpolated Yiddish exchanges between Shylock and Jessica create a unique intimacy between the two of them, emphasizing their separateness from the city around them. Shylock is volatile in his treatment of his daughter, chiding her about the state of a kitchen pot, slapping her face anxiously when he thinks about the carnivalesque dangers outside the house, but also embracing her tenderly and singing with her the Hebrew song 'Eshet Chayil' (Edelman 265–6). The poignant melody of the song and Jessica's evident distress intensify the audience's apprehension over Shylock's vulnerability in the face of her imminent abandonment of the 'sober house'. Even Lancelot Gobbo listens with tears in his eyes. Lancelot Gobbo, however, is the link to one of the most disturbing scenes of Nunn's production: Shylock is ushered into the louche world of the nightclub by Bassanio, while Gobbo performs his speech from Act 2 (the struggle between the fiend and his conscience) as a piece of stand-up comedy. Shylock is both humiliated and disgusted and leaves abruptly, only to be further offended by the raucous merrymaking of the masquers. Nunn might well have been aware of Auden's judgement that 'Shylock is the outsider because he is the only serious person in the play' and Venice resents that seriousness (Auden 84).

The domestic sphere of Shylock and Jessica is contrasted with Portia's golden world of Belmont, effectively created by production designer Hildegard Bechtler. An exotic Klimt-style mural dominates the back wall, while the totemic caskets are displayed in a tiered glass cabinet. Despite the opulence, Portia's despondency is immediately apparent in her embittered rejection of her would-be suitors, displayed on a slide-show by Nerissa. Portia is a strong-willed woman whose situation is precarious: 'a living daughter curbed by the will of a dead father' (*MV* 1.2.23–4). Nunn makes the directorial decision to excise Portia's casual racism: she appears attracted to the glamorous Morocco and Nunn cuts her concluding couplet: 'A gentle riddance. Draw the curtains, go. / Let all of his complexion choose me so' (*MV* 2.7.78–9). Kenneth Rothwell suggests that Nunn links the casket plot with Venice and Shylock's story through metaphor – where gold and silver caskets conceal 'an inner cache of menace and death' (Rothwell 204) – and through the oath sworn over the ring: 'Which, when you part from, lose or give away, / Let it presage the ruin of your love' (*MV* 3.2.172–3). Bassanio will, of course, be unfaithful to his oath; the potent significance of the ring connects Bassanio with Jessica, who, allegedly, has exchanged her father's betrothal ring 'for a monkey' (*MV* 3.1.108). Only Shylock, it seems, will be faithful to his bond – 'an oath in heaven' (*MV* 4.1.224).

The cinematography of the trial scene, and particularly the consistent use of the close-up, undoubtedly increases the intensity of the exchanges between Shylock and Portia: as Rothwell observes, '[the] gazing camera morphs into an invisible narrator that defines and redefines the *diegesis*' (205). Where the wide-angle shot reveals the hostility of the court, the close-up takes the audience into Shylock's sober and dignified arrival at the proceedings. As Goodman defined it in rehearsal, '[by] the time [Shylock] has arrived at the Duke's court he has made a pact with God, and enters the room cold and committed' (O'Connor 139). Two aspects of Shylock's persona stand out in sharp relief here: his respect for the Venetian law and his determination to pursue his 'losing suit' (*MV* 4.1.61). He has been mocked and goaded in the public street for his apparent attachment to his 'ducats'; when Antonio requests the loan, Shylock reminds him 'many a time and oft / In the Rialto you have rated me / About my moneys and my usances' (*MV* 1.3.103–5). At this point, though, he chooses to reject three times the borrowed sum and revert to the terms of the original bond. It is worthless, as he knows – mere 'carrion flesh' – but it is 'dearly bought' (*MV* 4.1.40, 99); the bond epitomizes the weight of contumely and injustice he has had to contend with and it also signifies the injury to his own flesh and blood in the abduction of his daughter. To Goodman, this was Shylock's sole opportunity for justice:

[It's] important that Shylock is a very clever, canny man. He's read the Old Testament in all its rich proverbial allegories and stories. He's a market trader at the highest level – that sense of playing the long game, almost mental chess [...] He thrives when faced with complex situations. Emotionally, he rubs his soul with joy when people take him on. He's held his sense of injustice back [...] but now he can actually look at it, deal with it [...] He enjoys taking them on in a way that he never did before.

(Goodman 167)

Nunn succeeds in creating a still moment of genuine exchange during the 'quality of mercy' speech, overcoming the difficulties and potential cliché of familiarity. Portia (Derbhla Crotty) sits directly opposite Shylock to deliver the words solely to him; there is an absence of rhetorical flourish in her delivery; she also takes him aside to say privately, 'Shylock, there's thrice thy money offered thee' (*MV*

4.1.223). There is conflict in Portia, however: the camera shows her to be highly aware of the emotional farewell between Antonio and Bassanio, as well as the way in which Bassanio would willingly sacrifice 'wife and all the world' to save Antonio. She appears deeply perturbed, indeed changed, by the events unfolding before her. The judgement imposed on Shylock is harsh – even the Duke remits it – and it is notable that she refers to him only, and repeatedly, as 'the Jew' once she has uttered the decisive 'Tarry a while!' Equally, her anger and astonishment against Bassanio when the ring is delivered to her prepares the audience for her own revenge in the final scene. The unanswerable question of whether Shylock would slash open Antonio's breast is less ambiguous in Nunn's production, where the close-up shows Shylock shaking and perspiring as he first approaches Antonio. He is unable to strike the fatal blow and backs away as if to gain courage. As he advances for the second time, Portia desperately produces the legal tome – there is no suggestion here that her argument has been pre-decided. Antony Sher's Shylock in the 1987 RSC production was altogether more brutally willing to execute Antonio; indeed, Shakespeare scholar Warren Chernaik walked out of the production in dismay and revulsion at the spectacle of a Shylock 'fully capable of butchering Antonio in open court'. Sher's portrayal seemed to Chernaik to '[encourage] audiences on a visceral level to loathe Shylock' (Chernaik 37, 36). Under Nunn's direction, the poignant moments in the scene are connected with Shylock's religious identity: the dignified departure of Tubal, and Shylock's final gesture of dropping his yarmulke and tallith into the weighing scales as he leaves the court, defeated.

The return to Belmont is muted: Nunn makes sweeping cuts to the love-duet between Lorenzo and Jessica and, as Rothwell sees it, Portia is 'never more sadistic than when she torments Bassanio' over the loss of the ring (Rothwell 214). But the final moments are Jessica's: as Lorenzo receives the deed of gift forced from Shylock, she falls to her knees and intones phrases of 'Eshet Chayil', the Yiddish song heard earlier. Nunn cuts and transposes the final lines from the play, adapting the text by removing Gratiano's double-entendre and concluding simply with Portia's 'It is almost morning'. In Nunn's pre-war context, Jessica's emotional devastation cannot fail to connote the grief and suffering to come. As John Gross has opined, after the Holocaust 'the play can never be quite the same again. It is still a masterpiece; but there is a permanent chill in the air, even in the gardens of Belmont' (352).

Howard Jacobson, *Shylock Is My Name* (2016)

Howard Jacobson, Booker Prize–winning British novelist, was one of the first writers commissioned to contribute to the Hogarth series of Shakespeare Retold novels, an ambitious project conceived as part of the Shakespeare 400th anniversary celebrations. Hogarth selected for their initial titles *The Merchant of Venice*, *The Taming of the Shrew*, *The Winter's Tale* and *The Tempest* (by, respectively, Jacobson, Anne Tyler, Jeannette Winterson and Margaret Atwood), publicizing their 'literary transformations' as 'a mission to publish the best new writing of the age', following in the tradition of Virginia and Leonard Woolf, founders of the Hogarth Press. There is no indication why their choice includes two of Shakespeare's most notoriously problematic comedies. Adapting *The Merchant of Venice*, albeit relocating it in a different time and place, could never be a neutral activity; the play is freighted with the inescapable knowledge of historical antisemitism and, in particular, Nazi genocide. Marjorie Garber, addressing questions of Shakespeare and modern culture, rightly observes that 'the play worries us. Worries us individually and collectively. Worries us as readers, as performers, as teachers, as scholars, as students. Worries us as members of the modern world' (128). Rather than anxiety, Jacobson, in discussion, talks about his anger with 'the way the play has been read' (Jacobson and Poole 25), but he also describes his 'joy' in reimagining Shylock. He is unambiguously clear that he would not censor anything in Shakespeare; for him, *The Merchant of Venice* is not an antisemitic play:

> To me, it's inconceivable that Shakespeare would be an anti-Semite [...] He is drawn towards those who fill others with horror and create bigotry and antagonism in others – he always is. And he goes to find the human in the object of other people's

disdain. And he does that with Shylock [...] he finds the man. This is the man and he renders him as a man capable of the deepest feelings.

(Jacobson and Poole 24)

To Jacobson, *The Merchant of Venice* is inescapably the story of Shylock: 'a character to celebrate' (Jacobson, 'Villain'). The anguished conversation with Tubal over the loss of his betrothal ring – his turquoise – gives the audience access to a new insight into the stigmatized and alienated character:

Whatever we have been thinking of Shylock so far, the ground seems to open beneath him here, not to swallow him but to grant us rare access into his history, his antecedent affections, the man he was before he became – and maybe why he became – the man he is now.

(Jacobson, 'Villain')

This is not to say that the novel does not confront questions of Jewish identity and contemporary antisemitism head on. Simon Strulovitch, as the novel's updated Shylock, does not experience ghettoization, but he is bitterly aware of 'the ancient stain' (Jacobson, *Shylock* 15). When his non-Jewish first wife Ophelia-Jane divorces him – for not being tragically Jewish enough – she accuses him of extracting his 'pound of flesh', a slur that wounds him deeply. And he is fully cognisant that the affluent people around him see him as essentially alien, despite his public role as notable art collector and philanthropist. Certainly, an undercurrent of antisemitism exists among the pampered and privileged: Plurabelle and D'Anton crack stereotypical racist jokes and D'Anton dismisses and prevents Strulovitch's planned gallery of Anglo-Jewish art.

The novel is set in the twenty-first-century milieu of Cheshire's 'Golden Triangle' – an exclusive world of the super-rich. In this context, Antonio is D'Anton, melancholy and epicene art dealer, whose chief pleasure in life is vicarious: he assumes responsibility for his (heterosexual) friends and their sexual entanglements. Barney is clearly Bassanio, while Gratan, a deeply boorish and rebarbative non-league footballer, replicates the aggressive antisemitism of Gratiano. Gratan has acquired a degree of notoriety for performing a Nazi salute on the football field and he has 'a thing' for Jewish women (Jacobson, *Shylock* 43). Portia is a restless and dissatisfied rich girl, bizarrely named Anna Livia Plurabelle Cleopatra A Thing Of Beauty Is A Joy Forever Wiser Than Solomon Christine; she is busy overturning the eccentric terms of her father's will. Meanwhile, Jessica is Strulovitch's daughter, sixteen-year-old Beatrice: rebellious, sexually precocious, openly scathing of her father's protestations of Jewishness when he chooses to live an entirely secular life. But Simon Strulovitch has discovered a hitherto unknown attachment to his Jewish roots, triggered by Beatrice's willingness to embrace – in his eyes – the most objectionable sexual partners. Witty, often sardonic, parallelisms abound. But Shylock is ineluctably himself:

> [There] isn't an equivalent to Shylock. Shylock is too towering a figure. So I had to do Shylock. How do you bring back Shylock? I didn't want to do anything fancy, I don't do magic realism, I just wanted him to be there – no questions asked. He's just there [...] He's always been there.
>
> (Jacobson and Poole 19)

In Jacobson's powerfully compelling opening, Shylock appears as a sepulchral presence in a graveyard: 'Of course Shylock is here, among the dead. When hasn't he been?' (Jacobson, *Shylock* 4). He mourns his beloved Leah and finds a bleak consolation in talking to her: 'Alive, she had been everywhere to him. Dead – he long ago determined – she will be the same' (5). Strulovitch is unsurprised by Shylock's presence; his Jewish imagination 'sets no limits to geography or topography' (5). Shylock's 'husbandly sorrow and fatherly wrath' is the mirror-image of his own situation – his second wife, Kay, is in a comatose state following a stroke. Shylock is not, strictly speaking, a revenant; rather he is transhistorical, a perpetually haunting presence who never finds assuagement of his grief. Extended late-night conversations between Shylock and Strulovitch provoke the lapsed modern Jew to probe his assumptions about his Jewish identity, the nature of assimilation and why, in particular, he is passionately opposed to his daughter's non-Jewish boyfriends.

The Merchant of Venice is, above all, a play of money. It is not surprising, then, that the '[r]ichly left and richly independent'

Plurabelle rejects the terms of her father's will and devises her own version of the casket test: on her twenty-first birthday she attends a swingers' party, throws the keys to each of her three cars into an ice bucket and waits to see what emerges. Fights break out over her BMW Alpina and her Porsche Carrera, but no one is interested in the modest Volkswagen Beetle in which she is hiding. She later announces that her 'ornamental virginity' might be auctioned on her TV show. So far, so comic: Plurabelle is never going to be a victim of patriarchy; Beatrice, on the other hand, suffers her father's anxiety and rage. Following his anguished nocturnal discussions with Shylock, Strulovitch invents his own version of Shylock's bond: if Gratan genuinely desires to marry Beatrice, he must prove his sincerity by agreeing to circumcision – a neat reversal of the Venetian state demanding that Shylock should be Christianized. By the end of the novel, Gratan and Beatrice have escaped to Venice and D'Anton agrees to act as proxy. Mirroring Antonio's self-sacrifice, he will undergo the procedure on Gratan's behalf if Beatrice fails to return at an appointed date. Strulovitch's daughter is a truculent and ungovernable teenager, but inevitable comparison sheds an unflattering light on Jessica. Beatrice is intelligent: she startles D'Anton by challenging him with a question on Rembrandt's chiaroscuro effects; she chuckles over her father's rage at her youthful waywardness – on one occasion he has dragged her away from a party by her hair, objecting vociferously to her preference for 'chthonic arseholes' (79).

The all-important bond links Strulovitch and Shylock, returning the reader to the source text and to the perennial, unanswerable question: '[how] merry was your bond?' (147). At the centre of the novel, the two men debate the momentous events of the Venetian courtroom with Shylock deflecting Strulovitch's probing with searching questions of his own: '[did] I know what I wanted in full earnest? [...] Was I acting out my desires or theirs?' (151). Shylock's insights establish two crucial points: first, that he has no alternative other than the pursuit of his bond – 'Antonio forfeits and what ensues must ensue – I must have my bond. Speak not against my bond. I am now become *the thing he made me* – my bond' (150, my italics); second, that Antonio longs to be 'ennobled' by the tragic destiny he nearly acquires: 'the tragedy he had always sought out for himself I very nearly gave him – although he was undeserving [...] I lifted him out of farce' (151). Shakespeare's text is woven through Shylock's reflections and his exchanges with Strulovitch, often in a wry and ironic tone. Strulovitch is uncomfortably aware that 'it was rare to hear someone say, "The villainy you teach me I will execute"' in an exclusive Italian restaurant (152). The novel has a trenchant ability to 'talk back' to Shylock while, simultaneously, Shylock 'talks back' to the play.

Among numerous textual echoes, two in particular reveal Jacobson's narrative technique and the novel's relationship with its source. The first is a teasing example, a reference which surely would return the reader questioningly to the text. Shylock, brooding painfully over the night of Jessica's elopement, muses over 'the fathomless impertinence of Antonio's "yet"' (124). The hypocrisy of Antonio's moralizing over money is summed up in the 'yet' (*MV* 1.3.59): he assumes a right to spit on Shylock, 'yet' his love for Bassanio licenses his willingness to take Shylock's money. Jacobson finds in a single word of Shakespeare's text a world of significance. A different type of intertextual referencing occurs when Plurabelle, D'Anton and Barney discuss the intractabilities of their situation. Barney – disadvantaged because he has lost Plury's ring – argues that Strulovitch will not back down from his demands: '[The] Jew will not back down. I've never heard of a Jew who will [...] It's against their religion [...] They have hearts of stone. Try standing on a beach and ordering the tide to go back – that's what it's like persuading a Jew to change his mind' (219). His hyperbole recalls the language of the Venetian courtroom:

I pray you, think you question with the Jew.
You may as well go stand upon the beach
And bid the main flood bate his usual height;
[...]
You may as well do anything most hard
As seek to soften that, than which what's harder –
His Jewish heart!

(*MV* 4.1.69–71, 77–9)

The verbal echo has the effect in the novel of emphasizing the careless antisemitism of this wealthy and entitled trio. They have effectively procured the underage Beatrice to satisfy Gratan; they are happy to trade centuries-old prejudices.

The bond itself, however, produces the most climactic and resonant encounter between source text and Jacobson's novel, producing a telling contrast between Shylock and Strulovitch and a startling dénouement. In Jacobson's 'Act Five', D'Anton has taken the place of the absent footballer and consented to submit himself for adult circumcision; Strulovitch attends the preceding legalities. This is the final opportunity for Strulovitch to back down. Plurabelle draws attention to the humiliation and potential danger of the procedure; Shylock extracts from D'Anton an admission that the terms are just. He then addresses his companion and alter ego Strulovitch:

> 'Then', he said, 'must the Jew be merciful ...'
> Strulovitch knew exactly what he had to say in return [...]
> 'On what compulsion must I?' he asked.
> Whereupon Shylock said what he too had to say. 'The quality of mercy is not strained; it droppeth as the gentle rain from heaven ...'
>
> (265)

This is a brilliantly powerful reversal of expectation: a rejection of Portia's 'Sunday school' platitudes (Jacobson and Poole 29) and a return to the original question of Shylock's intention. Earlier, Shylock has raised the biblical example of Abraham and Isaac: would the father have sacrificed his son, as God had commanded (Jacobson, *Shylock* 178)? Shylock's argument is that the question itself is 'illegitimate [and] unanswerable': he opines that nothing in Abraham's story suggests that he could kill his child; equally, nothing in Shylock's story would suggest that he could be a man of blood. A determined and absolutist revenger might have proceeded, of course, accepting the consequences of Venice's death penalty. Shylock is not that revenger, although he knows 'how it is to be brought to the threshold of murder' (182). But in Plurabelle's dissipated and vacuous world, Shylock attempts to persuade Strulovitch that compassion towards an undeserving enemy is a moral good. Strulovitch is unpersuaded: unlike Shylock, he pursues his bond unrelentingly. Shylock's eloquence has disturbed Plurabelle's unthinking antisemitism, however: 'God, I love this man, she thought. I fucking love him' (268). Her veneration, unsurprisingly, leaves Shylock unmoved; he simply corrects her assumptions:

It is morally and historically wrong not to know that Jesus was a
Jewish thinker and that when you quote him against us you are
talking vicious nonsense. Charity is a Jewish concept. So is mercy.
You took them from us, that is all. You appropriated them. They
were given freely, but still you had to steal them.

(270)

Closure has perhaps been achieved for Shylock in an ironic reversal
of moral authority that operates on a number of levels as the
notion of substitution proliferates and is dismantled. D'Anton has
substituted himself for Gratan but meretriciously, since he was
circumcised as a child. Plurabelle, cognisant of the secret, is morally
repugnant in claiming superiority over Strulovitch; as Shylock's
parallel, Strulovitch has struggled from his daughter's birth with
the 'concept of covenant' (38, 9); he proceeds further than Shylock
in his desire for vengeance but, defeated, is 'content'.

Lanier argues that the tendency of the first Hogarth adaptations
is to 'revise their Shakespearean source narratives into tales of
redemption' (Lanier, 'Hogarth' 242). For Strulovitch and Beatrice
there is certainly the chance of a new beginning: Beatrice deserts
her unworthy lover and returns home. In the final exchange of the
novel there is tentative resolution: 'It's enough you're here.' 'It's
enough for me too' (Jacobson, *Shylock* 277). Strulovitch perceives
a resemblance to Shylock in her 'strong unforgivingness'. For
Beatrice, as a proud and self-determining young woman, coming
home was always a possibility; Shylock, however, can never know
Jessica's ultimate fate, and his final thought, as he fades from view,
is that 'Jessica was not and never would be fine' (272). For Shylock
'there is no now' – Shakespeare's play offers no role for Shylock in
Act 5. The threat of conversion, the loss of his money, all lie in a
projected world beyond the text. As Shylock confesses to Strulovitch,
'I hanker, as you will easily imagine, for a resounding exit line' (70).
Jacobson's reinvention is, in Lanier's term, 'reparative' (Lanier,
'Hogarth' 247): Shylock gains the moral victory, denied him at
the end of *The Merchant of Venice*, in his appropriation of the
'quality of mercy' speech. But he remains a figure of unfathomable
and eternal loneliness; equally, Strulovitch's dilemmas over his
Jewish identity remain turbulent. On the macrocosmic cultural
and political scale, antisemitism, if not as injurious as in the Venice

of the 1590s, still exists in the modern world of Jacobson's novel. In her discussion of Shylock, Marjorie Garber draws on Adorno's notion that post-Holocaust art demonstrates a 'withering away of the alternative between lightheartedness and seriousness, between the comic and the tragic' (146). The concept of a 'third possibility' offers a helpful approach to Jacobson's adaptation: the underlying tragedy of *Merchant* is infused through the novel but charged with the possibility of transformation. Adaptation offers 'another kind of discourse' (Garber 147) as though 'an old play can nag away in the mind and make something new happen' (Burrow 16).

6

Hamlet

This chapter explores two twenty-first-century, highly politicized adaptations of *Hamlet*: *The Al-Hamlet Summit* and *Haider*. In both Al-Bassam's play and Bhardwaj's film, the action moves inescapably towards destruction as the protagonist struggles in vain against systemic corruption. The twenty-first-century reinvention of Ophelia, on the other hand, subverts convention, reimagining Ophelia as an empowered survivor of Elsinore.

Sulayman Al-Bassam, *The Al-Hamlet Summit* (premiered 2002)

Sulayman Al-Bassam (b. 1972) is an Anglo-Kuwaiti dramatist and theatre director; born in Kuwait to a British mother and a Kuwaiti father, he received most of his formal education in Britain and, although fluent in Arabic, chooses to write in English. His dual nationality gives him a unique position within the cultural world of Kuwait. As Holderness explains, Al-Bassam is committed to his country's cultural progress while 'acutely conscious of the nation's need for radical political reform and cultural change' ('From Summit' 128). Al-Bassam's artistic and intellectual inheritance is a complex one: from independence in the early 1960s, Kuwait pursued a modern and liberal programme as an autonomous nation state. The Iraqi invasion of Kuwait (1990) created a conservative backlash, however; as Katherine Hennessey observes, prominent Islamists perceived this as divine retribution for 'liberal and materialist pre-war lifestyles' (253). For Al-Bassam himself, the 1990s was a period of education in Britain and the founding of his London-based theatre company (Zaoum, 1996–2001); his artistic influences were strongly European and he identified intellectually with post-modern Europe, 'blissfully insouciant of my alienness'. The 'magnesium flash' of 9/11 conclusively shifted his perception of himself and his creative world:

> In the fallout of the terrorist attacks on Manhattan [my] looks, my language, my name became sources of interrogation and suspicion. I was poised between two cultures with a sense of identity defined as much by non-assimilation and non-belonging as by any unified narrative of tribe, culture, language, or history.
>
> (Al-Bassam, 'Shakespeare' 124)

But, as Al-Bassam himself suggests, '[bad] times for living: rich pickings for theatre' ('Shakespeare' 125): drama of political urgency, subversive and dangerous theatre finds a 'perfect bedmate, co-conspirator and alibi' in Shakespeare (Al-Bassam, 'Bard').

In terms of historic discourse with Shakespeare, Arabic literature operates within a complex and multifaceted context of English, French and Eastern European appropriation. For writers beginning their careers in a post-colonial era, British influences were already in the past. In the early twentieth century, French translations of Shakespeare – and particularly nineteenth-century adaptations featuring Hamlet's victorious survival – had coexisted alongside colonial education and Lamb's *Tales of Shakespeare*. By the 1970s, arguably the most influential appropriations of *Hamlet* for Middle Eastern writers were Kozintsev's film and Kott's widely translated *Shakespeare Our Contemporary*. Litvin cites the example of 1980s Egyptian playwright Mahmoud Aboudoma, producing a reimagining of *Hamlet* (translated as *Dance of the Scorpions*). Aboudoma had no direct experience of Shakespeare's text; his perception of 'Hamlet' had been mediated by and refracted through numerous allied texts. In Litvin's helpful definition he had encountered Shakespeare through a 'global kaleidoscope' of sources:

Unlike postcolonial appropriation theory, the global kaleidoscope model does not claim to generalise about the *purpose* of rewriting a respected literary work or to predict the direction that such a rewriting might take. Instead [it] provide[s] a framework [...] within which to consider the individual rewriter's imbrication within a multifaceted and dynamic tradition of Shakespeare use. In particular it draws attention to the great variety of actual sources through which an appropriator acquires a 'source' text.

(Litvin, 'Vanishing' 81)

In other words, Middle Eastern appropriations of Shakespeare do not inevitably conform to a binary model of 'talking back' to the Empire but offer 'a means for discussing diverse post-colonialities' (Loomba and Orkin 19). Modern Arabic writers, living in turbulent times, operate within murderously oppressive regimes: state censorship, as described by Al-Bassam, has the authority to approve or proscribe texts, police rehearsals, cut scenes or cancel entire plays. The choice of Shakespeare as a vehicle for seditious critique is governed by two radically different factors: first, the hefty weight of 'cultural capital' – the unchallenged authority of Shakespeare. From an oppositional perspective, though, Shakespeare is the 'heaving underworld of illicit meanings, transgressive actions, and contentious critique' (Al-Bassam, 'Bard'). For Al-Bassam, Shakespeare's world is strikingly analogous to the current Arab situation:

Both are turbulent, uneven worlds of Rulers and Ruled in which religious authority and corrupt oligarchs reign supreme over a largely feudal and tribal social fabric. Both are worlds in which the power of language, poetry, and storytelling are imbued with incantatory, transformative powers – in the case of Arabic, this power has sacred roots, anchored as it is in the Holy Qur'an. Wars, conspiracies, hooded assassins, criminal oppression, questions of kingship, statehood, national and individual identity are all daily fare in today's Arab world.

(Al-Bassam, 'Bard')

In this context, there is no place for a romantically melancholic nor an existentialist, philosophic Hamlet. For Al-Bassam, the play can readily metamorphosize into 'the birth of Islamic religious fanaticism fuelled by domestic corruption and western opportunism' (Al-Bassam, *Al-Hamlet* xix).

Additional layers of adaptive nuance exist in Al-Bassam's decision to write in English while overseeing translation into Arabic. As Al-Bassam explains, Arabic is a diglossic language with differing forms depending on social context – 'a supremely Shakespearean linguistic model' (*Al-Hamlet* xxi). Al-Bassam encouraged the cast to suggest changes in rehearsal so 'the Arabic performance texts became living palimpsests that accrued the input, graffiti and inflection of many scribes' (xxi). The shifting, contingent state of the performative text offers the perfect metaphor for the *Hamlet* Al-Bassam creates. What might be described as his *Hamlet* artwork began, first, in 2001 with *Hamlet in Kuwait*, an adaptation commissioned for the tenth anniversary of Kuwait's liberation. In response to the 9/11 attacks, this text was reworked as *The Arab League Hamlet* – both adaptations based on Shakespeare's text. *The Al-Hamlet Summit* marked a significant change of direction; rewritten and set in a contemporary Middle East, the play was first performed in English at the Edinburgh Festival (August 2002), where it won the Fringe First Award for Excellence and Innovation in Writing and Directing; performed in Cairo (2002), the play won Cairo's International Festival of Experimental Theatre, Best Director and Best Performance Awards. The Tokyo International Arts Festival commissioned an Arabic-language version of the piece and this version (premiered in Tokyo, 2004) has toured widely across the world. *The Al-Hamlet Summit*, then, has unfolded through a series of politically charged, changing performative texts. How far the play succeeds for a British audience has been questioned by the author himself. Arab audiences actively desire controversy from serious theatre and 'are very quick to extract political meaning from theatrical signifiers' (Al-Bassam, 'Am' 86). The response of London audiences to his *Arab League Hamlet* proved disappointing; the transgressive urgency of his appropriation failed to reacculturate:

> I had wanted them to feel the same voyeuristic thrill that the Arab one had felt in listening to the forbidden word, hearing the forbidden thought, and witnessing the forbidden act [...] and,

above all, the same degree of implication in the events presented to them on stage.

(Al-Bassam, 'Am', 87)

The drama opens in the seemingly neutral world of the political summit, the conference chamber as a '*huis clos* that parodies the so-called "transparency" of today's political processes and a deadly arena of internal conflict' (SABAB). It is a featureless space with six named desks, the paraphernalia of microphones and a large back projection of an Arabic leader. Later, the screen magnifies the emotions and actions of the characters as well as relaying the familiar visions of TV news – burning tanks, explosions, civil war. Hamlet has returned home on the death of his father, but the succession is already determined. Claudius's demonstration of absolute power is confident and commanding: his marriage to Gertrude, the threat from Fortinbras and the rejection of Hamlet's request to return to university are all dealt with summarily. Internal dissent will be brutally crushed – seditious leaflets circulate an account of the murder of Old Hamlet:

POLONIUS
I've got 300 men working round the clock gathering up the leaflets.
CLAUDIUS
Forget the leaflets, burn the townships, all of them – I want them all burnt by dawn.

(*Al-Hamlet* 8)

Resistance continues throughout: a car bomb is detonated during the opening of the New Parliament, but Claudius's concern is only for the safety of his oil pipeline. The carnage and fraught instability is overseen and facilitated by the urbane and sophisticated figure of Arms Dealer, who sidles into every act of the play. He epitomizes the promiscuity of his trade, supplying weaponry to Claudius, Hamlet, Ophelia and Fortinbras; in the Arabic version he is the only character to speak in English.

For modern audiences, the alterity of Shakespeare's *Hamlet* derives, significantly, from the play's eschatological dimension.

For Al-Bassam, equally, the religious imperative and the numinous pervade the drama, shaping feeling and action; the desire for political justice does not preclude spirituality. The five-act structure is both Shakespearean and Arabic – the names of each act are those of the five daily prayers in Islam. As Ewan Fernie has argued, '[*Hamlet*] opens up a spiritual horizon for deconstruction in terms of the Prince of Denmark's traumatic reorientation towards otherness' (194). Belief as a shared audience response is now lost to British audiences, whereas Middle Eastern audiences are familiar with the ubiquitous routines of religious worship. The death-infused nature of Al-Bassam's *Hamlet* is apparent from Hamlet's prayer at his father's grave: his urgent desire for action is expressed in apocalyptic imagery:

HAMLET
Let the skies fall in and the seas be set ablaze, let the material world collapse [...] make hell fires burn fiercely and bring paradise near: but [...] inspire me with your command, show me my labours, I hold my life in no esteem, I carry not an atom's weight of good [...] inspire me with your command, inspire me with your command –

(*Al-Hamlet* 12)

The echoes of Hamlet's response to his father's ghost are audible: Hamlet, too, exclaims, 'I do not set my life at a pin's fee' (*Ham* 1.4.65). But the 'Ghost' in Al-Bassam's play is the sinister Arms Dealer who acquaints Hamlet with the truth of his father's death, thereby sealing Hamlet's destiny. The chiliastic imagery recurs in his love poems to Ophelia: when 'paradise is brought nearer this earth / On that day, know that I am looking for you' (18). Hamlet is again alone by his father's grave as Claudius presides over the opening of his New Parliament and, in soliloquy, echoes the despair and futility of 'O that this too too sallied flesh' (*Ham* 1.2.129). Here, again, the Arms Dealer woos him: 'we could be friends. You need someone to confide in and I know what it is like to be isolated' (*Al-Hamlet* 21). Hamlet's self-accusations recur later when he soliloquizes over a pistol: he finds in himself 'nothing heroic [...] just a futile mediocrity' (29). Claudius's anguished soliloquy ('O my offence is rank', *Ham* 3.3.36) is paralleled by Al-Bassam but transformed into a cry of despair that the corrupting forces of the West are abandoning him. Shakespeare's Claudius is all too aware that 'the corrupted currents of this world' are transitory and absolute judgement awaits him after death. Al-Bassam's Claudius worships a god of merciless materialism:

> Oh God: Petro dollars. Teach me the meaning of petro dollars.
> I have no other God than you. I am created in your image, I seek guidance from you the All Seeing, the All Knowing Master of Worlds, Prosperity and Order.
>
> (*Al-Hamlet* 40)

He appeals to a deity of 'gluttony and endless filth' who has supplied him with the plutonium, the loans, the 'world shafting bank' (40, 41). Claudius 'cannot bear to be myself, cannot, cannot bear it'. He has willingly become the 'monstrous marionette of the West's creation' (Stafford-Mills 19) and, in abjuring his own religion, has found only betrayal:

> I do not try to be pure: I have learnt so much filth, I eat filth, I am an artist of filth, I make mounds of human bodies, sacrifices to your glory. I adore the stench of rotting peasants gassed with your technology.
>
> (*Al-Hamlet* 40–1)

Ophelia, too, embraces the apocalyptic: when Hamlet turns away from her, suspicious of treachery, Ophelia seeks out the Arms Dealer, requesting a bomb. Her fidelity to Hamlet and her sexuality are ridiculed in the scene corresponding to the play-within-the-play: Hamlet, dressed as an Abbasid warrior, complete with hobby horse, declaims a brief hysterical monologue, threatening all the members of the court and suggesting that Ophelia should offer sexual services to the army. Thereafter, Ophelia appears, veiled, on screen, pronouncing her final pre-recorded words:

> I have tried to speak the language of women,
> I have tried to forgive, on many nights I severed my tongue
> But my silence bleeds from my mouth.
> [...] I will express with my body
> [...] I go to my God pure in my soul in my dignity I am pure.
>
> (49)

It is, of course, Gertrude who witnesses and announces Ophelia's horrific death as a suicide bomber. The final bloodbath is initiated by Hamlet – now appearing in the style and dress of a radical Islamist leader and assuming control of his inheritance: 'I Hamlet, son of Hamlet, son of Hamlet and the rightful heir' (52). News reports intercut Claudius's rallying speeches, revealing Gertrude's death – protecting her son – Laertes' death and the last encounter, between Hamlet firing mortars from the Mosque and Claudius firing from the Palace. For Hamlet, there is no grieving Horatio, no 'flights of angels', but rather a bleak political insight that the 'history of other nations' is inscribed in his people's blood: 'This perception of truth too late, / Is hell' (55). Fortinbras appears, promising a completed pipeline and new beginnings, just as the play's one constant character reappears: Arms Dealer.

Al-Bassam's overriding objective in recontextualizing *Hamlet* was always a campaigning one: to 'increase dialogue between cultures' (Dent). Theatre 'challenges the accepted world views and breaks the mirrors of authority. Shakespeare understood that power very well' (Dent). Appropriating Shakespearean tragedy can inspire new insights into the human cost of unappeasable political circumstances: '[the] tragic is a poetic and dramatic discourse that [...] ventures into a darker, more obscure territory, into a confrontation with irreconcilable imperatives' (Litvin, 'Tragedy' 853). As Holderness has observed, Al-Bassam's adaptive engagement with *Hamlet* has produced 'new and unforeseen meanings' (*Al-Hamlet* ix).

Haider, dir. Vishal Bhardwaj (2014)

Twenty-first-century political adaptations of *Hamlet* share an urgency and bitterness: their vision is one of ingrained corruption where the increasingly isolated protagonist pays a terrible price for opposing tyranny. Both Bhardwaj and Al-Bassam judged *Hamlet* to be the apposite text to dramatize the violence and trauma of present-day political conflict. As Douglas Lanier contends, filmic adaptation of *Hamlet* theorizes tragedy itself, every film offering its own distinctive interpretation of what makes the play tragic (*'Hamlet'* 584). Further, in comparison with a psychological reading, 'films that stress the corruption of the system against which Hamlet pits himself tend to offer a much darker view of the play's tragedy' ('*Hamlet*' 585). *Haider* was Bhardwaj's third Shakespearean tragedy to be transmediated into modern Indian culture, following his successful art-house adaptations: *Maqbool* (2004), an Urdu- and Hindi-language version of *Macbeth*, set in contemporary Mumbai, and *Omkara* (2006), a Hindi-language *Othello*, set in Uttar Pradesh. Mark Thornton Burnett observes that Bhardwaj presents a test case for 'how the auteur might operate according to Indian paradigms' as well as inviting reflection on Shakespeare's place within different nation states (Burnett 56). Adapting Renaissance tragedy in an Indian context is an act of transculturation that raises questions about tragedy as a genre. Trivedi explains that the tragic view of life was non-existent in India before the introduction of Western traditions: 'the concept of tragic fall and waste of human potential was alien to a world view which was largely governed by the laws of karma, and in which the role of art was to represent and valorize the harmonization of man with the universe' (881). It is worth noting that Bhardwaj's inspiration for *Maqbool* came not from the source text but from Kurosawa's *Throne of Blood* (1957): '[that] was when I got a glimpse of the power of Shakespeare's writing (and Kurosawa's cinematic interpretation, equally powerfully)' (quoted in Chaudhuri, 'What' 102). Bhardwaj commenced his professional career in music and composition, so his filmic aesthetic is one where a bricolage of musical effects can supersede the primacy of the visual or textual – 'more acoustic auteur than virtuoso of mise-en-scène' (Rodgers 500). The role of Takemitsu's music in Kurosawa's Shakespeare, or Shostakovich in Kozintsev's *Hamlet*, suggests that, in any study of filmic adaptation, 'dynamically inter-connected forms of auteurism are significant forces to recognize' (Burnett 58). This discussion will focus on the challenges of appropriating a revenge ethic in a politically sensitive and volatile context, and Bhardwaj's use of distinctively Kashmiri performative traditions of music and dance.

Bhardwaj describes the Kashmiri situation as 'the biggest tragedy of modern Indian history' (*Haider* vi), citing co-writer Basharat Peer's autobiographical *Curfewed Night* (2008) as a profound influence on the film. He chose to set *Haider* in 1995, a period of peak militancy: '[wanting] to observe the human tragedy that a regular middle-class family went through' (Singh). The ubiquitous militia, with their paraphernalia of heavy weaponry, roadblocks and detention camps, invade everyday life. To Bhardwaj, 'Kashmir becomes Hamlet' (Singh); the land itself a tragic victim: '[Kashmir's] beauty is blinding [...] the suffering is silent, lurking in the air, piercing your soul' (vii). This creates a macrocosmic context for the sexual jealousy and fratricide of Khurram (Claudius): Bhardwaj reveals quite how easy it is for an unscrupulous individual to exploit violent times. As in *Hamlet*, individuals and relationships are drawn into the web of political subterfuge and betrayal. Parvez (Polonius) is a senior police officer deeply involved in the Indian Army's campaign to recruit local volunteers to inform on militant separatists in their own communities. In the opening frames of the film, he is seen mercilessly shooting three young freedom-fighters at point-blank range; later, he orders the murder of Haider to protect Khurram. Salman and Salman, comic analogues of Rosencrantz and Guildenstern, are also corrupted by the political situation: they spy on Haider at Parvez's instruction and betray him to certain death. Haider's father, Hilaal, is a doctor attempting to practise his profession according to the humanitarian principles of disinterested medical care – 'I am for life', he quietly claims as he organizes an emergency operation on the local insurgent commander. But he is betrayed by his brother and arrested in a dawn raid where he is forced to watch his house and his patient blown up. Incarcerated in a military prison, he has become one of many 'disappeareds'.

As Amy Rodgers observes, the film 'relies heavily on extradiegetic and intradiegetic instrumental and vocal music to express narrative turbulence' (501), and two sequences are particularly striking: the Jhelum river song and the performance of 'Bismil' (analogous to the play-within-the-play). The Puriya Dhanashree song 'Jhelum dhonnde kinaara' is the soundtrack to a montage of scenes in which Haider pursues his fruitless quest to find his father. The song, performed by Bhardwaj himself, is a tribute to the beauty and sorrow of the river Jhelum; the music begins as Haider and Arshia (Ophelia) set out by boat: 'Jhelum, Jhelum, searching a shore / [...] The waters of the river Jhelum / Have turned saline / [...] Who to ask for how much longer / This pain we must continue to bear.' As the repeated refrain builds in intensity, Haider can be seen producing a photocopied photograph of his father to show military officials, all of whom shake their heads. In a poignant gesture, he compares photographs with an old woman searching for her lost son; they silently weep together. A newspaper headlines a story of bodies found in the river; small gatherings of silent protesters hold photographs and banners pleading for the return of lost sons, fathers and husbands. Shakespeare's play-within-the-play is also acculturated into local tradition: Bhardwaj 'knew the mousetrap has to be a big big song number for me [...] We're so culturally rooted in music and dance' (Bhardwaj, 'Decoding'). Elaborately costumed male dancers perform an exuberant, intricately choreographed dance to the song 'Bismil' in the style of Kashmiri folk tradition, *Bhand Pather*, where myths and stories unfold through performance. Haider himself performs as chief narrator, interpolating his private narrative of Khurram's treachery, as Hamlet does. The striking background of the ancient ruins of the Martand Sun Temple, the ranks of traditional sitar players and the stylized gestures of the dancers create a unique interface between source text and Bhardwaj's creative adaptation.

The evocative poetry of Faiz Ahmed Faiz similarly recontextualizes Shakespeare's text. Accompanied by Arshia, Haider returns to the ruins of his burned-out home. Idealized recollections of childhood happiness intercut the scenes of devastation. In one poignant vignette, a fragment of poetry is smilingly recited by his father, Hilaal, to see whether his young son can complete the quotation. The lyric poem, or *ghazal*, is Faiz's 'Let the petals fill with colour' (*Haider* 37); it is repeated in a far more menacing context when Roohdaar (as the Ghost) cites the same phrase to seize Haider's attention and act as confirmation that he has come with a message from Haider's father. In *Hamlet*, the torments of purgatory are implied through the periphrastic speeches of the Ghost; in *Haider*, a montage of all-too-earthly torture and interrogation is revealed through Roohdaar, who announces himself as Hilaal's soul. Hilaal, chained and unshaven, is revealed quietly murmuring the – highly appropriate – second verse of the poem, '[the] prison is a sullen ghost'. Roohdaar explains to Haider that Hilaal's voice 'would echo in the night ... a balm to our agony' (115). Hilaal's message, according to Roohdaar, is vengeance: 'take revenge for a foul and unnatural murder' (113). It is in truth a message from the dead, as Roohdaar's narrative reveals that Haider's father has been tortured and thrown into a river to die. Bringing together the respected left-wing Pakistani poet, Haider's recollections of childhood and the hidden world of political punishment indigenizes Shakespearean affect in powerfully resonant ways. But the injunction to revenge is complicated by the mysterious ambiguity of Roohdaar: he appears, swathed in white and grey garments, against a snow-covered landscape; he is actively involved in the insurgency. Does he urge Haider to vengeance for his own purposes? The identical, unanswerable, question pertains to *Hamlet* and *Haider*: would a loving father command his son to be damned as a murderer? *Haider*, like *Hamlet*, is threaded through with the past, generationally and historically. Hilaal's father, the elderly Dr Meer, observes that India's independence was won by Gandhi by peaceful means: 'revenge does not set you free. True freedom lies beyond violence. Remember. Revenge only begets revenge' (89). As this is interpolated as a recollection from the past, the effect is as though two distinct messages come from the dead, one pursuing revenge, the other warning against it. Ghazala repeats the same words to Haider in their final and highly charged scene – unknown to Haider, she is already wired into a suicide vest (possibly provided by Roohdaar). Haider states that he will never surrender to Khurram and must revenge his father's death; Ghazala speaks his grandfather's words warning against revenge – but she was not present when the words were initially spoken, so a disturbing, quasi-supernatural effect is created. When she walks into the graveyard to confront Khurram, she is ready to detonate herself. She is seen to be a woman in complete despair, but her strongest motivation is the imperative to save her son from certain death. Like Gertrude, her dying gestures all focus on her son. When Haider, bleeding heavily from his own wounds, rushes after her, his intention is to kill Khurram, but the echo of '[freedom] lies beyond revenge' prevents him and he limps away, leaving the scene of slaughter behind him. Bhardwaj explained in interview that his revised decision that Haider should not inevitably die arose from his political judgement: 'he overcomes his feeling of revenge. It makes him a bigger character. It leaves hope for Kashmir. For everything' (Bhardwaj, 'Decoding'). Political reappropriation can create a fragile new vision out of horror.

Ophelia in the twenty-first century: survival and revival

Ophelia speaks less than 5 per cent of the language of *Hamlet* and appears in only five of nineteen scenes, but, in recent decades, she has become one of the most frequently appropriated images

associated with the Shakespeare industry – Ophelia bedlinen
is one of the more bizarre examples. This is due in part to the
adaptogenic nature of the source text and the ambiguities accruing
around Ophelia and, equally, to feminist intentions to liberate
Ophelia from the romanticized but dutifully passive role prescribed
for her. The Victorian legacy, perpetuated through male-centred
criticism, awarded Ophelia pathos rather than agency. By the end
of the twentieth century, however, Ophelia had been thoroughly
reappropriated and reinvented, freed from operating as a prototype
of female insanity or 'essentialized notions of femininity' (Peterson
and Williams 2).

It was probably Hazlitt who set in motion the nineteenth-
century Romantic and Victorian reification of Ophelia as a
beautiful, altogether fragile, object: 'Ophelia is a character almost
too exquisitely touching to be dwelt upon. Oh rose of May, oh
flower too soon faded!' (Hazlitt, *Characters* 85). Ophelia's virginal
innocence and finely tuned sensibility became aestheticized and
eroticized in Millais' iconic painting (1851–2), an early Pre-
Raphaelite work that established the iconographical tone for the
many succeeding pictorial versions of Ophelia's 'truly feminine
death' (Showalter 81). Carol Kiefer's work establishes Ophelia as
the 'single most represented subject of English literary painting'
(quoted in Kiefer 12), permanently fetishized as the beautiful
corpse bedecked with flowers. French artists (Delacroix and
Redon, for example) and poets also adopted Ophelia's death as an
inspirational subject. The Symbolist poet Rimbaud wrote his lyrical
poem 'Ophélie' as an ekphrastic response to the necro-eroticism
of the paintings rather than to the play. In critical terms, A. C.
Bradley, at the beginning of the twentieth century, perpetuated the
Romantic interpretation: Ophelia's 'childlike nature' introduces a
'pathetic beauty, which makes the analysis of her character almost
a desecration' (Bradley 136). More recently, Lacan famously
commenced his seminar on *Hamlet* by announcing his intention
to discuss 'that piece of bait named Ophelia' (11). He signally
fails to address Ophelia herself; indeed, she is entirely negated as
'the exteriorized and rejected [phallus]' (23). Elaine Showalter
rescued Ophelia from perpetual Lacanian absence in her ground-
breaking study of the representation of Ophelia, in particular the
appropriation of Ophelia as emblematizing female derangement.
The ethical stance of Showalter's argument underpins later feminist
reappropriations: as Showalter explains, 'to dissolve [Ophelia] into

a female symbolism of absence is to endorse our own marginality; to make her Hamlet's anima is to reduce her to a metaphor of male experience' (79). By recontextualizing and critiquing representations of Ophelia, Showalter shows how pictorially and performatively Ophelia epitomizes each culture's distinctive construct of female sexuality: '[there] is no "true" Ophelia [...] only a Cubist Ophelia of multiple perspectives, more than the sum of all her parts' (92). Empowered theatrical Ophelias began to emerge with second-wave feminism. In Melissa Murray's agitprop verse drama *Ophelia* (1979), written for and performed by the women's theatre group Hormone Imbalance, a lesbian Ophelia despises Hamlet and elopes with her female servant, Branwen, to join a guerrilla commune, returning to Elsinore to execute the royal family. Murray's Ophelia is bold and self-determining: 'Hamlet: Madam, I love you. / Ophelia: Get you away from me' (M. Murray). By the end of the twentieth century, feminist readings of Shakespeare, together with the rise of Young Adult (YA) fiction as a distinct genre, paved the way for the reimagining of *Hamlet* from Ophelia's perspective, a radical rejection of Hamlet's interiority as 'the vortical subject of the play' (de Grazia 5). As a number of critics (Megan Lynn Isaac, Abigail Rokison) have observed, *Hamlet* is ripe material for the YA reader: moody adolescent dislikes his stepfather and fights with his mother; Ophelia's ambitious father bullies his daughter for his own advancement. Arguably, there are two distinct manifestations of Ophelia in the late twentieth century: in 1994 American psychologist Mary Pipher published *Reviving Ophelia: Saving the Selves of Adolescent Girls*, a series of case studies predicated on the 'destructive forces that affect young women' (Pipher 20). Pipher is concerned with showing ways in which cultural forces undermine female confidence, causing mental and emotional collapse, appropriating Ophelia as a metaphor for the adolescent crisis of identity; YA fiction, on the other hand, offers an infinitely more rebellious model. Four female-authored novels (Lisa Fiedler's *Dating Hamlet* (2002), Lisa Klein's *Ophelia* (2006), Rebecca Reisert's *Ophelia's Revenge* (2003) and Michelle Ray's *Falling for Hamlet* (2011)) share key tropes:

- Ophelia is the triumphant survivor of the tragedy.
- Ophelia is intelligent, assertive, resourceful, courageous.
- Ophelia enjoys a fulfilled sexual experience with Hamlet.

- Ophelia is openly defiant of her father's authority.
- Ophelia chooses to feign madness, and sometimes death, in order to survive the dangers of the court.
- Ophelia metamorphosizes into the heroine of a Shakespearean comedy, using disguise to escape the dangers of Elsinore.
- Ophelia as first-person narrator recounts and controls her story.

Lisa Fiedler's *Dating Hamlet* (2002) is undoubtedly the most light-heartedly ludic adaptation. The moral and emotional weight of *Hamlet* is significantly lessened by the reimagining of key details and by the narrative strategy of establishing Ophelia as first-person narrator. The motif of Ophelia's absent mother is often significant in these novels: here, Ophelia is skilled in the science of herbology because she has inherited her mother's written observations on plant lore and potions. Ophelia takes charge throughout; Hamlet is indecisive and melancholic. She sees the ghost, assists Hamlet in his plan of revenge, and they rehearse the 'nunnery' scene together. When threatened with rape by the guard, Barnardo, she escapes by drugging him and then landing an effective punch to his jaw. Later, after Hamlet has been sent to England, Ophelia is sexually threatened by Claudius himself and puts into action her plan of feigned madness followed by an apparent 'drowning'. Laertes, here, is a fellow plotter; the fencing scene is choreographed so that neither Laertes nor Hamlet is harmed; the poison is temporary. Gertrude, innocent of Claudius's scheming, is treated with the antidote; Claudius, left to the judgement of the invading Fortinbras, is left to die. Ophelia and Hamlet escape joyously to Verona. Selective fidelity characterizes Fiedler's text: quotations from *Hamlet* echo through key scenes but with radically changed tonality. The 'nunnery' scene, for example (Fiedler 81–5), intersperses Shakespeare's language with Ophelia's parenthetic comments and a certain amount of winking and concealed by-play between the youthful pair. Equally, Ophelia is still identified with the totemic flowers, but here they signify her superior botanical knowledge. Fiedler's text succeeds as a YA novel by pitting the young lovers against the machinations of the court; they emerge triumphant and sail away from Elsinore to their own happy ending.

Lisa Klein's *Ophelia* (2006) is also a first-person narrative that focuses on the survival of Ophelia, but the prefatory prologue reveals that the play's tragic outcomes are unaltered; nobody knows of Ophelia's survival except Horatio. Part 1 (1585–1601) functions as a prequel: Ophelia learns the highly restrictive courtly codes governing young women while internally rebelling. Proficient in Latin, she reads tales of courtly love with Gertrude; she also discovers Mechthild, a reclusive wise woman. Mutual passion between Ophelia and Hamlet results in a secret marriage and then pregnancy. Klein's tone is altogether darker than Fiedler's: Ophelia is deeply troubled by Hamlet's obsession with revenge and is conscious that it undermines her love for him; when she sees that Laertes is similarly 'sick with the contagion of revenge' (Klein 198) she realizes that she must take control of her own destiny. Again, the skills of the female apothecary are crucial to Ophelia's escape, together with her own daring and the ever-useful concealment of male disguise. Part 3 (1601–2) is unexpected and unusual, departing entirely from the source text. This final section takes place in a French convent, where Ophelia seeks refuge while she awaits the birth of her child. After the corruption and violence of the court, Ophelia is subject to a world of female authority. The individual novices tell their own tales of escape from sexual threats; the religious life offers safety and, for some, religious ecstasy. The final episodes of the novel describe Ophelia's joy at the birth of her son and the unexpected arrival of Horatio – clearly in love with Ophelia, he offers the promise of a new life. Unlike Fiedler, Klein's adaptation remains faithful to the greater intensity and darker emotions of the original. The addition of the sequel enables Ophelia's survival and motherhood but also opens a door onto a wider spectrum of female lives. Ophelia is offered a meaningful life with the sisterhood, not as a nun but as their apothecary.

Rebecca Reisert's *Ophelia's Revenge* (2003) weighs in at over 500 pages and is a blockbuster, action-packed novel, seizing the reader's attention from the outset:

> By my sixteenth birthday, I'd murdered two kings, my father, my brother, a queen, a prince and my husband.
>
> (Reisert 3)

This Ophelia has spent an innocent childhood in the castle's neighbouring village, a useful narrative strategy that enables her to judge aristocratic corruption with clear eyes. Once established at Elsinore, Ophelia soon discovers that she has the ability to see all the ghosts of the castle, including Yorick, who becomes her confidant and informer. Old Hamlet still reigns here – brutal and womanizing, with an elder son, Prince Holgar, who is cast in the same mould. Young Prince Hamlet is far from the warrior king required by his father: artistic, intellectual, melancholic. But when Holgar flings himself from the castle battlements in a fit of drunken bravado, Hamlet is the sole male heir. Old Hamlet, determined to father more sons, intends to murder Gertrude and marry Ophelia. Decisive action is required and Ophelia is ready and willing. The local herbwife provides poison for the murder of Old Hamlet; Ophelia subcontracts the deed to Claudius, who duly assumes the kingship and marries Gertrude. The teenage Ophelia is initially besotted with Hamlet, although her childhood friend, Ragnor, now a sea-faring adventurer, is clearly a powerful rival. Revelation dawns on Ophelia when Hamlet light-heartedly reveals that he has sent Rosencrantz and Guildenstern to their deaths: his lack of concern sickens her and she concludes that he could never be a just and moral king. Ophelia's feigned madness and death, the fatal duel and the deaths of Claudius and Gertrude follow with predictable inevitability. There is one key plot change: the ghostly Yorick has engineered the entire process in revenge for his own death, which was caused by Hamlet as a child. Ophelia is imprisoned by Erik Strong Arm (Fortinbras) while he determines whether she could be pregnant with Hamlet's child (and she is). But, ever resourceful, she escapes in servant clothing and joins Ragnor on a ship bound for England, anticipating 'a fine life [with] the freedom to be a woman and not a princess' (Reisert 519).

Michelle Ray's *Falling for Hamlet* (2011) opens with an uncompromising epigraph:

'Frailty, thy name is woman' – William Shakespeare
'Willy, thy name is sexism' – Ophelia

Michelle Ray is the only writer among the four discussed to recontextualize the entire drama in the current age. Her setting is a fictionalized Danish court in the full gaze of social media, ubiquitous surveillance and the cult of celebrity. The novel owes much to Almereyda's modern filmed version with Julia Stiles playing Ophelia as a young art student. Indeed, Jennifer Hulbert sees 'Shakespearean "It" girl, Julia Stiles' as creating a twenty-first-century Ophelia – a 'synecdoche for all teenage girls' (Hulbert 201). Ophelia, here, is on trial – both by an invented equivalent of the FBI and by television audience. The novel is structured through Ophelia's televised interview with Zara, clearly referencing Oprah Winfrey, and the intrusive questioning that she endures to escape a public witch-hunt. The officers of the DDI (Danish Department of Investigations) insult, bully and threaten her, but she lobs their insults back energetically:

BARNARDO
Are you always this mouthy?
OPHELIA
No. You just bring out the best in me.

(Ray 344)

Interestingly, in this present-day recontextualization, Ray chooses to incorporate extended paraphrases of the source text in a way which is both naturalistic and emotionally convincing:

Are you kidding me? Not even a month. The shoes she walked in behind my father's casket aren't even worn in. Did she want to save money by using the leftover food from the funeral [...] Goddamn it! My uncle? [...] Any animal would have mourned longer. Marrying my uncle? He's no more like my father than I am like ... like Superman.

(Ray 91)

Similarly, the fear of damnation that informs *Hamlet* is effectively transformed to a modern, agnostic perspective: 'What's in the afterlife – if there is one? That's the scary part. That's what keeps us living out our long painful lives [...] Fear of something worse makes us too scared to do anything' (Ray 122). Ray balances the intense interiority of Hamlet's suffering and Ophelia's emotional turmoil with the incessant public interrogation of 'celebrity' lives; Ophelia watches the intrusive TV reporting of the search-and-rescue mission to recover her body after her fake drowning. The final inevitable bloodbath leaves Ophelia threatened with prosecution. She is exonerated once the all-powerful Zara has decided to swing her TV audience against Claudius. Although she has survived, Ophelia's own epilogue is muted – more so than the historicized appropriations: 'I've learned to trust very few people [...] I've learned not to believe everything I see on TV [...] I've learned that I do believe in ghosts. [...] The rest is silence' (Ray 348). Ray's modern adaptation is trenchantly satiric: the novel critiques modern social and political mores but allows Ophelia to survive through an adroit manipulation of the tear-jerking confessional TV appearance. She is both vulnerable and solitary. But she succeeds in escaping to a new future in Paris.

All four of these twenty-first-century Ophelias, then, defy the limitations of their patriarchal cultures, drawing on female alliances (and, often, knowledge) not simply to survive but to create new futures, distant from the corrupting world of the court. In a neat intertextual reference, Ray's modern Ophelia reads a textbook on Millais, thereby signifying that this Ophelia has been rescued from Pre-Raphaelite iconography: present-day Ophelias are no longer simply the object of the male gaze. Although scripted, these novelized reimaginings share characteristics with online fanfiction: the revisionary adaptation of canonical texts is arguably where fanfiction begins. Michelle Yost offers a helpful definition: 'individual reflections and interpretations of old stories, updated to entertain others in the community without concern for profit or distribution' (194). Several online versions of *Ophelia's Diary* offer unlimited possibilities for 'talking back' to Shakespeare. Iyengar and Desmet find, similarly, that YouTube remediations reveal 'intense, emotional identification with Ophelia as a fictional person resembling the artist in age and gender' (68). The importance of school and college examination curricula should not be underestimated: *Romeo and Juliet*, with the largest online presence, is the most frequently examined Shakespeare text (a choice undoubtedly influenced by the popularity of Luhrmann's film). The digital platform is inevitably subject to obsolescence, however: as Michael Best establishes, computer codes need to be maintained or sites become extinct (Best 574). *Hamlet* attracts YouTube parodies, mashups and memes, all of which suggest a sophisticated process of recognition and cultural reinvention. Facetious parody such as 'Ophelia's Sassy Gay Friend' presupposes a degree of knowledge of the original, a paradox whereby the clip is avowedly anti-elitist while drawing upon Shakespeare –

the apotheosis of cultural icons. Adaptive parody dismantles the cultural icon while keeping the play alive. Ophelia's radically revived twenty-first-century identity testifies to the 'ambivalence of Shakespop [...] its capacity to serve the cultural status quo and its potential – incrementally, tentatively – to transform it' (Lanier, *Shakespeare* 109).

7

Othello

This chapter examines three treatments of *Othello*, one of the most frequently performed and adapted of Shakespeare's plays. Focusing on an *Othello* extract, the first section considers how far eighteenth-century editors might be regarded as adaptors. Moving to the Victorian period, the second section explores a burlesque version of *Othello*, staged in the same year as the Slave Emancipation Act. The final section looks at a silent film adaptation produced almost a century later, reflecting on how filmmakers embraced Shakespeare as a means of bringing respectability to a medium still to be welcomed into the realms of 'high culture'.

Othello and its eighteenth-century editors

To look across the critical apparatus of the three series of Arden Shakespeare is to survey a century of attitudinal change towards issues such as gender, class, race and nationality and, in so doing, to realize the necessity of keeping the early modern text in tune with the modern. Updating an edition inevitably involves some adaptive practices; as Bate and Massai point out, 'Editors and adapters, usually considered as two distinct figures, are in fact very similar: they both interact with a playscript to adjust it to the different exigencies of the receiving audience' (131). These 'exigencies' might include modernizing the text's spelling and grammar, adjusting footnotes to take account of what a new generation of readers needs to know, or rewriting the introduction to properly reflect the scholarly thinking and performance record of the day. In the past few decades, the burgeoning area of editing and textual studies has paid close attention to the eighteenth century, an era usually associated with the rise of the Shakespeare editor and the emergence of 'a mode of interpreting Shakespeare which privileged putatively "transcendent" reading over the vicissitudes of live performance' (Henderson 22). While Restoration dramatists had already engaged energetically with editing Shakespeare's plays to suit evolving theatrical tastes and conditions, it was not until the 1700s that 'named' editors came into being. Examining the sequence of complete-work editions, from Nicholas Rowe's in 1709 through to Edmond Malone's in 1790, reveals the increasing professionalism of Shakespearean editing, as ever-expanding prefaces were employed to justify textual methodology and to discuss the vexed issue of what were often referred to as the 'old copies' or 'ancient' versions of Shakespeare's plays: the quartos and the First Folio.

Othello is unique in being the only Shakespeare play to be published posthumously in two distinct full-length versions (the 1622 quarto, followed by the First Folio in 1623). One of the editors of the *New Oxford Shakespeare* calls attention to how these two texts 'disagree over about a thousand substantive verbal variants' (Taylor et al., vol. 2, 3137), underlining the challenges inherent in producing a single-text edition. E. A. J. Honigmann, the textual editor of the Arden 3 Revised Edition, fixes on 5.2.1–25 to exemplify his 'editorial thinking' (370), a speech picked out for scrutiny by several other modern commentators weighing up the quarto–Folio variants. This section settles on the same extract to consider six major editors and their complete-work editions: Nicholas Rowe (1709), Alexander Pope (1723–5), Lewis Theobald (1733), Samuel Johnson (1765), Edward Capell (1767–8) and Edmond Malone (1790). More specifically, it examines three areas of editorial procedure that attend to adapting the text for the contemporary reader: evoking the stage on the page; ensuring clarity of meaning; and preserving and promoting the aesthetic qualities of the writing.

The stage on the page

In the 1700s, the increasing availability of print Shakespeare meant that more and more people experienced the plays on the page, and editors played an important role in assisting their dramatic imaginations. Nicholas Rowe, the first named editor of Shakespeare's works, brought his own experience as a successful dramatist to bear on his editorial enterprise, for the first time marking act and scene divisions throughout and providing *dramatis personae* at the start of each play; he also commissioned woodcut illustrations of the works in performance – a visual stimulus for the reader, which, according to some scholars, 'may reflect actual performances' (Vaughan, *Othello* 95). The *Othello* illustration depicts the moment directly following the suffocation of Desdemona; the hero, costumed as an eighteenth-century British army officer, is shown with his arms spread wide in what appears to be a gesture of extreme anguish as the dead Desdemona lies lifeless on the bed, one breast exposed – a detail which recalls the Restoration relish for vulnerable female flesh laid bare. Placed opposite the play's title page, the eroticized image would doubtless have shaped how readers pictured the drama as it unfolded in the mind's eye.

One other significant innovation in Rowe's edition is the addition of stage directions to his Fourth Folio base text. He extends the initial directions for 5.2 ('*Enter* Othello, *and* Desdemona *in her bed*') by providing the fictional stage direction '*A Bed-chamber*' and making explicit for the reader that Desdemona '*is discover'd asleep in her Bed*'; he also adds the direction '*Kissing her*' at the line 'I'll smell thee on the Tree', here importing the quarto stage direction: 'He kisses her'. Pope built on Rowe's theatrical stage directions, specifying that Othello enters '*with a light, and a sword*', both stage props serving to literalize the imagery of the passage, as well as prompting the first-time reader to anticipate (wrongly) that the protagonist will, indeed, 'scar that whiter skin [...] than snow'. If, as the century wore on, editors would look increasingly to the early Shakespeare texts to establish their own version, stage directions remained a domain apart, treated 'with a latitude not exercised in relation to a play's speeches' (Dustagheer and Woods 3). Malone, for example, though he placed great value on the quarto and Folio editions of Shakespeare, nonetheless regarded the stage directions found there as inauthentic in that they were 'furnished by the players' (Malone, vol. 1, part 1, lviii).

Reading across the centuries

The linguistic landscape of the eighteenth century was sufficiently altered from that of a century earlier to make reading Shakespeare a challenging endeavour, and editors set about assisting the reader's comprehension by deploying a range of textual and paratextual strategies. Modernizing spelling, grammar and punctuation was one obvious way to make the text more 'readable', a process of updating that 'has been regarded by some commentators as a form of adaptation' (Kidnie 163). Various other reader-assistive strategies might be considered adaptive in nature in that they involve the editor's own literary sensibilities: emending textual obscurities; identifying and correcting 'errors' attributed to early modern carelessness; supplying explanatory notes and annotations; compiling glossaries (even a word definition is not influence-free). According to Lukas Erne, Samuel Johnson was the first Shakespeare editor to undertake 'Herculean labors to illuminate the countless words and passages that are far from self-explanatory' (67). As a skilled lexicographer and author of the first *Dictionary of the English Language* (1755), Johnson was more than qualified to take on the task of making the 'authour's meaning accessible to many who were frighted from perusing him' (Johnson, vol. 1, D6r), and one of the ways he accomplished this was by supplying detailed explanatory notes. Mindful of the reader experience, he provides the following guide to using the textual apparatus:

> Notes are often necessary, but they are necessary evils. Let him, that is yet unacquainted with the powers of *Shakespeare* [...] read every play from the first scene to the last, with utter negligence of all his commentators. [...] And when the pleasures of novelty have ceased, let him attempt exactness, and read the commentators.
>
> (E4r)

Johnson's notes on 5.2 include those of his predecessor, Theobald. However, while he records verbatim some of Theobald's commentary on the line 'Put out the light, and then put out the light', he omits observations drawn from the editor's personal experience of the play on stage. A similar move away from the theatrical can be detected in Johnson's own comments on the scene. He identifies Othello's soliloquy as 'obscure' in its 'abruptness' before explaining what he takes to be the meaning of what the speaker 'says [...] in his mind' (vol. 8, 455). Here, the soliloquy is treated not as a dramatic device, whereby ideas and feelings are expressed aloud to the audience, but as interior thought; the speech, then, remains in the speaker's head, ready to be transmitted to that of the reader.

Critical apparatus grew bulkier with each successive edition as editors concerned themselves less with making the text intelligible for the reader and more with the editorial process itself. Editors engaged with an increasingly wide assortment of texts, placing ever greater store on the first quarto and First Folio versions of plays. Capell was the first to compose his text from scratch, executing a painstaking collation of the early texts rather than marking up that of the editor before him. The variants of 5.2.1–25 must have proved especially exacting; take, for instance, the metaphor of the rose, with its connotations of virginity and olfactory resonances. Capell's selection of the First Folio's 'pluck'd thy Rose' over the quarto's 'pluckt the rose' is one example of how the choice of one three-letter functional word over another can significantly alter meaning and impact. As Massai observes in her perceptive variorum close reading of the extract, 'the deictic pronoun foregrounds Desdemona's physical proximity to Othello', whereas the generic 'the rose' 'distances him from the immediacy of the sensorial experience his words evoke' (Massai 71). Capell's subsequent opting for the First Folio's 'I'll smell thee on the Tree' over the quarto's 'I'll smell it on the tree' is in keeping with his earlier choice of 'thy rose', creating an erotically charged stage moment and, at the same time, echoing Othello's earlier railing at Desdemona: 'O thou weed / Who art so lovely fair and smell'st so sweet / That the sense aches at thee' (4.2.68–70). However, Capell moves back to the quarto to include the stage direction (not provided in the First Folio) that Othello kisses Desdemona, an editorial decision that has stood from Rowe to the present day, perhaps because kissing is 'a culturally more discreet' act than the 'indiscreet and oddly unquantifiable act of smelling' (Massai 72).

Following Capell, Malone produced an edition considered by most scholars to represent 'a step change in scholarship and method' (Ritchie and Sabor 34), one that made no concessions to the casual reader. If, as Johnson warned, some Shakespeare readers found that the 'mind is refrigerated by interruption' (vol. 1, E4v), they would not have fared well with this editorial 'step change': the text of 5.2.1–25 is spread over four pages, with the proportion of notes far outweighing the dramatic text (Malone, vol. 9, 619–22). Like Capell, Malone based his text on a collation of the 1622 quarto and the 1623 Folio, only departing from his predecessor in his treatment of the rose image. Though he follows Capell in choosing the Folio's personal pronoun ('thy rose') over the quarto's more distancing definite article ('the rose'), he then returns to the quarto, preferring 'smell it' to the Folio's 'smell thee', thereby lessening the sense of somatic intimacy. At the same time, he departs from his editorial predecessors in favouring the quarto version's 'once more', a decision that captures the diffuseness of the act of smelling more than the Folio's 'one more', which summons an action distinct enough to be counted.

Scrutinizing Capell's and Malone's linguistic choices for this scene reveals, then, how editing is far from a neutral process. Indeed, by the middle of the eighteenth century, the tendentiousness of the editor was already a target for satire. Henry Fielding's prose fantasy, A Journey from This World to the Next (1745), mocks the editorial process through an imaginary dispute between two great Shakespearean actors, Betterton and Booth, over the reading of one line from 5.2: 'Put out the light, and then put out the light.' Failing to reach a consensus, they appeal to Shakespeare himself, who, with a shrug, declares: 'Faith, gentleman, it is so long since I wrote the line, I have forgot my meaning' (Fielding 41).

Textual aesthetics

Shakespeare's early named editors subscribed to the somewhat nebulous concept of aesthetic value as one of their guiding principles. As an admired and established poet, Pope was supremely confident in his own aesthetic judgement, implementing a system of annotation that drew the reader's attention to how he had separated the literary wheat from the chaff:

Some suspected passages which are excessively bad [...] are degraded to the bottom of the page [...]. Some of the most shining passages are distinguish'd by comma's [*sic*] in the margin; and where the beauty lay not in particulars but in the whole a star is prefix'd to the scene.

(Pope, vol. 1, xxii–xxiii)

As one recent textual scholar puts it, Pope 'acted as Shakespeare's artistic partner, rather than his textual servant' (Murphy 96), a partnership that included smoothing out metrical infelicities and selecting textual variants to present Shakespeare in what the editor regarded as his Sunday best. In a century which saw readers grow ever more sensitive to indecorousness, Pope's textual makeover also entailed ridding the plays of potentially offensive language; as one modern scholar highlights, the 'real rationale' behind Pope's relegation of dubious passages 'seems often to be an aesthetic objection to Shakespearean banter, quibble and vulgarity' (Walsh 25). And Pope was not alone in attempting to exonerate Shakespeare from the charge of coarseness. Thomas Hanmer, one of Shakespeare's less distinguished editors, maintains in his preface that most of the 'low stuff which disgraces the works of this great Author' was interpolated by the players, following Shakespeare's death, in an attempt to 'please the vulgar audiences by which they subsisted' (iii–iv). In a similar vein, Francis Gentleman, the editor of Bell's popular acting edition of Shakespeare's plays, explains in the Advertisement that the acting copies printed therein have been relieved of what 'may justly be attributed to the loose quibbling, licentious taste of his time' (A3r).

Moving very decidedly away from the aesthetic approach, Johnson states in his preface that Shakespeare's language was not 'designed for the reader's desk' (D2r) and warns against promoting the plays by 'select quotations' (A3r) – a warning that may also have been aimed at the flourishing anthology market that grew up in the second half of the century. Explicitly distinguishing himself from the poet–editor Pope, Johnson goes on to explain: '[t]he poetical beauties or defects I have not been very diligent to observe [...]. The reader, I believe, is seldom pleased to find his opinion anticipated; it is natural to delight more in what we find or make, than in what we receive' (D7v).

The eighteenth-century editorial project endeavoured to provide the reader with as intelligible and 'authentic' a version of the national poet as recoverable. Such an endeavour might appear far removed from adaptive purpose and praxis; after all, an adaptation is usually defined by its divergence from the source text, whereas an edition is commonly taken as the source text itself. Yet, as this section has exemplified, editorial practices nonetheless 'adapt Shakespeare, making him conform to a particular editorial vision' (Fischlin and Fortier 17) shaped by the cultural, social and moral parameters of the day.

Charles Mathews, *Othello, the Moor of Fleet Street* (1833)

Shakespeare's plays stood at the very centre of nineteenth-century social and literary culture: they enjoyed a privileged place in theatre repertoires, served as edifying reading material for the young and provided inspiration for a range of transmedial adaptations. Yet among the myriad outward manifestations of Victorian reverence for the man and all his works, there was one that revealed a somewhat more ambivalent attitude: the Shakespeare burlesque or 'travesty'. Fast-paced and resolutely raucous in tone and action, these stage entertainments appropriated the 'serious' Shakespeare texts and played them for laughs. Whether this clash of popular and high cultures threatened the iconicity of Shakespeare or ultimately reaffirmed it is one of the central questions posed by this carnivalesque genre, one already taken up by John Poole, author of the first full-length Shakespearean burlesque to be performed on the public stage. In the preface to his highly successful *Hamlet Travestie* (1810), Poole comes down strongly on the side of affirmation, writing self-deprecatingly:

> Homer and Virgil have both been the subjects of strong burlesques, but they are still read with unabated admiration [...] and it would be an insult to the high character of our Poet, were it supposed that the wreath is so loosely twined around *his* brows as to be endangered by so mere a trifle [*Hamlet Travestie*].
>
> (J. Poole vi–vii)

Also included in Poole's paratext are mock-scholarly annotations of the burlesqued playscript, forming a witty spoof on the editorial tradition developed over the eighteenth century and the high seriousness of contemporary Shakespeareans: the 'false lights, and the fanciful and arbitrary illustrations, of Black-letter Critics and Coney-catching Commentators' (J. Poole viii). Evident here is Poole's conviction that the main target for burlesque treatment is not Shakespeare himself but those who attempt to take charge of him. As the author of the definitive study of Shakespeare burlesques observes: '[b]y its own admission [...] the burlesque actively intervened to protect Shakespeare from his true detractors' (Schoch 4).

Given that the dynamic of the burlesque rests on the deliberate undermining of the elevated and the grave, Shakespeare's tragedies were an obvious choice for burlesquers. Familiarity was also an important selection criterion: audiences needed to have at least a basic grasp of the prior text if they were to detect and savour the shift from high seriousness to broad comedy, hence why the most frequently performed tragedies were favoured by the parodists (*Romeo and Juliet*, *Hamlet*, *Othello* and *Macbeth* proved especially popular). *Othello, the Moor of Fleet Street* was the first burlesque treatment of Shakespeare's *Othello* to be staged. If twenty-first-century perspectives on race and gender now make *Othello* one of the least amenable tragedies to parodic treatment, this was not so much the case in the early Victorian period. *Othello*'s comic potentiality has been remarked upon as far back as Thomas Rymer's *A Short View of Tragedy* (1693), which concluded that '[t]here is in this Play, some burlesk, some humour, and ramble of Comical Wit' (146) and continues to be acknowledged by some modern Shakespearean scholars. Yet if, as Michael Bristol contends, the play 'lends itself very well to parody, burlesque and caricature' (181), these comic possibilities are rarely developed in modern productions; the play remains one of the most adaptogenic of the canon partly because adapters have chosen to minimize its comedy and maximize its tragic force to explore urgent issues such as multiculturalism, institutional racism and gender inequality.

Othello, the Moor of Fleet Street, thought to have been composed by the comedian Charles Mathews (though authorship is not entirely certain), was first performed in 1833: a highly significant year, both in terms of British politics and the history of *Othello* in performance. Following closely on the heels of the 1832 Reform Act, the Slave Emancipation Act of 1833 took another legislative step towards democratization and universal human rights. Legislation notwithstanding, the racist ideology that had kept the institution of plantation slavery firmly in place for centuries remained a powerful force in British society, as was evident from the theatrical fortunes of Ira Aldridge, the first black performer to appear on one of the patent-theatre stages. When, in March 1833, the great Shakespearean actor Edmund Kean collapsed while performing the role of Othello at the Theatre Royal, Covent Garden, Aldridge accepted an invitation to take his place. Although he was warmly received by audiences and certain areas of the press, some of the day's influential journals responded to the stand-in with bitterly hostile and racialist attacks, generating negative publicity which might well have contributed (along with a flu epidemic in London) to lamentably poor box-office takings and the consequent closure of the production after only two performances.

Just a few months prior to Aldridge's ill-fated appearances at the prestigious Theatre Royal, *Othello, the Moor of Fleet Street* had opened close by at the rather less prestigious Adelphi Theatre. One of the generic characteristics of such burlesques was the downgrading of characters' social status and living conditions, enabling *Othello* parodists such as Mathews to conjoin blackness and menial status, thus keeping in place long-embedded intersectional hierarchies. Set among the urban underclass, the hero, said to be modelled on a real-life figure (see the introduction to Draudt's edition, 28), is cast as a crossing-sweeper. As the title announces, the play-world is relocated from Venice to London's Blackfriars, with a brief jaunt to the Old Bailey serving as the move to Cyprus. In common with most burlesques, *The Moor of Fleet Street* relies heavily on social stereotyping to provoke an immediate response from the spectator, which, along with the speed created by the relentless rhymes and rhythms of the script's dialogue and song lyrics, helps generate a brisk dramatic tempo. How far Shakespeare's *Othello* deconstructs or colludes with racial stereotypes has long divided critics, though there is no denying that, in the first two acts at least, the high esteem in which Othello is held in Venice, his rhetorical facility, his calmness in the face of provocation, and his self-styling as a man whose sexual appetites are now 'defunct' (*Oth* 1.3.265) all run counter to seventeenth-century stereotypes of the African. Mathews' Moor, on the other hand, conforms to crude racial stereotypes from start to finish. In being subjected to the burlesque tradition of social relegation, Mathews's Othello has none of what G. Wilson Knight termed the 'Othello music', a rhetorical diminishment that is especially noticeable in his dealings with Desdemona. In his first speech, he defines her as a 'drab' (Mathews 2.2), an expression that accords with Rymer's view that 'a *Moor* might marry some little drab' (Rymer 92) but would never rise to the status of a general, as Shakespeare would have it. He is also quick to attribute blame to his wife. In a scene burlesquing the Shakespearean Othello's appearance before the Senate, the Fleet Street Moor tells the Lord Mayor that Desdemona is the 'cause of all this breach' (Mathews 3.51), his phrasing echoing the judgement passed by Shakespeare's hero only in the play's concluding act. And the exotic storytelling of Shakespeare's hero is transformed into a musical parody, concluding with the linguistically nonsensical 'Tooral looral lay, te rol rumpti nay, / Tweedle deedle rem! ri fol rumpti doodle em!' (3.47–8).

A genre ill-suited to the lexical and rhetorical subtlety that characterizes Iago's treatment of Othello in the source text, the Fleet Street double-dealer's manipulative power extends little further than plying the sweeper with alcohol, a strategy only practised upon the Moor's subordinate, Cassio, in Shakespeare's version. The burlesque's most overt racism imposes itself when Othello returns home in an advanced state of inebriation, singing:

Bukra wives, dey like Old Nick,
Very fair to face, sir.
Very black dey do de trick
Dere hubbies to disgrace, sir;
Sing ching clink qua, for woman's flaw
De African have speedy law.

(7.21–6)

Shifting from his usual colloquial English, shared by his white working-class compatriots, to a black dialect reminiscent of the blackface minstrel, the song succeeds in transforming Shakespeare's noble Moor into a brute whose roots lie in a culture that sanctions murder as a punishment for sexually errant wives. Here, as elsewhere in *The Moor of Fleet Street*, the audience is left in no doubt that Othello is a black African, an identity that runs counter to the 'tawny' Moor played by Edmund Kean. This famous actor's performative skin-whitening helped erase any affiliation of the hero with plantation slavery and eased early nineteenth-century anxieties about the play's bi-racial marriage; Kean's acting career did, after all, coincide with the writing career of Charles Lamb, who, in an essay extolling the delights of Shakespeare on the page, wondered whether a spectator of a stage *Othello* 'did not find something extremely revolting in the courtship and wedded caresses of Othello and Desdemona' (Lamb, *Works*, vol. 2, 27–8).

Celebrity players such as Kean were themselves often the satirical target of burlesquers, as is evident in Mathews's stage direction advising that Othello's speech to the Senators be '*spoken in the manner of Kean*'. Its opening line, 'Most potent, very reverend, grave' (3.35), is a slight, though nonetheless comic, rearrangement of Shakespeare's 'Most potent, grave, and reverend signiors' (*Oth* 1.3.77) – one that is clearly intended to mimic the point in the play when Othello appears at his most eloquent. The actor cast in the role of the burlesque Othello, John Reeve, the Adelphi's most popular low comedian, would doubtless have exercised all his dramatic skills in impersonating the 'high culture' delivery of the patent-theatre actor; indeed, a review in the *Spectator* suggested that the 'vulgar burlesque of *Othello*' had been produced mainly for the sake of 'introducing imitations of Kean and Macready [who played Iago to Kean's Othello]' (quoted in the Draudt edition, 26, n. 53).

The Moor of Fleet Street's resolution sees comedy triumph over tragedy. Despite various threats of murder and mayhem, nobody dies, and a rousing finale restores harmony in the play-world at the same time as ratcheting up the metatheatricality. Playgoers are reminded, 'No Patent shop is this, and we / Are not the Patent folk' (7.74–5), a declaration that presupposes a largely middle-class audience with at least an awareness of the 'legitimate' Shakespeare practice being held up to ridicule. Perhaps, then, one of the chief attractions for the burlesque audience was to inhabit two socio-cultural milieus at once: the Adelphi on the Strand was, after all, just a few minutes' walk away from the patent Covent Garden and Drury Lane theatres.

Nowadays, nineteenth-century burlesques are rarely revived, a neglect attributed by some scholars to their characteristic topicality, colloquialisms and 'in-jokes', all of which render them incomprehensible to future generations. In his invaluable edition of *The Moor of Fleet Street*, for instance, Manfred Draudt reveals a heightened concern with the decipherability of the slang lexicon, glossing phrases such as 'diddling', 'save his bacon' and 'a dozen bob a day', despite their being perfectly familiar to present-day native speakers. Yet if the unintelligibility case can sometimes be overstated, there is no doubt that the enduringly popular adaptive strategy of contemporarization can render a reworking culturally obscure for future audiences, consigning it – if it survives at all – to a secondary place alongside its textual predecessor. However, when it comes to *The Moor of Fleet Street*, it is primarily the play's treatment of race that renders it beyond the pale of performance in the twenty-first century. Desdemona's final speech, delivered directly to the audience's women, declares, 'Ladies, I hope you'll like my love, / He's far more fair than black' (7.82–3). More than a simple echo of the Duke's pronouncement in Shakespeare's version (*Oth* 1.3.291), the line serves as a metatheatrical reassurance that there is a white actor in control beneath the black make-up – a dramatic tradition that would take more than another century to dislodge.

Othello, dir. Dimitri Buchowetzki (1922)

The retronymic denotation of the 'silent film' calls attention to its identity as a thing of the past, a cinematic form rendered obsolete by the technological advances which ushered in the era of the 'talkies'. Up until the early years of this century, silent Shakespeare films looked destined for archival obscurity, discounted by most literary scholars for their lack of spoken dialogue and snubbed by cinephiles for aping the conventions of the stage rather than embracing the new techniques of cinema. In recent years, however, early screen Shakespeare has attracted considerable attention from both film and literature specialists. Judith Buchanan, one of the foremost experts in the field, estimates that there were between 250 and 300 silent Shakespeare adaptions made between 1899 and the emergence of the sound era in 1927, of which around forty survive (*Excellent* 1–2). It is an estimate that underscores the importance of Shakespeare to early filmmakers, one that came about partly because of cinema's struggle to be recognized as a 'proper' art form: adapting plays of great cultural cachet was one means of gaining respectability. Additionally, the familiarity of Shakespeare's storylines and characters suited the wordless aesthetic. Prior knowledge meant that audiences could follow the narrative with relative ease, at the same time as enjoying the novelty of seeing the stories played out in a new medium, one that offered a verisimilitude that had been keenly sought – but never achieved – through the pictorial, 'archaeological' approach of late-Victorian stage managers.

One reason why cinema has tended to be excluded from the highest echelons of creative endeavour is its association with the commercial and the popular. Making movies has always been a costly enterprise and that the silent film industry flourished at all was down to the willingness of those with the economic wherewithal to invest in marketable productions. That film adaptations of Shakespeare were by necessity dialogue-free meant that audiences did not have to grapple with the verbal difficulties posed by Early Modern English, thus increasing their commercial appeal. Intertitles (also termed title cards) could carry judiciously selected quotations from or paraphrases of the inherited text, enabling twentieth-century audiences to follow the action unimpeded by linguistic obscurities. Thanks to its portability, the intertitle also encouraged a vigorous international market; as Russell Jackson points out, 'the substitution of title cards in the language of the country where they were shown made films easy to export' (3). The history of *Othello* on the pre-sound screen is typical of the transnational reach of silent Shakespeare, with British, Danish, French, German, Italian and American productions all appearing in the adaptation timeline (details are available at http://bufvc.ac.uk/shakespeare/). These range from the 'momentary visual "quotations"' (Buchanan, 'Shakespeare' 471) of the early 'one-reelers' to films of an hour or more, made possible by developing technologies; they also demonstrate an impressive diversity of adaptive approaches, some anticipating future trends in screen Shakespeare, such as modern updating, pastiche, animation and the production-within-a-production.

According to the British Universities Film and Video Council website, eighteen silent film versions of Shakespeare's *Othello* had already been produced by the time Dimitri Buchowetzki's *Othello* was released in 1922. Out of this number, only five survive, the

American version of Buchowetzki's six-reel *Othello* being the most accessible and, with a running time of sixty-five minutes (a few minutes shorter than the original German version), the longest of them all. Starring the popular screen and stage actors Emil Jannings (Othello) and Werner Krauss (Iago), it played to appreciative movie audiences on its New York release in 1923 and was well-received by the critics. Later responses, though, have been somewhat more hostile. The author of the first major study of silent Shakespeare, Robert Hamilton Ball, pronounced it 'tasteless and unimaginative' (279), and more recent film scholars, though a little less damning in their judgements, have declared it 'a magnificent wreck' (Rothwell, *History* 25) and 'grandly overblown' (Buchanan, *Excellent* 7). Shot mainly in Berlin film studios, Buchowetzki resisted the glamour of location filming (first tried out in a twelve-minute Italian version of *Othello*, released in 1909), opting instead to signify Venice through the occasional verbal or visual gondola reference and letting one outdoor shot of a fort's crenelated roof stand for Cyprus. Boasting some impressive tableau shots, the film is certainly grand in setting and architecture, employing a broadly expressionist cinematography. Where Rothwell considers that its 'streak of realism makes it too literal-minded for greatness' (*History* 25), a more recent commentator reads the director's decision to adopt an expressionist style as offering 'a firm challenge to the idea that adapting the Anglophone playwright means surrendering to the cultural values, aesthetic or other, according to which his original work was produced' (Semenza, 'Globalist' 336–7).

It could, indeed, be argued that the absence of spoken language frees the silent film adaptation to some extent from Shakespeare's perceived cultural supremacy; at the same time, as Buchanan and others have observed, it is this same absence that causes many to regard the very idea of 'silent Shakespeare' as oxymoronic. As the visual sophistication of early cinema grew, so the continuing lack of audio dialogue became ever more noticeable and incongruous, prompting Shakespeare's screen adapters to experiment with mitigating strategies, one such being the use of intertitles. Buchowetzki's *Othello* includes close to 200 intertitles, approximately 10 per cent of which are devoted to exposition, with the rest presenting individual speeches or dialogue; these are either copied directly from the playtext or, more typically, paraphrased in what one critic described as 'appalling, invented

Renaissance Argot' (Guneratne 162). As Lois Potter observes, although the 'sheer length of the English captions [...] looks like homage to the source [...] the adaptation is extremely free' (98) and, in some instances, includes additions which substantially alter the play's meaning. One case in point is Othello's pronouncement via intertitle that he is the 'son of Egyptian prince and Spanish princess'. Emphasized by underlining, this specific detail of the hero's bi-racial origins could be seen to render him less 'other', a means of 'playing down miscegenation, perhaps to explain to American audiences that Othello is not a negro' (Ball 281); however, as more recent critical commentators point out, this intertitular information sits somewhat incongruously with Emil Jannings's 'very black make-up' (Hatchuel and Vienne-Guerrin 5). As well as textual additions, there are also substantial textual rearrangements. For instance, Othello's 'I am your own for ever', spoken to Iago at the close of 3.3, becomes 'I am bound to you for ever', delivered not as a chilling signifier that the speaker is completely in thrall to the play's 'demi-devil' but as an expression of gratitude for Iago's safe-keeping of Desdemona during the voyage to Cyprus. The inherited text is also moved around in order to promote clear visual links between scenes and to clarify the action; the handkerchief, for example, is introduced as a bridal gift at an early point in the narrative, with Othello delivering a dire warning to his wife of the consequences of mislaying it. As events take their course, so we see the magical handkerchief, minus its sexually suggestive strawberries (not easy to picture in black and white), pass through the hands of Emilia and Iago before ending up back with its original possessor. By this stage a sign of a wife's infidelity, it provides one of the most memorable moments of the film, as Othello takes the erstwhile love token and tears it to shreds with his teeth.

Extreme performance gestures akin to this handkerchief-shredding have earned Buchowetzki's *Othello* a good deal of critical opprobrium. Ball gives a wholesale denouncement of the acting, deeming it no more than 'extravagant mumming and mugging [mouthing words]' (Ball 279); most critics have followed suit, blaming perceived failures on the actors' inability – or unwillingness – to adapt to filmic performance codes. For sure, *Othello* is a drama wherein the chief power of both hero and villain derives from their impressive, if distinctly different, command of rhetoric – a strength which is especially challenging to convey in a non-speaking medium. Buchanan considers Jannings's performance to lack 'the necessary nuanced physical eloquence to compensate sufficiently for the character's lack of language' ('Shakespeare' 479) and there is no doubt that, even allowing for what some see as Buchowetzki's commitment to the stylistic distortions of expressionism, the actor's screen presence sits uneasily with the celebrated 'Othello music'. Iago's linguistic deftness is perhaps more successfully captured through Krauss's bodily stance and gestures, as persuasive speech is replaced with the caressing, stroking, leaning against, smoothing down and cradling of those he seeks to manipulate. And, just as in the final stages of the play, when Iago's manipulation of Othello has worked so effectively that he feels he can safely 'save [his] speech' (*Oth* 4.1.280), so in the film, immediately prior to Desdemona's murder, Iago is seen to 'save' his physical exertions. In a medium-long two-shot, a trembling, enraged Othello faces the camera, his lieutenant standing right next to him, stock still and bolt upright, his back to the camera. Reaching for the sword that hangs phallically below his waist, Othello at first places it in Iago's hands but, following an intercut shot of the sleeping Desdemona, takes the murder weapon into his own hands – Iago's villainous labouring is done.

If Buchowetzki's adaptive methods are shaped to a greater or lesser extent by the limitations of pre-sound cinema, they are also assisted by the exciting interpretive and performative capabilities of the rapidly evolving medium. The technique of cross-cutting, for example, provides a succinct means of creating suspense, as in the case of Othello and Desdemona's marriage ceremony cross-cut with that of Brabantio's calling up 'special officers' in response to hearing that his daughter has fallen into the 'gross clasps of the moor!' Similarly, frequent cross-cutting of scenes featuring the newly-weds' lovemaking with those of Iago scheming to destroy them creates an immediate, acute sense of irony. Also made possible by the technological affordances of film is the superimposed projection of Othello's dream onto the curtain draped behind the couch on which he sleeps. Picturing Desdemona with her hair flowing more freely than at any other point in the film, embracing Cassio with unconcealed erotic fervour, Buchowetzki translates Iago's studiedly casual line 'With her, on her, what you will' (*Oth* 4.1.34) into the psycho-sexual vision it conjures up in his interlocutor. And if the movie camera facilitated new ways of capturing the close-up and personal in *Othello*, so it also captured the play's wider political worlds through its capacity to shoot convincing crowd scenes from a variety of perspectives. Dismissed by some as otiose (Rothwell quipped, '[n]ever have so many extras done so much to accomplish so little' (*History* 26)), they nonetheless serve to underscore Othello's military prowess, as the masses clamour for him to remain in charge of defeating the Turkish foe – a threat kept in the filmic foreground throughout the narrative. Moreover, punctuating the film's action as they do, the crowd scenes maintain the tension between the hero's domestic and martial lives, adding an extra dimension to his marital breakdown and fall from grace.

At the close of Buchowetzki's *Othello*, the body count is not substantially adrift from that of the source drama, though the characters on the director's fatalities list do not correspond entirely with those on Shakespeare's. Emilia – played as young and impressionable more than worldly wise – is spared, left alive to reflect on the havoc she has witnessed; however, in a reversal of the play's finale, Iago dies at the hands of Othello, who, having labelled his lieutenant a 'Spartan dog' (a repurposing of Lodovico's phrase at 5.2.359), stabs him in the back. Buchowetzki, then, delivers the satisfaction of a hero avenged and a villain punished, realizing, perhaps, that the deep unease a theatre audience feels at Iago's refusal to 'speak word' (*Oth* 5.2.301) would not translate readily to a medium in which no one ever does.

8

King Lear

This chapter explores three twentieth-century appropriations of *King Lear*. For both Bond and Smiley, adaptation functions as critique; engaging in highly confrontational dialogue with Shakespeare, they reject platitudes about unchanging verities yet discover that 'his plays still work for those who live in this later time of revolution'. Kurosawa's *Ran* localizes and recontextualizes Shakespeare, melding Jacobean tragedy with Japanese history and performance tradition. All three reimaginings attest to the malleability of the hypotext, creating vital and troubling visions of individual suffering within a wider context of familial and social violence.

Edward Bond, *Lear* (1971)

Edward Bond (born 1934) is widely regarded as an *enfant terrible* of the modern British stage: radical and uncompromising. His dislike of Britain's establishment theatre has resulted in his plays being performed more frequently in Europe than in London, and his eightieth birthday, in 2014, passed unmarked by Britain's media. Bond's family background – labouring working class – and the disruptions of the Second World War meant that he received very little in the way of formal schooling; indeed, he is on record as saying that his effective education consisted of one memorable evening seeing Donald Wolfit play Macbeth:

[For] the very first time in my life [...] I met somebody who was actually talking about my problems, about the life I'd been living, the political society around me. [...] There was just this feeling of total recognition. I *knew* all these people [...] this in fact was my world.

(Bond, 'Drama' 5)

Reaching adulthood in the mid-twentieth century could be seen as a mixed blessing; the possibility of greater social mobility weighed against the inheritance of the post-war world with its revelations of Nazi atrocities and Stalinist 'Terror'. The Iron Curtain and the threat of nuclear destruction was felt acutely; the late 1960s saw the escalation of American war in Vietnam and, in Britain, conflict on the streets of Northern Ireland. In Shakespearean terms the 1960s saw *King Lear* 'usurp[ing] the throne securely occupied by *Hamlet*', emerging as 'the keystone of the canon' (Ryan, '*King Lear*' 1). Shakespearean critics such as Jan Kott found existential futility in *King Lear*; a tragic grotesque 'that exposes the absurdity of apparent reality' (Kott, *Shakespeare* 133). For Bond there is no question of such nihilism; his theatre is 'prescribed by the political situation in which it is created' (Bond, *Plays* xi); the audience should be forced to engage with 'things it would normally run away from in fear, turn away from in embarrassment' (quoted in Hirst 24). Bond's attitude to the theatre audience certainly shapes the way in which he appropriates *King Lear*: he objects vigorously to 'the worshipping of that play by the academic theatre [which] I think is a totally dishonest experience'. For Bond, it is 'artistically lazy' to admire Lear's suffering: '[it's] nice and comfortable. You don't have to question yourself, or change your society' (Bond, 'Interview' 24). Bond is frank in his admiration of Shakespeare's play, seeing it as the text from which he has 'learned more [than] from any other play', but he is also clear that 'we now have to use the play for ourselves, for our society, for our time, for our problems' ('Interview' 24).

Bond's play begins and ends with violent death and with the symbolically divisive wall, a bleakly contemporary signifier connoting the dangerous and inexorable barrier of the Iron Curtain. At the opening of the play, Lear, with his courtly retinue, is making an official visit to inspect the wall, his two daughters, Bodice and Fontanelle, uttering meaningless clichés: 'so enjoyable and informative', 'Such an interesting day' (Bond, *Lear* 2). The wall clearly exacts a terrible toll – work is enforced by the army because conditions are appalling and men are dying – but Lear states his stubborn belief in its efficacy:

> I started this wall when I was young. I stopped my enemies in the field, but there were always more of them […] So I built this wall to keep our enemies out. My people will live behind this wall when I'm dead. You may be governed by fools but you'll always live in peace. My wall will make you free.
>
> (3–4)

When the body of a dead labourer is discovered, Lear insists on convening an immediate and flagrantly unjust trial; a blameless worker is accused and sentenced. Conflict immediately ensues: Lear is intemperate and irascible, insisting, 'I must be obeyed!' (6); his daughters attempt to countermand the summary death sentence. But Lear shoots the accused worker himself while expressing his belief that he has loved and cherished his people, employing Christ-like imagery in his deluded self-veneration: '[my people] are my sheep and if one of them is lost I'd take fire to hell to bring him out' (7). Theatre historian and critic Katharine Worth wrote of the first production that the wall effectively disrupted 'the familiar Shakespearean ambience', compelling the audience 'to think in Bond's terms' (178). Certainly, Bond's opening scene synthesizes a recognizably despotic Shakespearean Lear with the paranoia of twentieth-century totalitarianism.

Bond has always been on the receiving end of damning reviews for the violence of *Lear*: 'unspeakable and unprintable tortures [and] sadistic exultation in them' (J. Barber 13). But the violence of Bond's play emerges from Shakespeare's text while conveying Bond's vision of the brutalizing nature of contemporary society – to Bond there is certainly an ethical imperative in adaptation:

> I write about violence as naturally as Jane Austen wrote about manners. Violence shapes and obsesses our society […] People who do not want writers to write about violence want to stop them writing about us and our time. It would be immoral not to write about violence.
>
> (Bond, *Lear* lvii)

Bodice and Fontanelle are certainly as disturbing as Goneril and
Regan: they ally to depose their father, using their husbands to war
against Lear's armies. However, they are clearly in control, plotting
against their respective husbands, as well as against each other, and
expressing their sexual frustrations with 'grim comic flippancy'
(Hay and Roberts 121). Following the defeat of Lear and his forces,
the mutilated body of Lear's advisor, Warrington, is brought to the
sisters for further torment. Bond intensifies the scene's darkly comic
grotesquerie by emphasizing the sisters' playful delight in torturing
their prisoner. Bodice, who has already ordered that Warrington's
tongue should be cut out, sits on a shooting stick commanding
events while paying close attention to her knitting. Fontanelle leaps
around hysterically, shouting and jumping on Warrington:

> FONTANELLE
> Kill his hands! Kill his feet! Jump on it – all of it! [...] Kill it!
> Kill all of it! Kill him inside! Make him dead! [...]
> BODICE [*knits*]
> Plain, pearl, plain. She was just the same at school.
>
> (14)

Bodice concludes the torture by prodding her knitting needles into
Warrington's ears: 'I'll just jog these in and out a little. Doodee,
doodee, doodee, doo' (15). A degree of moral normality is established
through the soldier: on the one hand, he willingly obeys orders to
gain promotion – 'Yer wan' 'im done in a fancy way?' (13) – but
his asides contribute a necessary counterpoint ('What a pair!'), and
he offers the mutilated Warrington some blunt consolation at the
end of the scene, paralleling the servants' care for Gloucester in the
Quarto *King Lear*.

The play's first audience might well have anticipated the blinding
of Warrington given the dramatic parallels between the scenes, but
it is Lear's eyes that are removed, by 'scientific device', later in the
play in a chillingly mechanical scene. A frame is placed over Lear's
head – it is sardonically described as a crown – and a fellow prisoner
explains his method: 'you extract the eye undamaged and then it
can be put to good use. It's based on a scouting gadget I had as a
boy' (63). As Katharine Worth explains, this transference allows
Bond to make Lear a Sophoclean, prophetic figure with insight
and authority. Worth's comments on the Royal Court production

of *Lear* shed a valuable contextual light on the response of Bond's first audiences: the black humour offers 'a way into the horror, [an] interim response to behaviour that seems to defeat understanding and reason' (Worth 179). The laughter distances, 'but not so as to let us forget that what Bond is showing us has been "real" in our time; this is a much cleaned up version of the obscene events of Nazi concentration camps' (Worth 179). Bond's appropriation challenges audiences to reconsider attitudes to violence in canonical texts; to what extent is it hypocritical to recoil against modern theatre while accepting uncritically the known and anticipated violence of Shakespeare's text? Is the violence of the source play qualitatively different?

In Bond's play, it is Cordelia who is responsible for the imprisonment and torture of Lear, a dramatic shock to anyone seeking an emotionally redemptive catharsis or a mimetic relationship with the source text. Bond commented in interview that Shakespeare's Cordelia seemed 'an absolute menace' (Bond, 'Drama' 8): here she is not Lear's daughter but the pregnant wife of the Gravedigger's Boy. Initially a vulnerable, tearful figure, she witnesses soldiers murder her husband, is then raped by the soldiers, miscarries her child and becomes a freedom fighter commanding the rebel forces – ironically, determined to maintain the divisive wall. The radical reinvention of Cordelia casts a telling light on the ways in which Bond focuses on Lear himself. Following the initial defeat in battle, Lear is seen 'ragged, tired, dirty and frightened' (Bond, *Lear* 16), rescued from his wasteland experience by the Gravedigger's Boy. Attracted to the simplicity of the peasant life, Lear's feelings divide between remorse for his past and self-pity:

> I could have a new life here. I could forget all the things that frighten me – the years I've wasted, my enemies, my anger, my mistakes. [...] I'm tormented by regrets – I must forget it all – throw it away! Yes! Let me live here and work for you.
>
> (25)

The brief idyll cannot last, and Lear is captured, imprisoned and tried by Bodice and Fontanelle. Throughout his trial Lear appears mad but with the lunacy of new insight and a newly acquired compassion. Alone in his cell he is visited by haunting presences: the ghost of the Gravedigger's Boy, to whom he shows a tender pity, and apparitions of his daughters as frightened young girls. He speaks gently to them, expressing a Blakean vision of what life might be:

> We won't chain ourselves to the dead, or send our children to school in the graveyard. The torturers and ministers and priests will lose their office. And we'll pass each other in the street without shuddering at what we've done to each other.
> [...]
> The animal will slip out of its cage, and lie in the fields, and run by the river, and groom itself in the sun [...]
>
> (40)

The tableau of the old king with his children has a quiet poignancy, rapidly dispelled by the ensuing chaos of civil war and the defeat and capture of the two sisters by Cordelia and her political ally and lover, the Carpenter, followed by the summary execution of Fontanelle and Bodice – the latter bludgeoned to death. In a scene of bizarre grotesquerie, Shakespeare's 'let them anatomize Regan; see what breeds about her heart' is literalized as an official autopsy 'to satisfy the authorities'. Lear frames incoherent questions – 'where is the ... where ...?' (59) – and, in an 'almost religious moment of mystery' (Gritzner 54), sees an unexpected beauty in the violated body:

> She sleeps inside like a lion and a lamb and a child. The things are so beautiful. I am astonished. I have never seen anything so beautiful [...] If I had known this beauty and patience and care, how I would have loved her.
>
> (59)

Audiences have found these scenes almost intolerable, although one astute critic, writing of the play's revival in 1983, justified the brutalities as 'even more topical now and will become more so as man's inhumanity gains subtle sophistication' (quoted in Roberts 24).

The short final act of Bond's play reveals Lear back in the former home of the Gravedigger's Boy. An embattled state of military oppression evidently still exists, but Lear has acquired moral authority and humility: 'I'm not a king. I have no power. [...] I came here when I was cold and hungry and afraid. I wasn't turned away and I won't turn anyone away' (74). Crowds gather to hear his gnomic prophetic utterances; in symbolic parables he talks about freedom and the abuse of power. But Lear's final confrontation with Cordelia, although passionately argued, does not achieve his desired effect:

> Listen Cordelia. [...] I've learned this, and you must learn it or you'll die. Listen Cordelia, [...] Our lives are awkward and fragile and we have only one thing to keep us sane: pity, and the man without pity is mad.
>
> (84)

Bond's moral is the inescapable cycle of violence: 'if you behave violently, you create an atmosphere of violence, which generates more violence' (Hay and Roberts 129). The final gesture of the play shows Bond's complete departure from Shakespeare's tragedy; Bond cannot accept a philosophy of resignation: 'the social moral of Shakespeare's *Lear* is this: endure till in time the world will be made right. That's a dangerous moral for us. We have less time than Shakespeare' (*Lear* xxvi). At this point of the first production, the audience saw the wall for the first time: 'a great earthy monster threatening us as well as the characters' (Worth 178). In front of the wall is the aged, ineffectual but determined figure of Lear: taking a shovel, he starts to remove the earth and dismantle the barricade. He seeks justice and atonement: '[my] Lear makes a gesture in which he accepts responsibility for his life and commits himself to action' (quoted in Roberts 25). He is killed by a single pistol shot and falls; workers depart, leaving the body lying on the ground. One looks back – the only frail possibility of hope at the end of the drama. In the appeal for political action rather than aesthetic resignation, Bond's adaptation 'builds on an epic vision that asks more from its audience than clapping and going home to bed' (Dobson and Rivier-Arnaud 72).

Ran, dir. Akira Kurosawa (1985)

Since the first screening of *Ran*, in 1985, there has been considerable critical discussion of the film, frequently described as Kurosawa's masterpiece and a supreme example of Shakespearean adaptation.

Yet it was initially reviewed by Peter Ackroyd as 'Shakespeare drained of its poetry, stripped of its human dimensions, and forced within a schematic framework derived from quite different attributes or preoccupations' (37). This is a perspective which demonstrates how far adaptation studies have developed beyond Ackroyd's reluctance to consider that *King Lear* might translate effectively to different cultural traditions. Kurosawa had certainly trained in a context far from Western film practice: he began his career as an artist in the early years of the Second World War and produced his first film as Japan surrendered to the USA. His artistic roots lie in the stylized conventions of Noh theatre and Babuku puppetry rather than mid-twentieth-century Western realism. Knowledge of Shakespeare, though, was 'firmly enshrined in orthodox Japanese culture' (Collick 187), and Kurosawa's *Throne of Blood* (1957), a samurai *Macbeth*, and *The Bad Sleep Well* (1960), a modern *Hamlet*, establish the importance of Shakespeare to Kurosawa's auteurial vision. This discussion of *Ran* will focus on ways in which Kurosawa's adaptation fuses aspects of *King Lear* with specifically Japanese tropes, in particular the downfall of the Samurai warlord; Tsurumaru and the motif of blindness; and the contrasting portrayals of Lady Kaede and Lady Sué. Kurosawa's title evokes the destructiveness of endless conflict rather than the tragedy of the individual. The etymology of the monosyllable *Ran* is complex but is generally taken to connote 'chaos' or 'turmoil', possibly 'desolation of the soul' (Rosenthal 87).

Kurosawa's historical setting is Japan's *sengoku* period (1392–1568), a time of civil war between rival clans. Initial inspiration came from stories of Motonari Mōri, the sixteenth-century warlord whose three sons exemplified filial loyalty; when Kurosawa contemplated an alternative narrative, where the sons proved undutiful, 'the similarities to *Lear* occurred to me' (quoted in Cardullo 28). Lord Hidetora, the patriarchal head of the Ichimonji clan, is the quintessential Samurai warlord: '[his] long white hair and beard billow in the wind; his hawkish eyes shine in his sun-tanned face – the magnificent vision of a great warrior who has survived hundreds of battles' (Kurosawa 7). In appropriating *King Lear*, Kurosawa, like Jane Smiley, felt a need to supply a backstory:

What has always troubled me about *King Lear* is precisely that Shakespeare gives his characters no past. We are plunged directly into the agonies of their present dilemmas without knowing how they got to this point [...] In *Ran* I tried to give Lear a history. I tried to make it clear that his power must rest upon a lifetime of bloodthirsty savagery.

(quoted in Cardullo 27)

Significant correspondences between *Ran* and *King Lear* emerge from the opening scene, the division of the kingdom. In *Ran*, the headship of the house of Ichimonji is bestowed upon the eldest son, Taro. Jiro and Saburo, second and third sons, receive their own castles and retainers but owe allegiance to Taro; Hidetora, meanwhile, will retain 'the title and forms of lordship' as well as his own battle-hardened warriors. The flattery of the eldest son rivals the hyperbole of Goneril and Regan, while the youngest, Saburo, speaks with scathing honesty, describing his father's decision as madness and reminding him that his sons might inherit his own martial ethos: 'You have lived without mercy or pity. But Father, we, too, are children of this degraded age of strife' (Kurosawa 16). The opposition of this youngest and best-loved son humiliates Hidetora, who peremptorily rejects him. When loyal servant Tango (Kent) attempts to make peace and persuade Hidetora to revoke his decision, he is also summarily dismissed. Parallels continue when Lord Fujikami offers his daughter's hand to the banished Saburo, stating his admiration of Saburo's honesty, whereas the rival suitor, Lord Ayabe, withdraws from marriage negotiations. Hidetora, meanwhile, is mocked by the songs of his Fool, Kyoami, and humiliated when he sees his concubines kneel deferentially to Taro's wife, Kaede. The film's structure, similarly, owes much to Shakespeare: Hidetora's self-imposed banishment from Taro's castle is followed by the joint refusal of the two sons to accommodate their father's rowdy retainers; Hidetora's madness and exile in the Azusa plain precedes the brief and poignant reconciliation with Saburo. There are verbal echoes in Jiro's suggestion that Hidetora no longer needs his own retainers and that he should return to Taro and apologize to him.

The film's most arresting sequence and significant departure from Shakespeare is the siege of the third castle: 'a vision of the apocalypse rendered with the highest artistic perfection' (Kott, 'Edo'). Hidetora has sought refuge for himself and his retinue and is unprepared for the attack that comes from the combined forces of Taro and Jiro. The battle scenes are both distanced and harrowing – Kurosawa's decision to replace the realist sounds of warfare with Takemitsu's classical soundtrack has a dissociating effect where graphically disturbing scenes of massacre are accompanied by melancholy, lyrical melodies. Similarly, waves of attacking archers are seen with their brilliantly coloured red and yellow banners in a precise choreography at odds with the graphic scenes of slaughter. Naturalistic sound only returns with the murder of the eldest son, Taro. Eventually the castle keep is fired; Hidetora and his closest servants accept the inevitability of defeat. The sumptuously attired concubines engage in mutual *seppuku* while the surviving son Jiro waits with his ally Kurogane, knowing that Hidetora must commit suicide to avoid shame. Indeed, Hidetora prepares to die, grasps his sword belt but, finding that he has no weapon, staggers, visibly traumatized, from the castle keep and through the massed ranks of soldiers. He escapes to a 'very wilderness of insanity' (Kurosawa 52); the barren plain and violent storm symbolize his mental torment. The battle is the cathartic climax of Hidetora's samurai life of slaughter and conquest, forcing him to confront the brutal reality of this martial world.

Kurosawa, like Bond and Smiley, chooses to maintain the motif of blindness, metaphorically and physically, while making subtle differences: as Hidetora suffers in the storm, Tango and Kyoami usher him into a modest straw hut where he experiences a further epiphanic revelation. Within the shadowy interior an androgynous figure can be seen – the blinded Tsurumaru, brother of Lady Sué. As Hidetora trembles, the young man reminds him of his story: 'I was just a child, but how could I forget one who gouged out my eyes [...] the day you burned down my father's castle?' (62). Kurosawa's variation on the Shakespearean theme is a fascinating one: the horror of the deed is replicated, but the perpetrator here is the Great Lord himself, and the victim is an innocent child. Tsurumaru confesses that he cannot attain the Buddhist state of grace practised by his sister but can, nonetheless, offer 'some hospitality of the heart' (62) by playing his flute. The use of the Noh flute in this intensely emotional scene is, as Collick explains, 'a direct reference to the warrior Noh *Atsumori* in which the ghost of a samurai is disguised as a flute playing reaper' (Collick 184). Hidetora is devastated and runs from the hut into the night. As Kurosawa explains, 'only by

confronting his evil head on can [Hidetora] transcend it and begin
to struggle towards virtue' (quoted in Cardullo 27).

The highly stylized world of Noh drama has further significance
in the depiction of the two female characters of the film: Taro's
wife, Kaede, appears at first to be beautiful and submissive with
her exquisite formal dress and decorous gestures. Yet she is a figure
combining aspects of Regan, Goneril and Edmund, with her own
project of revenge. Beneath her 'beautiful immobility' lies a terrible
history:

> I was born and bred in this castle, which used to belong to my
> father. Then I left it to marry you. My father and brothers, all
> unaware because of our marriage, were murdered by your father,
> Hidetora [...] This is the room where my mother committed
> suicide.
>
> (Kurosawa 29)

She states, chillingly, 'I have waited for this day ever since.' But
her campaign is not yet concluded: when her brother-in-law Jiro
announces the death of Taro, presenting her with the victor's
trophy of helmet and top-knot, she appears to congratulate him on
his triumph. Then, in a highly dramatic gesture, she leaps at him,
unsheathes his sword, holds the point of the weapon to his neck
and threatens to kill him. When Jiro protests that Kurogane was
responsible for Taro's death, she mocks him and hurls herself upon
him, kissing him passionately. As he falls beneath her kimono, she is
seen to lick drops of blood from his neck in a disturbingly vampiric
way. Later, she feigns tears, demanding to become his wife rather
than his mistress. Quietly crushing a small butterfly fluttering beside
her, she requests the death of Lady Sué. Kurogane is ordered to bring
the head of Sué preserved in salt but presents Kaede with a stone
fox head – a symbol of her evil. When, finally, Kurogane is about to
execute Kaede, she states her satisfaction: 'I wanted to see this castle
burn and the house of Ichimonji ruined [...] I wanted to see all this!'
(106). Lady Sué is the antithesis of Kaede, epitomizing spirituality
and karmic acceptance. She is first seen praying to the setting sun, 'the
Western Paradise [...] the Amitabha', and she greets Hidetora with
gentleness and respect despite the atrocities he has committed against
her family. In her philosophy 'everything has been preordained in our

previous lives ... All things are the heart of the Buddha' (32). Like Cordelia, she is killed by a random soldier willing to obey pointlessly vicious orders; attempting to escape Kaede's murderous intentions, Sué turns back to rescue her brother's much-loved flute and is killed.

The wilderness exile of Hidetora owes much to Act 4 of *King Lear*: the intense pain of remorse and reluctance to be reunited with the banished child; the role of nature exemplified in the crown of flowers worn by Lear, and the helmet of wild grasses Kyoami weaves for Hidetora. Kyoami as the Fool retains an important role to the end; he weeps over Hidetora's fate, shouting, 'All human beings cry when they are born. They die after they have cried enough' (78) in an obvious echo of Lear's words to Gloucester (*KL* 4.6.174–9). Similarly, Hidetora's first words to Saburo are 'How cruel you are! How could you pull me from my grave?' (Kurosawa 96) just as Lear objects to Cordelia, 'You do me wrong to take me out of the grave' (*KL* 4.7.45); both fathers offer to take poison; both are persuaded of the sincerity of their child by tears, not words. Saburo's death is arbitrarily cruel – he is shot as he crosses the Azusa field, taking his father to safety. Hidetora collapses over his son's body and dies grief-stricken, leaving Tango to point the moral of the tragedy: 'the evil of human beings ... who believe their survival depends on killing others, repeated again and again throughout all time. Even God or the Buddha cannot save us from it' (Kurosawa 99). And, indeed, Jiro's army has now been decisively vanquished by Ayabe's soldiers; Jiro too must die the defeated warrior's death.

In the final frames of the film, the fragile figure of the blind Tsurumaru is seen tapping towards the edge of the high stone wall of his family's ruined castle. As he stumbles, his talismanic scroll of the Amitabha Buddha falls from his hand and he is seen alone, a small figure as the camera cuts away from him, silhouetted in the fading light of the sunset.

Jane Smiley, *A Thousand Acres* (1991)

The body repeats the landscape. They are the source of each other and create each other.

(Meridel Le Sueur, epigraph to *A Thousand Acres*)

Jane Smiley's *A Thousand Acres* was awarded America's prestigious Pulitzer Prize for fiction in 1992, acclaimed, by Pulitzer criteria, as a distinguished work 'dealing with American life' and widely reviewed in the US as 'quintessentially' American. Jack Fuller of the *Chicago Tribune* reviewed it as 'a true American tragedy [like] Arthur Miller's *Death of a Salesman*' (230). Connections with Shakespeare did not dominate initial discussion and, as Rozett observes, paratextual 'narratives of origin and explication' are 'conspicuously absent' (168). The novel can undoubtedly be read as an autonomous work of literature – a steely-eyed tale of a dysfunctional family; a dystopian vision of industrialized agribusiness and ecological catastrophe. Yet Smiley herself has described the process of composition as a persistent wrestling match with her primary source:

> It was pretty much a struggle all the way through. It was very grim for one thing. Then there was the aspect of having to think through all the details [...] And that felt like physical labor. I'd get up from writing and feel as if I'd been carrying rocks.
>
> (Berne 237)

Smiley shares with Victorian writers such as Cowden Clarke the desire to fictionalize the lacunae of the hypotext, focalizing newly invented material through a central female character. Yet where Victorian writers approach 'the Bard' with exaggerated respect, Smiley offers dialogue and opposition. Cowden Clarke concludes her 'Girlhoods' at the opening of the respective play; she invents prequels but effectively shuts down any possibility of further reinvention. Smiley's revisionist fiction appropriates the conflict of the play and moves beyond it; her six sections parallel the five acts of Shakespearean tragedy and add a coda, a postlude unique to the novel. Cowden Clarke cannot spring surprises on her readers; Smiley evidently can: the reading experience creates suspense and a chill of uneasy foreboding. Smiley's engagement with *King Lear* begins with resistance: 'a longstanding dissatisfaction with an interpretation [...] that privileged the father's needs over the daughters' (Berne 236); a desire to address 'the ways in which I found the conventional readings of *King Lear* frustrating and wrong' (Smiley, 'Shakespeare' 160). Two areas in particular antagonized Smiley: Lear himself, 'selfish, demanding, humorless, self-pitying' ('Shakespeare' 161), wholly incapable of change in his female relationships (Berne 237). Goneril and Regan, however, universally demonized, 'sounded familiar' ('Shakespeare' 161). Smiley challenges simplistic notions of universality, substituting an alternative interpretation of domestic conflict: 'I could not allow [Shakespeare's] universality, but instead [...] had to counter it with the universality of my vision' ('Shakespeare' 172). As Kiernan Ryan suggests, 'iconoclastic creative assaults on Shakespeare like Smiley's [...] are justified and long overdue', the 'alleged universality' being 'a myth contrived to disguise the patriarchal point of view as the common plight of humanity' (*Shakespeare's Universality* 8). In this respect, Smiley's adaptative method is appropriative and polemical. Her stated intention is to supply adolescent readers with 'a prophylactic against [...] guilt about proper daughterhood' ('Shakespeare' 173); in Anna Lindhé's words, 'accepting the post-text's invitation to experience and perceive the prior work in a different way' (18). This discussion will focus on the adaptive process itself; to cite Hutcheon's terminology, reading the adaptation '*as an adaptation*' (Hutcheon, *Theory of Adaptation* 6) exploring the initiating 'division of the kingdom', the storm and the conclusion of the novel.

If Smiley's inspiration for *A Thousand Acres* arose from her rejection of conventional readings of *King Lear*, the crucial spark to inspire the writing came from the winter landscape of Iowa:

[The] ideas about Lear's daughters and about agriculture had been knocking around in my mind for fifteen years or so, but the exact moment when they jelled was when I was driving down I-35 in northern Iowa in late March 1988. The landscape was cold, lit by a weak winter sun [...] the farm fields seemed enormous and isolated [...] The image of that bleak landscape remained throughout the writing of the book as a talisman to return to every time composition faltered.

(Smiley, *Thirteen Ways* 97)

For American reviewers, the specificity of Smiley's depiction of this rural scene achieved 'a kind of stunning nostalgia' (Carlson); the domestic world of canning and preserving, the obsession with scrubbing and cleaning, all evoke an ordered and virtuous universe, the realization of America's foundational myth of work, resourcefulness, prosperity. In *A Thousand Acres*, the myth of the irreproachable pioneer farmer is exposed as a lie: the ruthless masculine exploitation of the land has poisoned the well-water, causing premature death, toxic cancers and Ginny's many miscarriages. As Diane Purkiss suggests, this is a 'lost Eden', an Iowa which is 'Hell, not Paradise' (20). The ineluctable fact of the land dominates the opening of the novel: 'the immensity of the piece of land my father owned [...] no encumbrances, as flat and fertile, black, friable, and exposed as any piece of land on the face of the earth' (Smiley, *A Thousand Acres* 3–4). Larry Cook (Lear) has accumulated land opportunistically, taking advantage of failing neighbourhood farmers. It is, then, Larry's 'division of the kingdom', the 'thousand acres', that begins the novel.

Clearly the land is all-important to Shakespeare's protagonist: Goneril's portion is 'riched' with 'shadowy forests, [...] plenteous rivers and wide-skirted meads' (*KL* 1.1.64–5), and Lear, in his typically declarative style, assumes authority over the property for eternity: 'To thine and Albany's issue / Be this perpetual' (*KL* 1.1.66–7). The decision to divide up the kingdom seems to be widely known within the court, but the occasion, coinciding with Cordelia's betrothal, draws attention to a fundamental contradiction: how can Cordelia be granted 'a third more opulent than your sisters' (*KL* 1.1.86) as queen of a foreign power? How can Lear reasonably expect 'to set my rest / On her kind nursery' (*KL* 1.1.124–5)? Larry's equally decisive and unexpected announcement is also proclaimed in a public context. One of Smiley's key narrative choices is to refract the material of the tale through Ginny – Goneril – as unreliable first-person narrator. For Smiley, 'it is much more interesting to have a narrator who is uncertain of what she thinks should be done or what the future will hold' (Berne 237).

Ginny watches her father anxiously, attempting to forestall his drunken irascibility. Larry's edict, looking at his youngest daughter, Caroline, is that there will be a new corporation, dividing shares between the three sisters who, with their husbands, will 'run the show' (Smiley, *A Thousand Acres* 19). But, Caroline, like Cordelia, is planning to marry and move away from the farm to city life. Her guarded response is simply, 'I don't know', although Ginny is aware that Larry's scheme 'would deposit her right back on the farm' (21). The implication, common to both texts, is that the fabled division of the kingdom is a coercive means of securing the younger daughter's loyalty and preventing her freedom. Difference emerges through genre and the novel's ability to supply retrospective detail: the reader has already been introduced to an entire genealogy of women married young for their property, dying early, remaining, in the case of Larry's wife, nameless throughout the novel. Ginny herself, married at nineteen, has suffered a series of miscarriages, the last a private tragedy buried beneath the dirt floor of an old barn. Her sister Rose (Regan) is recovering from breast cancer. Caroline, conversely, brought up by her elder sisters, 'made good grades, conceived large ambitions, and went off as we had planned, [to] something brighter and sharper and more promising' (64). The seeds of future conflict have been sown: Ginny attempts to cajole Caroline into apologizing to their father but meets with initial refusal: 'I hate that little girl stuff' (34). Legal papers for transferring the property are drawn up; Caroline arrives, in conciliatory mood, but Larry slams the door in her face – a wordless rejection of his 'Loving Child' (64) but, like Lear's vitriolic renunciation, both capricious and despotic. This disturbing test of daughterly loyalty and the exercise of patriarchal will over adult women leaves neither Lear nor Larry in a sympathetic light.

Smiley emphasizes the domestic parallels between the protagonists in the immediate aftermath of the momentous abdication: Lear in peremptory mood – 'Let me not stay a jot for dinner; go, get it ready' (*KL* 1.4.8) – Larry similarly exacting: '[he] expected to come in at five and sit right down to the table' (Smiley, *A Thousand Acres* 47–8). Both men discover that the premature bequeathing of land denies them identity and purpose; both react with querulous and unpredictable behaviours. Lear, though, begins to question his identity: 'Does any here know me? Why, this is not Lear. [...] Who is it that can tell me who I am?' (*KL* 1.4.217, 221) – the beginnings of a traumatic dislocation which impels him to move beyond his egotistic certainties. Larry, on the other hand, is never seen to question himself or his judgement and retreats into a world of irrational actions and menacing silences. The storm marks the profoundest difference between Smiley's narrative and Shakespeare's tragic vision. The emotional tempest in Lear's mind drives him to embrace the naked vulnerability of the bedlam beggar; his concern for his loyal followers reveals a newly acquired empathy. In *A Thousand Acres*, Larry suffers none of this anagnorisis or peripeteia. On a night of mid-west 'tornado watch',

Larry confronts Ginny with a torrent of violent invective: '[you] barren whore! I know all about you, you slut [...] you're not really a woman, are you? I don't know what you are, just a bitch, is all, just a dried-up whore bitch' (181). The violence of his language triggers Ginny's memory of his uncontrolled physical attacks on her in childhood. The abuses of the past are also uppermost in Rose's challenge: 'well, Daddy, I know all about you, and you know I know' (182). In Smiley's reimagining, the climactic storm uncovers the darkest secrets: as Larry stumbles away into the torrential rain, Rose talks to Ginny for the first time about their father's incestuous abuse: 'We were just his, to do with as he pleased, like the pond, or the houses or the hogs or the crops' (191). In fact, Ginny has repressed this traumatic memory; it returns later when she returns to the former family home. The storm, then, focuses on the rape of Ginny and Rose rather than on Larry, who simply staggers around in the rain, shouting, until rescued by a neighbouring family: he is 'what an unheroic Lear looks like when viewed entirely from the perspective of a daughter whose life he has controlled' (Rozett 169). Smiley's decision to deprive Larry of any of Lear's wild grandeur or agonizing insights strikes a brutally pessimistic note: Larry is the product and prime exemplar of his exploitative world, which stultifies and prevents any feelings of remorse:

[He] did fuck us and he did beat us. He beat us more than he fucked us. He beat us routinely. And the thing is, he's respected. Others of them like him and look up to him. He fits right in. However many of them have fucked their daughters or their stepdaughters or their nieces or not, the fact is that they all accept beating as a way of life [...] This person who beats and fucks his own daughters can go out into the community, and get respect and power, and take it for granted that he deserves it.

(302)

As Martha Tuck Rozett proposes, Smiley moves beyond simply creating a tyrannical protagonist: '[her] project is nothing less than an iconoclastic dismantling of a literary tradition that embraces the flawed but magnificent tragic hero at the expense of the two-dimensional women characters who oppose him' (169).

To Smiley, the bleak ending of *A Thousand Acres* is 'a step away from the abyss [...] a movement away from the apocalypse' (Berne

237): her readers might disagree. Larry, certainly, is deprived of any tragic stature: seemingly lost in a word of raging dementia, he accuses Ginny and Rose of murdering their younger sister. Soon after the court case initiated by Caroline, he suffers a heart attack in a supermarket and dies in the cereal aisle. There is no contrition or recognition of the truth of the past, a situation which is intolerable to Rose, whose bitter resentment has infected her adult life:

> I wanted him to feel remorse and know what he did and what he is, but when you see him around town and they talk about him, he's just senile. He's safe from ever knowing. People pat him on the head and sympathize with him and say what bitches we are, and he believes them and that's that, the end of history. I can't *stand* that.
>
> (303)

In a similarly muted manner, the sexual jealousy between the two elder sisters is reduced to bathos: Ginny prepares poisoned liver sausage for her sister, but Rose never eats it; Jess, the object of their desire, returns to Canada; Ginny's husband, Ty, leaves for Texas. The narrator herself has found a new life in an urban scene that seems to possess all the alienated anonymity of a painting by Edward Hopper: living in a small apartment, working as a waitress, she finds reassurance in the everyday, impersonal exchanges with customers. The critical confrontation is the final one between the dying Rose and Ginny after some years of estrangement; the true 'afterlife' of the text. Despite their mutual mistrust, Rose wishes to leave the land to her sisters and asks Ginny to take care of her daughters; at thirty-seven she is left with her unappeased anger and a partial reconciliation with Ginny: '[All] I have is the knowledge that I saw! That I saw without being afraid and without turning away, and that I didn't forgive the unforgiveable [...] That's my sole, solitary, lonely accomplishment' (355–6). In *King Lear*, the ability and willingness to confront a painful knowledge is everything; Smiley repositions tragic tradition in leaving her characters stranded in their own rage or uncertainty. There can be no cathartic closure in the relationship between Ginny and Caroline, as the dark secret of abuse remains concealed by Ginny: the younger sister will never know the truth of her protected life within the family.

For ecofeminist critics, the true protagonist is the violated and industrialized land: the eponymous acres finally sold, bulldozed and reduced to a featureless dystopia – 'no lives are lived within the horizon of your gaze' (368). Ginny is left with an inner darkness: '[a] gleaming obsidian shard' – fragmented, deadly, yet illuminating – a 'weapon of resistance' (Strehle 224). Julie Sanders judges Smiley's adaptation to be 'equivocal to the end, darker and more ambiguous in its vision, penetrating further below the surface of the visible, than even its author's printed claims suggest' (Sanders, *Novel Shakespeares* 214). Smiley herself talks about learning from, and being transformed by, the adaptive process, describing such creative interaction as 'two mirrors facing each other in the present moment, reflecting infinitely backward into the past and infinitely forward into the future' (Smiley, 'Shakespeare' 173).

9

Macbeth

Macbeth is one of Shakespeare's most frequently adapted plays and one which has been more than usually susceptible to later writers 'talking back' to it. This chapter discusses how the creative practices of two dramatists and one filmmaker have developed a fresh, sometimes provocative, dialogue between the source text and their own times.

Eugène Ionesco, *Macbett*, translated by Donald Watson (1973)

In January 1972, a newspaper article declared: 'It must be International Macbeth Year: our hero is popping up more often than Father Christmases in a December Oxford Street' ('Macbeth' 11). Included in this theatrical plenitude was Ionesco's *Macbett*, a darkly comic take on Shakespeare's tragedy, now generally regarded as belonging to the 'Theatre of the Absurd', a dramatic term established by Martin Esslin in his landmark study *The Theatre of the Absurd* (1961). In it, Esslin focuses primarily on French-language plays by Beckett, Adamov, Ionesco and Genet, insisting that such works should not be judged by 'conventional' theatrical norms. In establishing a working definition of the 'absurd', Esslin draws on Ionesco's writings about Kafka: 'Absurd is that which is devoid of purpose ... Cut off from his religious, metaphysical, and transcendental roots, man is lost; all his actions become senseless, absurd, useless' (quoted in Esslin 5). It was an existential vision that Ionesco would explore in dramatic form throughout his career and one that can be keenly felt in his appropriation of Shakespeare's *Macbeth*.

Assuming Macbeth and his dramatic creator to be one and the same, Ionesco remarked in interview: 'Didn't he [Shakespeare] say of the world that "it is a tale told by an idiot" and that everything is but "sound and fury"? He's the forefather of the theatre of the absurd' (Bonnefoy 49). Here, then, the twentieth-century artist looks back to Shakespeare as a revered literary ancestor to validate his own avant-gardism, and, surely, the political nihilism, grotesque comedy and linguistic scepticism that characterize Ionesco's dramas might all be traced back to Shakespearean models. That is not to say that Shakespeare is a figure of homage. Speaking in interview, Ionesco spelled out that '*Macbett* was a conscious parody of Shakespeare' (Guppy 75), the change in the title's final letter signalling a departure from its iconic predecessor. In the programme notes for the first production of the play (staged at the Théâtre de la Rive Gauche in Paris), Ionesco wryly explained that the respelling was to prevent audiences from confusing his work with Shakespeare's. In truth, only an audience with no prior knowledge of *Macbeth* whatsoever could have fallen prey to such confusion. Though Ionesco's named roles can be matched with their Shakespearean counterparts without too much difficulty, his representation of them is radically different, as is the play's dramatic style and action. *Macbett* opens with Archduke Duncan, a cowardly, self-serving ruler, married to an invented Lady Duncan, a ruthless, scheming villainess. Reduced in number from three to two, the witches reveal themselves to be Lady Duncan and her lady-in-waiting in disguise before a murdering triumvirate is formed with Macbett, Banco and the Archduchess (unlike Shakespeare, Ionesco follows Holinshed in making Banquo and Macbeth co-conspirators). After Duncan's assassination, Macbett takes the throne, marries Lady Duncan and murders Banco; however, his rule is disrupted by the retransformation of Lady Macbett (the erstwhile Lady Duncan) into the 'first witch'. Left to host the wedding banquet alone, Macbett is surprised less by the ghost of Banco than by the reappearance of Lady Duncan. Now liberated from the grip of a witch who had imprisoned her and assumed her identity, the

Archduke's widow assumes her original role and title. Macol, who turns out to be Banco's son by a 'gazelle, transformed by a witch into a woman' (Ionesco, *Plays* 101), returns, overthrows Macbett and assumes power.

In a letter published in 1980, Ionesco wrote that '*Macbett* est un pamphlet contre la politique et même contre l'action' ('*Macbett* is a pamphlet against politics and even against [political] action' [my translation]) (Coleman 815), a statement very much in keeping with his and fellow absurdists' professed antipathy to political theatre. Some commentators have regarded as facile Ionesco's rejection of affirmative action and his representation of all political systems as inherently flawed; others, though, have questioned his anti-political stance, averring that the very act of 'giving voice to the widespread rejection of political life' marks him out as a 'political playwright' (Morgan 119). In fact, it is possible to read *Macbett* from both perspectives: its numbing verbal repetitions, for example, evoke a sense of stasis, suggesting the impossibility of moving beyond political systems, while the heightened attention paid to the sycophantic rhetoric and double-speak of authority could be read as a form of political consciousness-raising. Whichever view is taken, there is no doubting that Ionesco recreated *Macbeth* in his own society's image. As one early analyst of *Macbett* notes, the source text is reformulated to 'correspond to our contemporary visions and concerns, [...] in the garb of modern theatrical technique' (Kern 3).

Yet if Ionesco reformulates the play for his own time, he does so under the influence of earlier Shakespearean appropriations, most notably Alfred Jarry's *Ubu Roi* (1896), a *succès de scandale* generally regarded as a precursor to absurdist drama. While Rosette C. Lamont's assessment of *Macbett* as 'a reading of *Macbeth* through Jarry binoculars' (236) is perhaps overstated, Ionesco's play undoubtedly shares the earlier appropriation's relish of bizarre, cartoonish stagecraft and demotic dialogue. However, perhaps the greatest influence on Ionesco's reworking of Shakespeare came not from the theatre but from scholarship. In numerous interviews, Ionesco cites Jan Kott's monumental study *Shakespeare our Contemporary* (1961) as his inspiration, most particularly its reading of the politics of *Macbeth*: 'A bad king is on the throne, a noble prince kills him to free the country of tyranny, but ipso facto he becomes a criminal and has to be killed in turn by someone else – and on it goes' (Guppy 66). In *Macbett*, this bleak cycle of toppling and tyranny is encapsulated in Macol's victory speech, Ionesco's only substantial textual borrowing from Shakespeare (*Mac* 4.3.50–99). But where Shakespeare's Malcolm is 'false speaking' (*Mac* 4.3.130) when he declares his sinful predilections, Macol speaks true, his final speech brazenly affirming his moral turpitude and despotism. In its promise of yet another cycle of violent upheaval, Ionesco's ending chimes with the closing frames of Roman Polanski's 1971 film adaptation of *Macbeth* (another striking instance of Kottian influence), in which Donalbain limps his way to the Weird Sisters, taking the viewer full circle and back to the film's opening.

If *Macbeth* concludes with the restoration of regal order (albeit one that scholars often regard as equivocal), *Macbett* leaves the audience in no doubt that the violence already witnessed is set to be repeated. This concluding prospect is dramatically consistent with the relentless repetitions that contribute to the play's absurdist tenor. The drama opens with an exchange between Glamiss and the ironically renamed Candor, their mirror-dialogue suggesting an exaggerated version of Rosencrantz and Guildenstern:

GLAMISS [*turning to* CANDOR]   Good day, Thane of Candor.
CANDOR [*turning to* GLAMISS]   Good day, Thane of Glamiss.
GLAMISS   Now listen, Candor.
CANDOR   Now listen, Glamiss.
GLAMISS   It can't go on like this.
CANDOR   It can't go on like this.

(Ionesco, *Plays* 9)

Lead personages are barely more distinctively treated: stage directions state that Banco and Macbett '*are extremely alike. Same costume, same beard*' (23), a physical similarity carried through to their speech. In a bold assault on audience patience, Macbett's lengthy monologue concerning the horrors of war is almost directly followed by Banco's verbatim delivery of the same speech. Not only are audiences forced to listen twice to the bloody details contained therein, they are also obliged to witness, albeit in stylized fashion, the mass execution of the traitor Candor's 137,000-strong army, as '*by means of light effects, a guillotine will become visible, and then a whole series of guillotines*' (37), a stage direction met somewhat bathetically by hedge-trimmers in the Royal Shakespeare

Company's 2007 production at the Swan Theatre, Stratford-upon-Avon. As the powerful settle down to watch the 'entertainment' and sip tea, Banco takes charge, repeatedly *'pressing the button'* (38); as heads pile up in a basket, so they form an image expressive of 'the horror of proliferation' (Esslin 121), which haunts so much of Ionesco's drama. As this scene illustrates, the darkly comic violence of *Macbett*, whether spoken about or embodied on stage, inhabits the realms of the surreal, inviting comparison with the cartoon violence created by the avant-garde ensemble Monty Python, which appeared weekly on British television screens in the early 1970s.

The violence of *Macbett* extends to language itself, as verbal communication is harassed and pushed to the point of meaninglessness. Ionesco's defamiliarizing of everyday language was first heard in *Le Cantatrice chauve* (1954), inspired by the playwright's own attempts to learn English from a language primer. The linguistic scepticism evident in this early work continued to be a defining feature of Ionesco's writing up to and including his take on Shakespeare. The exhilarating metaphorical density of *Macbeth*'s poetry is replaced by over-worn clichés, idioms and proverbial phrases, a shift in verbal tenor that has been read as 'a deliberate affront to Shakespeare's rhetorical complexity' (Rozett 130). Macbett's recounting how it seemed as if 'the trees were trying to rip themselves up by the roots' (Ionesco, *Plays* 42) has none of the supernatural foreboding of Lennox's evocation of the 'unruly' (*Mac* 2.3.54) night of Duncan's murder, especially when followed by his flippant observation that 'we didn't come here to talk about stormy weather' (*Plays* 42). Similarly, the mesmeric alliteration and trochaic rhythm of Shakespeare's paradoxical 'Fair is foul, and foul is fair' (*Mac* 1.1.9) is rendered humdrum: 'I am quite close and far away' (*Plays* 48). The cumulative effect of *Macbett*'s emphatically quotidian dialogue – often made strange by repetition and metadiscursive phrasing – is to block out psychological complexity and, consequently, any affective impact on the audience. Speaking of *Macbett*, Ionesco observed: 'there is none of Shakespeare's compassion [...]. There is no remorse. All the characters are incapable of love' (Hess). This absence of feeling is chillingly apparent when Lady Duncan gazes at the body of the husband she has just murdered, remarking matter-of-factly: 'Dead, he reminds me of my father. I never liked my father' (*Plays* 81). Audiences familiar with *Macbeth* will, of course, recall the Lady's

'Had he not resembled / My father as he slept, I had done't' (*Mac* 2.2.13–14), a reflection that serves to complicate 'fiend-like' (*Mac* 5.9.35) as her defining epithet.

That the *Macbett* script examined in this section is translated from the author's original French must be kept in mind in any close reading, not least because the process of translation requires a degree of creative adaptation, involving both linguistic and cultural negotiations. As a translation of an appropriated source text read in translation, the *Macbett* considered here is, indeed, more than usually palimpsestic. Reading Ionesco's original French text alongside two English translations by Donald Watson and Charles Marowitz respectively reveals some notable variations. A case in point is Banco's 'Mais nous qui ne craignons rien' (Ionesco, *Théâtre* 135), spoken to Lady Duncan. Whereas Watson elects for a more or less literal translation, 'But we who fear nothing' (Ionesco, *Plays* 30), Marowitz inserts a slightly adjusted phrase from *Hamlet* (1.4.6): 'As for our own life, we hold it at a pin's fee' (Ionesco, *Exit* 24), an addition in tune with the dramatist-translator's own adaptive practice of intertextual collage. And where Watson follows Ionesco in transforming into prose those speeches of Malcolm's given to Macol in the closing moments of the play, Marowitz retains Shakespeare's blank verse form, seemingly more alert to the reader than the spectator. While blank verse is unlikely to sound appreciably distinct from prose in performance, its on-the-page appearance evokes the presence of the source text (something Ionesco's original and Watson's translation avoid by indicating the borrowed lines in a footnote).

Reviewing the RSC's 2007 production, Michael Billington rated *Macbett* a 'quirky, parodic footnote that represents the last gasp of Theatre of the Absurd' ('*Macbett*'). It is certainly true that the play was composed in the dog days of absurdism and equally true that it occupies a relatively marginal place in Ionesco's oeuvre and in studies of Shakespearean appropriations. Nonetheless, *Macbett* has not yet sunk into obscurity under the proliferating weight of Shakespeare-inspired dramatic writing. Going by John Gross's assertion that 'the only neo-Shakespearian plays with any life in them are anti-Shakespearian in spirit' (*After Shakespeare* ix), Ionesco's thoroughgoing disruption of *Macbeth* may well survive for some decades to come.

Mickey B, dir. Tom Magill (2007)

In the closing moments of Phyllida Lloyd's *Tempest* (Donmar Warehouse, 2018), performed within the frame of a women's prison, the leading actor-inmate bins her copy of the Shakespeare script and takes up a copy of Margaret Atwood's *Hag-Seed*, a fictional account of a production of the same romance staged in a US prison. If the incarcerated figures of the play world are now set free, the player-prisoner is once more in chains, theatrical escape restricted to the vicarious experience of a novel. Here, captured in just minutes of stage-time, is a multi-layered representation of what goes by the phrase 'Prison Shakespeare'. Programmes which engage prisoners with Shakespeare have developed rapidly since the mid-1980s and, as one scholar in the field notes, 'the phenomenon has grown to where performances of Shakespeare's plays by prisoners are an annual occurrence in many parts of the world' (Pensalfini 9). While some of these initiatives focus primarily on behavioural, habilitative and educative benefits rather than an end product, others place significant emphasis on aesthetic outcomes. One such initiative is the Educational Shakespeare Company (now rebranded as 'esc films'), whose feature-length film *Mickey B*, an adaptation of *Macbeth*, won plaudits from around the globe. Shot in Northern Ireland's Maghaberry prison with a cast made up exclusively of serving prisoners and prison staff, *Mickey B* started out as a local venture, intended for local audiences. That the film was eventually screened at festivals across the world and subtitled into French, German, Portuguese, Korean and Hebrew is a testament to how it reached beyond its immediate socio-political contexts to interact with audiences of diverse histories and cultures. The film's director, Tom Magill, himself an ex-young offender and an exponent of the work of Augusto Boal and Paulo Freire (whose theatrical approaches are generally known by the term 'Theatre of the Oppressed'), took on the project with very clear adaptive intentions and strategies in mind. In interview with adaptation scholar Daniel Fischlin, Magill insists that the most effective way of keeping Shakespeare alive 'is to find a relevant contemporary parallel setting, with similar power struggles and hierarchies, and relocate the story in that parallel setting' (Fischlin et al. 181). So, in *Mickey B*, a Scottish castle becomes a Northern Irish prison and the hierarchy of king and thanes becomes that of drug lord and minders, who rule by violence and intimidation. Duncan (Sam McClean) is the ill-fated drugs baron, Mickey B (David Conway) his minder/murderer. Ladyboy (Jason Thompson) is Mickey B's prison bitch, the 'queen of hate'.

While all Shakespearean adaptations are to some extent shaped by the circumstances of their making, a film produced in a maximum-security prison will be more than usually so. As Magill reflects, he 'wasn't [...] making aesthetic choices from an infinite palette of possibilities' (Fischlin et al. 174), and many of his creative decisions had to accommodate various political sensitivities while also working around some severe material constraints. That *Mickey B* opened opportunities for 'carnivalesque inversions of state power' (Bretz 581) was a worrying prospect for the prison authorities, hyper-conscious as they were that the drama scheme might be perceived by the public as a perverse rewarding of criminal behaviour. And if the choice of Shakespeare gave the initiative an edifying stamp of 'high culture', the updating of a play sometimes regarded as Shakespearean Grand Guignol was an additional cause for anxiety. Moreover, the representation of Maghaberry prison – no stranger to public controversy – was also concerning, not least because of the plan to set the film action in prison wings ruled by inmates. Negotiating these issues required significant artistic compromises, including minimizing screen violence, avoiding direct depictions of drug-taking, and fictionalizing the site (aptly renamed 'Burnam Prison'). The DVD of the film includes both the main feature and short documentaries charting its development, capturing what Hutcheon refers to as the 'process and the product' of adaptation (*Theory of Adaptation* 7). Perhaps with public sensibilities in mind, the documentary titled 'Category A: *Mickey B*' presents the adaptive process as a collaborative, creative one, with inmates discovering new skills and, in some cases, gaining in self-knowledge and self-esteem.

One of the most noteworthy features of *Mickey B* is that the participants were selected from the least conforming prisoners, those who had proven difficult to reach through work or education programmes. Inmates were initially wary of a project centred around drama; as one of the actors observes in the documentary, 'I thought it was a wee girl's thing', rapidly adding, 'I'm straight, get that down just in case.' The choice of *Macbeth* was, then, crucial for dispelling such preconceptions, set as it is in a world where manhood is predicated on being physically strong, aggressive and sexually potent – much as it is in male prison communities. The recontextualizing of the Lady as the prison bitch contributes tellingly to the film's representation of gender, with the hyper-awareness of male heteronormativity that emerges in the documentary especially evident in Ladyboy's exchanges with Mickey B. S/he mocks him as a 'wee blue eye' and 'a wee queer', taunting him with rhetorical questions, a colloquial rephrasing of the Lady's mockery of Macbeth's manhood.

Bearing in mind that the actor-inmates had little experience of theatre and tended to associate the stage with an effeminate 'high culture', the choice of film as the adaptive medium was a shrewd one. Cinema was one of the few artistic media familiar to the inmate-cast and, according to Magill, best suited to the prison culture of 'instant gratification' (Fischlin et al. 164). At the same time, it offered a permanent record of achievement, one that could be played in any place, at any time. With the camera preferred over the stage, the next decision was how to render accessible one of Shakespeare's most linguistically compact and complex texts. While some of the cast were confident readers (Sam McClean, one of the co-scriptwriters, asserts in the documentary, 'it's not like we're incompetent; we're capable of reading the lines'), others required language close to their own demotic. One scripting strategy was to retain some of the more straightforward Shakespearean lines and integrate them unobtrusively into the newly scripted dialogue. The Lady's phrase 'What's done, cannot be undone' (*Mac* 5.1.67–8), for example, becomes a fitting sententia for both the fictional world and that of its immediate production, serving both as a choric refrain and a macabre suicide note, scrawled across Ladyboy's mattress. In other instances, as Ramona Wray observes, 'quotation takes the form of parody [...]. Hence, before the murder of Duncan, Mickey B/Macbeth jokingly places a knife to Banknote/Banquo's throat, asking, "Is this a knife I see before me, the handle towards my hand?"' (355). A broadly collaborative approach to scripting also meant that the decision to retain certain source lines was sometimes prompted by cast members. Magill recalls how Anthony Hagans, the actor playing Satan (Seyton), wanted to keep the half-line 'The Queen, my lord, is dead' (*Mac* 5.5.16), prompting David Conway to follow suit with Macbeth's 'She should have died hereafter' (*Mac* 5.5.16). More typically, though, the Shakespearean text is paraphrased, so that, for example, Duncan's proverbial 'There's no art / To find the mind's construction in the face' (*Mac* 1.4.11–12) becomes 'You can never tell a man's mind from the expression on his face.' Early modern imagery is adroitly matched to twenty-first-century idiom, so that the Captain's graphic description of how Macbeth took Macdonald and 'unseamed him from the nave to th'chops' (*Mac* 1.2.22) is recontextualized and rephrased to become Mickey B beating the rival 'Cossacks' gang like 'a pound of mince on a butcher's block'. Some of what one scholar lists as 'impenetrable localisms' (Cartelli 32) (including to 'throw a warbler', a mishearing of 'throw a wobbler' – and a phrase found in a standard English dictionary) necessitated subtitular 'retranslation' of the already translated text, an aspect of the film's production that at once underlines the specificity of its socio-cultural location and its carnivalesque qualities: a working-class reappropriation has rendered a Shakespeare text partially incomprehensible to the literate and literary classes who, traditionally, have had ownership over it.

If the Shakespeare script was adapted for non-professional actors with literacy limitations, so some of the key elements of film were adapted to a prison environment. Magill made a virtue out of the unavoidable necessity of barking guard dogs, transforming what started out as nuisance noise into a means of transition from one scene to another, matching sound with images of canine ferocity, shot in high-angle close-ups. Also used for transitions were exterior shots of the prison's high metal fences and barbed wire, their cold steeliness carried through to the filming of interiors whose monotonal consistency is accentuated by means of acid-blue filters. The soundtrack is likewise gritty, forbidding and edgy, with both diegetic and non-diegetic sound seeming to echo the metallic properties of the prison. With filming confined to the prison grounds, cinematographic choices were inevitably constrained and, as if by virtue of necessity, *Mickey B* is dominated by close-ups and extreme close-ups. Magill has spoken of how he 'learned through many mistakes the power of close-ups' (Fischlin et al. 173), and this cinematographic learning works to evoke a sense of inescapable claustrophobia, akin to Macbeth's feeling of being mentally 'cabined, cribbed, confined' (*Mac* 3.4.22). Nowhere is this more evident than in Duncan's murder scene. Shot in a mock-up of a thirteen-by-seven-foot cell, the tightness of the space serves to intensify the taut directness of the blows inflicted by Mickey B's makeshift knife. However, perhaps mindful of the prison authorities' demand that violence should be moderated, the multiple penetrations are witnessed only in silhouette, with the aftermath shown more directly in the form of blood splatters on the cell wall, literalizing the blood imagery that permeates *Macbeth*. The strenuousness of the stabbing is conveyed by the diegetic sound of Mickey B's heavy breathing and by the spectacle of the body he leaves behind. The discovery of the bloody corpse is filmed from Duffer's point of view, the high-angle full shot presenting the dead drug lord in a manner recalling Christ in the tomb, an association strengthened by the discoverer's exclamatory 'Jesus!' Watching the murder scene alongside the documentary film makes the spectator more than usually conscious of the relationship between actor and role. Hearing Sam McClean's account of having to lie for several hours in the cold before the murder scene was completed (a narrative reminiscent of Lizzie Siddal's almost freezing to death as she posed for John Everett Millais' *Ophelia* in a bath of water) perhaps makes less 'real' the gruesome image of the butchered Duncan. A rather less comfortable dual perspective, though no less humanizing, is viewing the moment when Mickey B thrusts the blade into his victim alongside one of the documentary interviews in which a prison officer points out the possibility of 'murderers playing murderers'. In this instance, the viewer is made acutely conscious of the multidimensionality of the actor-inmate's identity: an actual prisoner, playing a fictional prisoner, playing a Shakespearean killer – albeit one yet to be convicted.

Magill's determination to update *Macbeth* inevitably led to some reaccentuation of the source text. The Weird Sisters are reimagined as bookies who deal in the prison currency of drugs and tobacco, the lexis of gaming replacing that of supernatural determination. And the Shakespearean ending is revised in a way that destabilizes any sense of rightful order being restored. The film's final scene pictures Malcolm playing chess with the 'buckets' (prison officers). Though he now wears his father's belcher chain (a crown equivalent), reclaimed from the neck of the defeated Mickey B, it is clear that the price of victory is collusion with the 'enemy', a fact underlined when, in response to the officer's question 'Are they all locked in their boxes?', he responds with 'Aye, where they belong.'

But if his reply has a ring of finality about it, it is unsettled by the presence of Duffer, who, aided by a mirror (a major motif in the film, recalling the source tragedy's preoccupation with doubleness), is viewing the scene through the hatch of the cell door, excluded from the power that he has helped Malcolm to gain. As the 'justice' tarot card flashes on screen, so the audience realizes that Duffer, the most egregiously mistreated personage in both film and play, is set on avenging the deaths of his wife and children. This final scenario is an individualized instance of the revenge ethic that shapes the structure of the film. The added figure of Steeky (Stephen McParland) acts as a choric narrator, opening and closing the film with '[o]ne man's revenge is another man's regret', a refrain that at once applies to the fictional world, the situation of many of the actor-convicts, and the tit-for-tat dynamics of the Troubles that so many of them have experienced.

In a follow-up to *Mickey B*, Tom Magill (now Artistic Director of esc films) is planning to turn his attentions away from vengeance and towards forgiveness with an adaptation of *The Tempest* entitled *Prospero's Prison*. While the production circumstances of this film project are rather different from those of *Mickey B* (Magill plans to use professional actors), it promises to continue the director's commitment to revisioning Shakespeare's plays through the lens of post-conflict Northern Ireland, guarding against them becoming 'solely [...] a cultural sermon for the middle classes and the dwindling ancient congregations at Stratford' (Fischlin et al. 194).

David Greig, *Dunsinane* (2010)

In an article exploring the enduring contemporaneity of Shakespeare's *Macbeth*, Michael Billington observes:

> It deals [...] with the destructive nature of unchecked power-lust and political ambition: it is no accident that the play has spawned a host of modern variations, from a 1955 gangster movie, Joe Macbeth, to a 1967 parodic play, Macbird, in which Barbara Garson wickedly implicated Lyndon Johnson in President John F Kennedy's assassination.

> ('Michael')

Adding to this narrative of modernization is *Dunsinane* by David Greig, one of Scotland's most critically acclaimed dramatists. While *Dunsinane* is Greig's only published appropriation of Shakespeare, his debut drama, *A Savage Reminiscence*, was a revisioning of *The Tempest*, a play he claims as his favourite, along with *The Winter's Tale* (Taylor). Yet if only two of Greig's plays to date are conspicuously connected to Shakespeare, he considers each of them to be 'some type of a rewrite of a Shakespeare play' (Taylor). Theatre critics and academics are not at one when it comes to identifying what 'type of a rewrite' *Dunsinane* actually is. Reviewers covering its London premiere in 2010 (Royal Shakespeare Company, Hampstead Theatre) and its Scottish premiere a year later (National Theatre of Scotland, Royal Lyceum Theatre, Edinburgh) named it a 'sequel', a creative category that has attracted quite diverse opinions in the field of adaptation studies. Julie Sanders proposes that prequels and sequels both 'have roles to play at different times in the adaptive mode' (*Adaptation* 22); Hutcheon, though, considers such forms as 'not really adaptations' (*Theory of Adaptation* 9). It must also be said that, while the majority of theatre critics are ready to label the play a sequel, some literary scholars are less willing; Graham Saunders, for example, contends that '*Dunsinane* is less of a sequel and more a speculative continuation of *Macbeth*' (119–20), a definition that is perhaps more fitting for a play which has more than a superficial engagement with the hypotext.

Dunsinane opens where *Macbeth* leaves off, with the English preparing for the final push against Macbeth's castle. Led by the English general Siward, supported by his Scottish lieutenant Macduff and his English lieutenant Egham, the troops occupy the dead king's former territory only to discover that his widow, Gruach, is still very much alive, well and determined to remain Scotland's queen. The main action of the drama focuses on English efforts to secure Malcolm's place on the Scottish throne amid persistent, sometimes violent, local resistance. As this brief synopsis reveals, *Dunsinane* features Shakespearean characters alongside newly minted ones, an adaptive strategy that keeps *Macbeth* in view even as it signals new creative directions. Greig has described his play as a 'response' to Shakespeare's drama (MacAlister), one that 'takes the same fragment of Scottish history and tells a different chunk of it' (Jones). This historical reaccentuation of an early modern English writer's vision of Scotland is immediately apparent from

the play's title. In replacing Shakespeare's eponymous hero with
the site of a historical ruler's defeat, Greig moves the audience's
generic expectations from tragedy to history, perhaps underlining
that *Macbeth* has tended to be read more as the former than the
latter. In what one critic has described as 'an act of repossession'
(Wallace 92), Greig's play responds to Shakespeare's appropriation
of eleventh-century Scottish history, tailored as it was to the
political circumstances of the early Jacobean period. In *Dunsinane*,
Macbeth is not, as Shakespeare represents him, a tyrannical ruler,
quickly toppled by righteous forces, but, as his widow insists, 'a
good king' who 'ruled for fifteen years' (Greig, *Dunsinane* 32),
an appraisal that better fits the historical figure, who reigned
from 1040 to 1057. Macbeth's queen is called by her historical
first name, Gruach, and it is perhaps in her portrayal that Greig's
response to Shakespeare's play can be most acutely felt. Whereas
Shakespeare's Lady suffers a psychological breakdown and takes
her own life (happenings which stem entirely from the playwright's
imagination), Gruach is sharp, wily and mentally resilient. A
central focus of the drama, Greig portrays her in such a way as
to challenge those aspects of Shakespeare's Lady that might be
seen to conform to seventeenth-century misogynistic stereotypes.
One especially memorable instance is when Gruach teases a young
English soldier:

BOY SOLDIER
    Is it true that you eat babies?
GRUACH
    Babies?
BOY SOLDIER
    They say you eat babies.
GRUACH
    They say the Scots eat babies?
BOY SOLDIER
    Oh – no – I mean –
GRUACH
    What do you mean?
BOY SOLDIER
    I was asking if it's true that *you* eat babies?
GRUACH
    Me?

BOY SOLDIER
    Yes.
GRUACH
    They say that?

(Greig, *Dunsinane* 59)

Here an audience needs to recall the Lady's declaration that she would pluck her nipple from her nursing baby's 'boneless gums' (*Mac* 1.7.57) to appreciate the humour which Greig employs to challenge Shakespeare's demonization of the Queen as maternally aberrant. The episode also engages with the mythmaking around the 'other' as Gruach plays on the Boy Soldier's national prejudices, warning him that if he swallows the drink she offers, he will 'turn into a bird' (61), a threat that gestures back to *Macbeth* and the persuasive connections it draws between the Lady and the Weird Sisters. Greig, in fact, dispenses with the supernatural altogether: there are no witches, just a risible superstitiousness that resides here in a poorly educated young man. Far from being affiliated with supernatural forces, Gruach is an entirely earthly military threat. Unlike Shakespeare's childless Lady, she has a son, Lulach, the historical Macbeth's stepson and, according to his mother, the rightful king of Scotland – a claim that generates much of the play's dramatic action.

As Saunders observes, *Dunsinane* is 'a more historically accurate play than *Macbeth*' (124), though that is not to say that its author held back from shaping history to suit his own dramatic purposes. Prior to the play's composition, Greig forecast that his next drama was 'very consciously about Iraq, although through the prism of [...] *Macbeth*' (Billingham 91). Premiering at a time when the political situations in Iraq and Afghanistan were at the forefront of international political debate, reviewers were quick to find contemporary parallels in Greig's drama: the George W. Bush administration's euphemizing of military realities in Malcolm's semantic sophistry; the twenty-first-century suicide bomber in the early medieval Hen Girl who stabs herself to elude capture (Greig, *Dunsinane* 119); the photo-images of US troops handing out treats to local children in the English soldiers who 'smile back – you know – for the children, / Offer out [their] hands to them with nuts or something' (39). However, as Greig himself observes: '[t]heatre reminds us constantly of the contingency, the changeability of things' ('Rough Theatre' 219), and when *Dunsinane* was staged in Scotland, performances were 'read very differently from the earlier ones at the Hampstead as a result of the socio-political backdrop of the newly re-elected Alex Salmond as First Minister of Scotland and the renewed cries for Scottish independence' (Price 19). Greig reimagines Shakespeare's *Macbeth* not only by 'claiming just a little bit of history from another point of view' (Wrench), but also by portraying a Scotland whose landscape, politics and language prove profoundly unsettling to the occupiers. As the anonymous young soldier explains in the choric monologue that opens the second act:

> Where everything that in England was normal –
> Summer, land, beer, a house, a bed – for example –
> In Scotland – that thing would turn out to be made of water –
> This is what you learn here – nothing is solid.
>
> (*Dunsinane* 39)

Here, as elsewhere in the play, Greig decentres the English consciousness and perceptions of the 'normal'. Siward and his soldiers have to get to grips not only with hostile terrain, but also with the complex tribal politics of its population; as Macduff warns the English general, '[t]here are many clans and families' (30) and to envisage them all working together with the English 'in pursuit of the kingdom's common interest' (32) is to fundamentally misunderstand Scotland, both past and present.

On stage, the play's depiction of Scotland's 'otherness' is perhaps most strikingly felt in its bilingualism. The playscript indicates that dialogue given in brackets is to be spoken in Scottish Gaelic, meaning that, from time to time, certain audience members are othered, their inability to comprehend one of Scotland's official languages sometimes excluding them from the play's comic moments. Greig's decentring strategy also works on a diachronic level. According to Sila Şenlen Güvenç, 'King James expressed his hostility toward his Gaelic subjects by calling their language and them "barbarous cannibals"' (104), good reason perhaps for why Shakespeare omitted any mention of the national language from *Macbeth* and why Greig chooses to reinstate it. In Greig's medieval Scotland, a character's ability to operate in more than one tongue correlates with how sensitive they are to the connotations of language – a force for power in the play world. At one extreme is Gruach, the only individual to move flexuously between Gaelic and English. Given to metalinguistic speculation, she often draws attention to what she perceives to be the quiddity of the two languages, telling Siward that seducing a man in English is 'like dancing wearing wooden shoes' (*Dunsinane* 69), a simile she later expounds through extended metaphor:

> Your English is a woodworker's tool.
> Siward.
> Hello, goodbye, that tree is green,
> Simple matters.
> A soldier's language sent out to capture the world in words.
> Always trying to describe.
> Throw words at the tree and eventually you'll force
> me to see the tree just as you see it.
> We long since gave up believing in descriptions.
> Our language is the forest.
>
> (76)

Here, in caricaturing English as prosaically denotative and Gaelic as mysteriously tenebrous, Gruach underscores why the monolingual Siward struggles to make sense of the land he strives to subdue. In observing that '[t]he sun could rise at night time and we could call it day' (34), she recognizes the arbitrary nature of the relationship between signified and signifier, something Siward obdurately refuses to accept. If, in the course of the play, Siward changes from a military man of restraint and decency to one who resembles Shakespeare's Macbeth in his descent into mindless violence (arguably one of the play's rare false notes), he remains constant in his refusal to acknowledge the power of the connotative over the denotative, the modal over the affirmative. His lack of linguistic agility places him in contradistinction to his ruler, whose fleet equivocations operate as a prime political tool:

> and so usually the way we manage this sort of thing in Scotland is by being careful not only not to tell lies – but also to be very very careful about the way we hear and understand words. So for example – if a person in Scotland says 'It seems a person has

died' we tend to hear that word 'seems' – 'seems' – and of course
that word makes a difference.

(Dunsinane 28)

As Sandra Clark observes in the Introduction to the Arden
edition of *Macbeth*, '[t]he theme of double-speak and linguistic
ambiguity pervades the whole play' (Clark and Mason 19), and
the same could be said of *Dunsinane*. Greig has remarked that
his 'guiding principle in adaptation is to try to discover the effect
which the original author was hoping to achieve' (Rodosthenous
10–11), and it is perhaps in his foregrounding of the unfixed nature
of language that he comes closest to doing so. While he offers a
knowing audience some impish nods to the Shakespearean text
when the sergeant tells a soldier to '[b]e a tree' (*Dunsinane* 10) or
when Gruach ponders the tenderness of cooked baby flesh, it is in
his portrayal of the shifty, quibbling Malcolm that he seems most
alert to what might be thought of as his own play's 'prequel'. Greig
takes what some *Macbeth* scholars view as Malcolm's capacity for
deceit and double-dealing, hinted at in his 'testing' of Macduff in
4.3, and makes it explicit. The verbal indirectness of *Dunsinane*'s
Malcolm, emphasized by his habitual use of the filler 'Mmm' in
response to uncomfortable truths or questions, seems to infect the
talk of several others, Scottish and English alike:

SIWARD
  You sound like you would prefer us to be defeated.
EGHAM
  Who said 'defeated'? I didn't say 'defeated'. Did you say
  'defeated'? I didn't say 'defeated'. I said 'leave'.
SIWARD
  'Defeated' – 'leave' – what's the difference?
EGHAM
  All the difference.

(Dunsinane 95)

As exemplified in the extract above, words in the playscript are
often placed in quotation marks (a typographical feature that could
be conveyed in various ways on stage); in such instances, meaning

seems to be suspended, hampering communication and rendering the very language system unsettlingly opaque.

Writing back to a play that has long held an elevated place in the Shakespearean canon is bound to be a daunting creative venture, and Greig has spoken about experiencing a moment of extreme panic just before *Dunsinane*'s London premiere:

> The audience was gathering and all of a sudden I felt so sick [...]. Blood drained from my body and I was thinking, 'What have you done? You've dared to write a sequel to Shakespeare and now it's being performed not only in England, but by the RSC.'
>
> (Taylor)

Yet as the opening-night reviews amply demonstrate, Greig's artistic daring created a thought-provoking and affective drama that deserves to be regarded as much more than a postscript to an illustrious forerunner.

10

Cymbeline

Cymbeline is a play noted for its generic hybridity, multiple
timeframes, rapidly shifting locations and complex plot, all of
which make it one of Shakespeare's most challenging dramas to
stage – and to adapt. This chapter examines the diverse ways in
which three creative artists have negotiated the play's challenges
to make it speak to the sentiments, fears and social concerns of
their own times.

David Garrick, *Cymbeline* (1762)

The celebrated actor, theatre manager and author David Garrick
(1717–79) was born at a time when the relationship between the
public and Shakespeare was growing increasingly close. 1709 saw
the publication of six folio-based volumes of Shakespeare's works,
edited by Nicholas Rowe, the first to be produced in portable
octavo form. Attractively illustrated by the engravings of François
Boitard, these editions came at a price, and it was not until the
1730s that cheaper, mass-produced print copies of Shakespeare
became easily available at affordable prices. In the mid-to-late
eighteenth century, when Garrick dominated the London stage,
the editing and performance of Shakespearean drama were closely
connected: the shaping of the plays to suit contemporary theatrical
conditions and tastes influenced printed editions, which in turn

provided the foundations for future performances. Several of Garrick's versions of Shakespeare were available in print editions, and present-day scholarly scrutiny of these has revealed that the actor–manager's reputation as the chief restorer of Shakespeare's texts was based largely on myth, created and sustained by Garrick's own canny self-fashioning and by his many admirers. Uncovering the Garrick 'myth' has yielded a more discriminating assessment of his contribution to the performance, production and editing of Shakespeare's dramatic writings.

The twentieth-century editors of Garrick's plays, Harry William Pedicord and Frederick Louis Bergmann, include eleven of the author's Shakespearean texts, classifying them as 'adaptations'; however, as Vanessa Cunningham points out, '"alteration" is certainly the preferable term [...] since throughout the eighteenth century "alter" was used far more commonly than "adapt"' (1). The extent to which Garrick altered the source texts was by no means consistent, nor did it follow any discernible pattern or direction over time, despite attitudes towards interfering with folio-based Shakespeare growing steadily more conservative as the century wore on. Garrick's *Cymbeline*, for example, is far less radical in its changes than his *Hamlet*, published a decade or so later. The author's reflections on his treatment of *Hamlet* cast interesting light on his approach to adapting the plays for the stage:

> I have ventured to produce Hamlet with alterations it was the most imprudent thing I ever did in all my life but I had sworn I would not leave the Stage till I had rescued that noble play from all the rubbish of the 5th Act I have brought it forth without the grave Diggers Ostrick & the Fencing Match the alteration was received with general approbation beyond my most warm expectations.
>
> (Garrick, *Letters*, vol. 2, 845–6; original punctuation retained)

One recent study of cutwork reads this letter as an expression of 'guilt about making changes to Shakespeare's texts' (B. R. Smith 10), though any such expression needs to be weighed against Garrick's dismissing parts of Shakespeare's most revered tragedy as 'rubbish' – pejorative language commonly applied to Shakespeare's works by Restoration adapters, whose editorial approach was sometimes far from reverential. Certainly, the correspondence is an apt illustration of Jean Marsden's assessment that '[i]n his dual role as adaptor and restorer, Garrick could both produce a play that appealed to the tastes of his audience and appear to score a point for England's literary heritage' ('Improving' 32).

Cymbeline is undoubtedly amongst Garrick's most restrained alterations of Shakespeare. Even early-twentieth-century critics, inclined to view any type of departure from the source text as an act of profanity, regarded the actor–manager's adjustments as 'nothing worth quarrelling about' (Odell, vol. 1, 371). In fact, set alongside previous reworkings of the romance, Garrick's seems the epitome of fidelity. Thomas Durfey's *The Injured Princess, or the Fatal Wager* (1682) capitalizes on the Restoration novelty of female performers by adding the threatened rape of a servant, Clarina, offering to playgoers the possibility of an exposed and violated female body on stage. Though Durfey's version is inimical to modern sensibilities in its downright misogyny, its frequent allusions to and occasional quotations from other Shakespeare plays lend it a distinctively post-modernist appeal, the text's *bricolage* mirroring in some respects the recapitulatory nature of the source play itself. Another author to try his hand at revising *Cymbeline* was William Hawkins, an Oxford professor whose main adaptive purpose was to reset Shakespeare's romance 'almost upon the plan of *Aristotle* himself' (Hawkins v), thus bringing it into line with the classical unities so aesthetically prized in the eighteenth century. Ineptly adjusted to fit the action of two days and confined to the sole location of Britain, Hawkins's *Cymbeline, A Tragedy, altered from Shakespeare* (1759) had limited stage appeal, and it would appear from the introduction to the printed edition that Garrick, in his role as manager of the Drury Lane Theatre, turned down the opportunity to produce it, obliging its author 'to take up his head-quarters at *Covent-Garden*' (Hawkins vii), the rival patent-theatre in London. Hawkins's *Cymbeline* ran for just six nights in 1759, to be followed just three years later by Garrick's own much more popular alteration.

Garrick's *Cymbeline. A Tragedy* was performed 163 times between its first performance in 1761 and the end of the century (Stone 311), a tally which attests to its author's instinct and sure-footedness as a drama practitioner. That his chief concern was with theatrical pragmatics is clear from the Advertisement to the printed edition of 1762, which asks 'Admirers of *Shakespear*' not to be discountenanced by the author's cutting of some 'fine passages', explaining that such excisions were necessary to bring the play 'within the Compass of a Night's Entertainment' (Garrick, *Cymbeline* A2); this 'compass' would have allowed for an assortment of performances, entirely detached from the main play in theme and genre, including farces, musical interludes, masquerades and dances. To create space for these theatrical extras, Garrick pruned 610 lines from Shakespeare's romance (around one-fifth of the total), with 524 being taken from the final act. That he cut a further forty or so lines after the first performance (Garrick, *Cymbeline* A2), presumably to fine-tune the timings, further testifies to his prioritizing of practicalities. The outcome of Garrick's stage edit was 'a leaner, cleaner, less complicated play' (Wayne, '*Cymbeline*: Patriotism' 397), effected by removing whole scenes (such as Posthumus' vision and the appearance of Jupiter), restructuring and resequencing others, and deleting narrative or verbal repetitions deemed dramatically unnecessary. In a couple of instances, Garrick seems to take note of calls for brevity made within the play world itself, such as when he cuts almost by half Iachimo's speech relating the story of the wager, as if responding to Cymbeline's urging to get 'to th' purpose' (*Cym* 5.5.178). Also removed were several of the play's classical references, a surprising editorial decision given the period's reverence for the classics. However, *Cymbeline*'s unusually high count of classical allusions could have been regarded as placing too great an emphasis on the Roman world at a time when the Britishness of the play was being foregrounded.

If some of Garrick's more substantial changes were prompted by the exigencies of stage time, others seem to have come from an astute awareness of the playgoer. Michael Caines identifies how 'Garrick [...] was highly successful in judging what the audience would take and what they wouldn't' (83), and his recrafting of *Cymbeline* is a telling example of his ability to adapt Shakespeare's text to suit the social, cultural and political sensibilities of the day. Always endeavouring to move away from the lingering Protestant suspicion of the theatre and to promote its respectability, Garrick strikes out some of the play's earthier language, including some of the sexually explicit puns and innuendoes that proliferate in the scenes with Cloten and the Lords. Also erased is Guiderius' declaration that if Fidele were a woman he would 'woo hard' (*Cym* 3.6.67), perhaps on account of the incestuous connotations often underscored by present-day critics (see Wayne, *Cymbeline* 91).

Squeamish spectators are also protected from the gory sight of Guiderius clutching Cloten's severed head and Imogen's subsequent smearing of her face with the blood of the matching torso. Another culturally sensitive excision is the references by both the Queen and Cornelius to testing potentially harmful drugs on 'cats and dogs' (*Cym* 1.5.38); vivisection was unlikely to have been well received in a period which saw the domestic pet firmly ensconced in the bourgeois household.

One other sentiment that Garrick seems to have been keen to embrace was that of British nationalism. In doing so, he was following the eighteenth-century inclination to shape what is nowadays read as *Cymbeline*'s internationalism into something more decidedly pro-British. William Hawkins, for example, discovered something 'truly *British*' (v) in the play, manipulating its ending to present 'the new ascendency of one race of empire-builders over their teachers' (Dobson 207). Given that Garrick's version played during the Seven Years' War with France, it is unsurprising that he pursued a similarly nationalistic line. The British nationalism fervently espoused by Shakespeare's Queen is removed, thus avoiding any uncomfortable suggestion that a patriot might also be the villain of the piece; likewise cut is the analeptic detail of Cymbeline's friendship with Augustus Caesar, making Rome unambiguously 'the enemy' as a consequence. For good measure, Garrick composes words to underline the power and status of the British king:

> and more than that,
> They have a KING, whose Love and Justice to them
> May ask and have their Treasures, and their Blood.

(Cymbeline 30)

Penned for Posthumus, the role earmarked for the actor-author himself, the praise is clearly intended to flatter the newly crowned George III – and who better than Garrick, a pillar of the British establishment, to deliver it?

Despite the 'alterations' outlined above, scholars of eighteenth-century Shakespeare are generally agreed that Garrick's adaptation is a relatively conservative one. However, there is one editing detail that seems at odds with such an assessment: the cutting and rewriting of the song spoken by the young princes to mark the supposed death of Fidele (*Cym* 4.2.257–80). The best-known lines in the play, they have long been regarded as Shakespeare at full poetic strength, appearing in intertexts by authors such as John Keats, Virginia Woolf, T. S. Eliot and Samuel Beckett. Generations of British schoolchildren encountered the song in *Palgrave's Golden Treasury* (1861), a verse anthology dedicated to the then Poet Laureate, Alfred Tennyson, himself a great admirer of *Cymbeline*. Productions that dare to excise verses so firmly rooted in the cultural consciousness will inevitably raise critical hackles. Reviewers of Matthew Dunster's *Imogen* (Globe, 2016), for example, though mixed in their responses to the substantially modernized source text, were unanimous in decrying the author's cutting of all but the first two lines of the threnody (Dunster 58). Why, then, did Garrick decide to retain a mere quatrain of this prized passage, two lines of which are rewritings borrowed from Hawkins's 1759 version? One reason might be that what Martin Butler terms the 'chillingly materialist' philosophy of the piece (23) was felt to be incompatible with the Christian orthodoxies of Georgian audiences. A more likely explanation, however, is that the poetic qualities of the text were not a paramount consideration in the editing process. As Tiffany Stern points out, for much of the eighteenth century, Shakespeare's words were 'the least valued part of his plays' (149), and they were by no means immune from disparaging aesthetic judgements. In common with many eighteenth-century literary commentators, Garrick was not an admirer of Shakespeare's rhyme (he refers to it as 'jingle' in the printed version of his 1748 *Romeo and Juliet*) and he may well have thought the alternating rhyme of the dirge unconducive to the more naturalistic style of performance he famously sought to foster; whether he would have included the song among the 'fine passages' he admits to having removed in the Advertisement to his *Cymbeline* is, then, debatable.

It would take until the end of the eighteenth century for the 'quasi-religious veneration for [Shakespeare's] very words' (Cunningham 76) to take hold, an inclination encouraged and facilitated by the proliferation of scholarly editions of the plays published in the course of the eighteenth century. As an 'authentic' Shakespeare came to be fixed in these texts and the language of the plays began to take on a sacred quality, so the freedom enjoyed by seventeenth- and eighteenth-century adapters of these works would be curtailed. Indeed, rather than regarding Garrick as the great restorer of Shakespeare's plays, he might more properly be viewed as one of the last few dramatists to engage creatively with them, still relatively free from the constraining forces of what would come to be known as 'Bardolatry'.

George Bernard Shaw, *Cymbeline Refinished* (1937)

George Bernard Shaw's engagement with Shakespeare was a highly complex one, both artistically and psychologically. From immersing himself in Shakespeare's plays in childhood to dramatizing his combative relationship with the playwright in the puppet play *Shakes versus Shav*, written and presented just a year before his death in 1950, Shaw had a seemingly indefatigable fascination with his theatrical forefather. Yet where Garrick contributed to making Shakespeare the 'God of our idolatry', Shaw put his journalistic and artistic weight behind bringing him back to earth, coining the term 'Bardolatry': the excessive, uncritical worship of Shakespeare. As drama critic for the *Saturday Review* (1895–8), Shaw practised what he preached, eschewing the reverential tone that pervaded most Victorian writing about Shakespeare. A bemusing mix of the serious and the facetious, his provocative pronouncements on Shakespearean text and performance made him something of a celebrity critic years before he made his mark as a dramatist in his own right.

Cymbeline Refinished is a meeting of late Shakespeare and late Shaw, though the latter's interest in making the romance stage-worthy began several decades earlier, as recorded in his lengthy correspondence with Ellen Terry. Included in this flirtatious epistolary exchange is Shaw's advice to Terry about performing the role of Imogen in Henry Irving's 1896 *Cymbeline* at the Lyceum, a production based on an edited version of the play denounced by Shaw as 'stupid to the last extremity' (*Shaw on Shakespeare* 69). It was a production that Shaw would come to blame for his initial disregard for the play:

> I must have got it from the last revival of the play at the old Lyceum theatre, when Irving, as Iachimo, a statue of romantic

melancholy, stood dumb for hours [...] whilst the others toiled through a series of *dénouements* of crushing tedium, in which the characters lost all their vitality and individuality, and had nothing to do but identify themselves by moles on their necks, or explain why they were not dead.

(Shaw, *Geneva* 134)

Years later, Shaw's scrupulous reading of *Cymbeline* led him to revise his view of the play and to reach the conclusion that the final act 'is not doggerel: it is a versified masque, in Shakespear's careless woodnotes wild, complete with Jupiter as *deus ex machina*, eagle and all' (*Geneva* 134). Notwithstanding this change of heart, he remained convinced that *Cymbeline* was intractable to twentieth-century performance, both in its theatrical demands and its romance elements, and *Cymbeline Refinished* stands as a testament to this conviction. Shaw explains the genesis of his adaptation in a letter to publishers R & R Clark:

It arose out of a proposal made at the last meeting of the Stratford-on-Avon committee to revive Cymbeline [*sic*]. I said that they had better let me rewrite the last act; and to my surprise they jumped at it. Curiosity, no doubt; but it stuck in my mind like a mosquito until I actually perpetrated the outrage.

(*Collected Letters*, vol. 4, 459)

While it would be reasonable to assume that the incorrigibly iconoclastic Shaw was being ironical in deeming his rewriting an 'outrage', his published views on the adaptation of Shakespeare indicate otherwise. In an article entitled 'On Cutting Shakespear', published in the *Fortnightly Review* in 1919, Shaw averred:

The moment you admit that the producer's business is to improve Shakespear by cutting out everything that he himself would not have written, and everything that he thinks the audience will either not like or not understand, and everything that does not make prosaic sense, you are launched on a slope on which there is no stopping until you reach the abyss[.]

(*Shaw on Shakespeare* 272)

As a thoroughgoing revisioning of the conclusion of Shakespeare's late play, *Cymbeline Refinished* appears to fly in the face of such vehement opposition to adaptation and, doubtless keenly aware of the gap between what he preached and what he practised, Shaw puts the case for his defence in the Foreword to the published piece: his rewriting is 'in response to an actual emergency', of an order entirely distinct from the 'crude literary butcheries' executed by the actor managers he frequently reviled (Shaw, *Geneva* 133).

Shaw's contention that *Cymbeline* 'goes to pieces in the last act' (*Geneva* 133) was not notably controversial: as Ann Thompson observes, the closing sequence of the play 'can *feel* long, and it has very often been abbreviated on stage' (204). Yet if cutting the performance time of the dénouement to about a third of the Folio version was undoubtedly a major imperative for Shaw, perhaps more pressing was his desire to strip away the idealizing elements of the romance and 'rewrite the act as Shakespear might have written it if he had been post-Ibsen' (Shaw, *Geneva* 136). Frank Harris, Shaw's close friend and one-time editor, quotes his subject's assessment of the impact of Ibsen on the dramatic tradition: '[o]ur Bard is knocked out of time [...] Hamlet is a spineless effigy beside Peer Gynt, Imogen a doll beside Nora Helmer' (Harris 249). In what might be seen as an experiment in theatrical time-travel, Shaw endeavours to knock the Bard back *into* time by removing all but eighty-nine lines of *Cymbeline*'s Act 5, thereby clearing space for his own creative modernization of the finale. The 'Refinished' of the title provides a novel addition to the vocabulary of adaptation: at surface level a clear statement of the job done, it also carries connotations of refining the source text to give it a more polished 'finish'; at the same time, the prefix of the word underscores the author's awareness that his may not be the definitive 'finishing' of the work, updating being an ongoing process (in fact, Shaw's working title had been '*Cymbeline* up to date', a title he probably realized would become 'out of date' all too quickly).

Through the process of what Gérard Genette terms 'proximation', Shaw brings the hypertext into closer proximity with the social, cultural and political conditions of his time, proving true to his avowal: 'My business is to incarnate the Zeitgeist' (*Collected Letters*, vol. 1, 222). Centring his post-Ibsen revisions around the role of Imogen, Shaw engages with the sexual politics of the day, and while the status of Shaw as a feminist writer is by no means uncontested, his treatment of Shakespeare's heroine certainly bears the hallmarks of a writer committed to gender equality. Shaw's correspondence with Terry provides a revealing insight into his reading of Imogen:

> All I can extract from the artificialities of the play is a double image – a woman *divined* by Shakespear without his knowing it clearly, a natural aristocrat, with a high temper and perfect courage, with two moods – a childlike affection and wounded rage; and an idiotic paragon of virtue produced by Shakespear's *views* of what a woman ought to be, a person who sews and cooks, and reads improving books until midnight [...] and is anxious to assure people that they may trust her implicitly with their spoons and forks [...]. If I were you I should cut the part so as to leave the paragon out and the woman in[.]
>
> (*Shaw on Shakespeare* 62–3)

In *Cymbeline Refinished*, Shaw appears to have followed his own advice to Terry in recasting the 'paragon' of Shakespeare's conclusion as an angry, resentful wife. And whereas Shakespeare's heroine is muted to some degree in Act 5 (only 5 per cent or so of her lines are spoken in the final act), she is the only character to gain lines in Shaw's version. Imogen's updated role not only speaks back to its seventeenth-century moment, it also rebukes what one critic termed the 'Imogenolatry' of the mid-Victorian period (Nevo 67), when she was deemed the cynosure of feminine virtue. Shaw harnesses the 'high temper' that he recognizes in Imogen to stage a scene of wifely recrimination. Rather than falling into Posthumus' arms at the point of their reunion, she instead challenges him, 'You dare pretend you love me' (Shaw, *Geneva* 143), before acknowledging Iachimo as the less despicable of the two men who have treated her as an object of barter:

> You at least
> Have grace to know yourself for what you are.
> My husband thinks that all is settled now
> And this a happy ending!
>
> (145)

Shaw leaves no trace of the 'conjugal tenderness' (Jameson, vol. 2, 60) so admired in the mid-Victorian era; rather, Imogen returns to the marital home more out of necessity than love:

CYMBELINE
God's patience, man, take your wife home to bed.
You're man and wife: nothing can alter that.
[...]
[*To Imogen*] Go change your dress
For one becoming to your sex and rank.
Have you no shame?
IMOGEN
None.
CYMBELINE
How? None!
IMOGEN   All is lost.
Shame, husband, happiness, and faith in Man.

(*Geneva* 148–9)

Rebuked by the patriarch-father, it is left to Guiderius and Arveragus, Imogen's long-lost brothers, whom she publicly pronounces her 'truest friends' (145), to restore her 'faith in Man'. Considerate and compassionate, their downright refusal to be heirs-in-waiting sets them apart from the homosocial values so negatively exhibited in the behaviour of Imogen's father, husband and would-be seducer.

In discussing Posthumus in the Foreword to *Cymbeline Refinished*, Shaw claims to have 'left most of his part untouched' (135). Notwithstanding the author's words, however, there is much in Shaw's redrawing that renders Posthumus a good deal less likeable than Shakespeare's protagonist, thus directing audience sympathy even more towards the heroine. In the 1890s, Shaw had found in Posthumus an 'anticipation of the crudest side of Ibsen's polemics on the Woman Question' (*Shaw on Shakespeare* 238), when he forgives Imogen for 'wrying but a little' (*Cym* 5.1.5); in *Cymbeline Refinished*, though, he refrains from developing this dawning self-awareness beyond preserving the soliloquy in which it appears. Though it is true that Shaw goes one step further than Shakespeare in having Posthumus forgive Imogen on stage *before* he has discovered Iachimo's trickery (Shakespeare's husband expresses forgiveness at a point when he believes his wife has been murdered on his orders and learns of Iachimo's deceit prior to their stage reunion), once relieved of the burdensome guilt of his wife's murder, he quickly falls back into a self-satisfied complacency, seemingly more concerned to reclaim the ten thousand ducats staked on Imogen's chastity than he is to recognize the gravity of his failure of faith. And when Posthumus defends his decision to order his wife's death by telling her it 'seemed natural' (Shaw, *Geneva* 145), he persists in regarding women as predestined to honour and obey their husbands in marriage. Perhaps, though, the greatest dent to Posthumus' likeability comes from Shaw's erasure of his highly affective lines to Imogen: 'Hang there like fruit, my soul, / Till the tree die' (*Cym* 5.5.262–3). Regarded by Alfred Tennyson as 'among the tenderest lines in Shakespeare' (vol. 2, 428) and by Virginia Woolf as guaranteed to 'send a shiver down your spine, even if you are in the middle of cold grouse and coffee' (8), these lines are preserved even in radical rescriptings of the play, such as that by David Grose and Emma Rice (2007). As one influential critic argued, these are 'ten words which do more than anything else in the whole play to bring him [Posthumus] in weight and value a little nearer to Imogen' (Spurgeon 293); Shaw's decision to remove them resists this rebalancing.

At the close of *Cymbeline Refinished*, Imogen resigns herself to 'go home and make the best of it / As other women must' (149), a dismal prospect in keeping with the anti-romantic tone of the piece. If the supernatural powers and fairytale tropes which feature large in the pre-text could lull the audience into accepting the 'infantile joys' (136) of reconciliation, Shaw's final act serves to block any such sentiments. Where Shakespeare prolongs the anticipation of loves restored and family members recovered to make the eventual reunion all the more joyful and touching, Shaw rattles through the revelations, truncating individual speeches and injecting a mundane realism into proceedings: Iachimo's recounting of his physical discomfort when hiding in the trunk overrides the erotic charge of the recollection; Posthumus' first reaction to hearing of Iachimo's attempt on his wife's chastity is to complain that he has been cheated out of his diamond ring; Cymbeline's concern that his daughter is improperly dressed prevails over any joy at finding her. Shaw's remoulded characters are, then, resolutely sublunary. In refinishing *Cymbeline*, Shaw brings the play much closer in mood to *Measure for Measure*, a play which he believed to be already in tune with the twentieth century. Just as Isabella's concluding silence in response to the Duke's proposal can be read as that of a female trapped in a patriarchal system which allows her little or no say over her own destiny, so Shaw's Imogen is left to accept the lot of the seventeenth-century woman, notwithstanding that, thanks to her two brothers' abdications, she appears to be next in line to Cymbeline's throne.

Though intended for performance at the Shakespeare Memorial Theatre, *Cymbeline Refinished* never reached its destination. As Shaw explains in a handwritten note at the foot of a page in a privately printed edition he sent to friends, 'Stratford funked my revision at the last moment', a loss of nerve that may have come from the coincidence of the abdication of Edward VIII in 1936 and Shaw's mischievous decision to have Guiderius and Arveragus refuse the privilege of primogeniture; the note continues, 'It had its first performance at the theatre near Swiss Cottage in London, and so far (Oct 1941) has not been used again' (*Cymbeline* 3). The production referred to here was a three-week run at the Embassy Theatre in late 1937, considered by one theatre critic to be a 'trimly modern *dénouement*', displaying plenty of Shavian wit and 'aggressively adult intelligence' ('Shakespeare and Mr Shaw' 14). But for all its virtues, it was nonetheless felt to raise 'the aesthetic objection that the texture of the rewritten act is different from that of the rest of the play', a problem that Shaw had sought to overcome by composing 200 or so lines of his own blank verse (a form he boasted came very naturally to him) to minimize the disjunction between early modern and modern. The next time *Cymbeline Refinished* would be lifted from the page would be in radio performances: one broadcast in the US in 1938 and another on the BBC's Third Programme in 1951. Although these are the final professional productions of the adaptation to date, it continues to find a place on the amateur stage. In 2016, a Los Angeles theatre company, Shakespeare by the Sea, staged a version of *Cymbeline* which interpolated a brief section from Shaw's act to show Imogen momentarily as a modern, feisty heroine. The impact of this selective grafting was to provoke audience laughter, a response which chimes with the prevailing view of Shaw's reimagining. As one recent commentator remarks, 'Shaw openly offers to improve upon a Shakespeare play, but it seems unlikely that we are to take *Cymbeline Refinished* as a serious substitution' (Bates 236). Serious or not, what Shaw himself described as a '*jeu d'esprit*' (*Geneva* 133) remains an audacious example of Shakespearean recreation, accompanied by a paratext that offers a stimulating – if not entirely trustworthy – account of the adaptive process.

Cymbeline, dir. Michael Almereyda (2014)

The history of *Cymbeline* on film is a short one: a twenty-minute silent movie, released in the US in 1913; Elijah Moshinsky's BBC television version, broadcast in 1983; and Michael Almereyda's low-budget *Cymbeline*, the first full-length adaptation for the cinema. Having first ventured into adaptation with *Hamlet* (2000), Shakespeare's best-known play, Almereyda's decision to choose one of the least known for his second adaptive project was, to say the least, a high-risk one. Acknowledging in interview the play's lack of screen antecedents, the indie auteur explained how he embraced the opportunity 'to start from scratch and make an exciting new movie' (Mears). But if *Cymbeline*'s relative obscurity brought artistic gains, it also brought losses, chief amongst them a lack of immediate audience appeal. Though it is the habit of adaptation scholars to steer clear of 'fidelity criticism', the fact remains that the attraction of screen Shakespeare for many viewers stems from what Hutcheon defines as 'the comfort of ritual combined with the piquancy of surprise' (*Theory of Adaptation* 4), a demanding combination to pull off when adapting one of the canon's less familiar works. Fears that *Cymbeline* might not attract many viewers can be detected in the distributer's decision (subsequently reversed) to retitle the film *Anarchy*, thereby associating it with the enormously successful television crime drama *Sons of Anarchy* (2008–14), as well as in the teaser-trailer's focus on car chases, shoot-outs and seductive female poses, all clearly targeted at mainstream audiences. Although retaining *Cymbeline*'s Early Modern English, the film delivers plenty of the modern movie staples promised in the trailer, as Almereyda creates what he has described as a 'willfully American version with

American characters and an American subtext' (Rome). Shakespeare's Britons are remade in the image of a New York motorcycle gang whose drug-related enterprises enable them to sustain a comfortable, if somewhat tawdry, bourgeois lifestyle. The main conflict of the narrative comes from the biker community's violent clashes with the corrupt and brutal regional police force – a tenuous equivalent of Shakespeare's Romans.

For Almereyda, adapting *Cymbeline* brought about 'a collision between contemporary reality and the world that Shakespeare was defining' (Mears). One of the contemporary realities of the screen *Cymbeline* is the ubiquity of digital devices; as one reviewer put it, the film has 'more tech gadgetry than an Apple store' (Rooney), with almost every character using a smartphone, laptop or iPad at some stage in the narrative. Updating the source text via the latest technologies has become an established inter-temporal trope of the Shakespeare movie, an instant means of signalling modernity at the same time as meeting the demands of cinematic realism. The hero of Almereyda's *Hamlet* is an amateur videographer who watches, creates and repurposes screen images to make sense of the media-saturated Web 1.0 society he inhabits. Set fourteen years later, *Cymbeline* charts the developments of Web 2.0, presenting a thesis which is, according to Douglas Lanier, 'rather more pessimistic about screen technology as a vehicle for alternative culture' ('Almereyda's *Cymbeline*' 240). On a purely pragmatic level, the film's technological equipment provides a here-and-now means of creating and communicating the falsehoods of the early modern play; on an interpretive level, it serves as a kind of yardstick for measuring the moral integrity of individual characters. Imogen rarely engages with the digital world of her own volition; she first appears gazing at a photograph of her lover, stored not as might be expected on her smartphone but in a picture frame. This initial association of Imogen with low-tech culture is matched by Posthumus' woodcut love token, the crafting of which is filmed in extreme close-up, affiliating him explicitly with the artisanal. Prior to this, however, he is shown to be an active user of digital devices when, in the all-male company of the wager scene, he shows Philario and Iachimo a photograph of Imogen as a child. Saved on his iPhone, this image underscores the capacity of technological devices to archive images from the past as well as of the moment; perhaps more significantly, it suggests Posthumus' inability to accept Imogen as a fully sexualized being – an indicator of the psycho-sexual vulnerability that Iachimo will soon exploit.

The film's main villain, Iachimo, played by the topliner Ethan Hawke, is the character most preoccupied with digital devices. His visit to Imogen sees him suited and booted, the figure of a young professional, completed by the leather-bound iPad which inflicts the first of several assaults on Imogen's happiness via the small screen: photoshopped pictures of Posthumus enjoying the company of a beautiful woman, the 'tomboy' of Shakespeare's text (*Cym* 1.6.121). Almereyda follows Shakespeare in having Iachimo subsequently explain away his fabricated reality as a ploy to test how far her 'affiance / Were deeply rooted' (*Cym* 1.6.162–3), thereby undermining the concept of 'photographic evidence', so often invoked as the acid test of truth. Iachimo's next exploitation of new media for deceptive purposes takes place in Imogen's bedroom, where, having secreted himself in a music-gear storage box, he emerges, iPhone at the ready, to document the room's furnishings before taking selfies and video footage as 'proof' that he has seduced the occupant. One of the most thought-provoking scenes in terms of looking and seeing in the digital age, the camera moves from long-shots of Iachimo, snapping images of the bedroom as he approaches the sleeping Imogen, to close-up two-shots as he positions himself next to the sleeper, ready to capture photographic 'evidence' of his sexual triumph. Yet the moment he touches the selfie icon and sees his own face in the frame (a moment synchronized with diegetic noise that unnerves him), he ceases to view the sleeping woman through a lens; instead, he looks directly at her, evoking the Shakespearean Iachimo's declaration that note-taking is unnecessary, considering that Imogen's image is 'riveted' (*Cym* 2.2.43) in his memory. From this point on, he appears disturbed, even distressed, by his own behaviour, Hawke's facial expression offering a distinct departure from the erotic desire or cynical control conveyed in so many stage performances of *Cymbeline*; it is also oddly out of sync with the more relaxed tone of the soliloquy delivered in voiceover, as if what is spoken is at odds with what is felt. In this performance, when Iachimo declares 'hell is here' (*Cym* 2.2.50), a phrase whose deictic has generated plural interpretations, the viewer is left in little doubt that the metaphor refers to his own mental state.

Iachimo's technologically faked 'evidence' would seem to
be an obvious means of making Posthumus' belief in Imogen's
sexual betrayal convincing for a modern audience; moreover, that
both lovers are duped by digital chicanery is consistent with the
film's initial association of them with a low-tech lifestyle and, by
implication, some degree of naivety. But although Iachimo arrives
armed with photographic evidence – conveniently synched to his
iPad – to claim his wager victory, its power to incriminate is barely
tested, the initial shots of Imogen's bedroom being the only ones
offered up in proof. These bedroom photographs provide a crisp
filmic synonymy for Iachimo's lengthy ekphrasis in Shakespeare's
text (*Cym* 2.4.66–91), though the way they are presented is perhaps
of greater significance than the images themselves. In a mise-en-scène
that positions the two rivals seated at opposite sides of a low table,
Iachimo uses Posthumus' skateboard to ferry the iPad photographs
across the table to his rival, placing together the objects with which
each man is most readily associated: a succinct metonymic image
to suggest that while they are distinctly different personalities,
they are bound by male kinship. Here, as Maurizio Calbi observes,
'the film seems to suggest [...] that the new medium is an updated
form of bonding between men, and that male connectivity *per se*
matters more than any visual content appearing on a screen' (11).
It is certainly the case that Almereyda's villain, like Shakespeare's,
fabricates Imogen's infidelity through a combination of material
proof (the bracelet) and an Iago-like gift for conjuring the erotic
from words alone. Potentially compelling though Iachimo's iPhone
visuals might be, they pale into insignificance alongside the authority
of speech. Retaining in its entirety Iachimo's account of kissing
Imogen's mole (*Cym* 2.4.134–8), the film asserts the enduring power
of the verbal to stir an emotion as strong as jealousy: millennial
men turn out to be no less homosocial or misogynistic than their
seventeenth-century forebears.

From this point on, technological devices function simply as a
means of updating the letters and maps of the early modern drama.
Imogen is the main victim of the present-day equivalents: she is
forced to read Posthumus' text-message denouncement of her as 'a
strumpet' on Philario's phone and is tracked down via her laptop's
browsing history by her predatory step-brother, Cloten. But for all
this, she maintains a distance from the technological world; she
manufactures 'proof' of her killing not through the easy route of

digital photography but through sending her cardigan, smeared with blood taken from a self-inflicted wound, by parcel-post. When she assumes her male identity and wanders into Belarius' run-down wood cabin (the dwelling equivalent of Shakespeare's cave), she finds herself in a home of kindred spirits. A similar model of the analogue television that appears in Imogen's bedroom is placed in the foreground of shots of Belarius' living area, broadcasting one of the movie's few uplifting screen images: Barack Obama, a figure of hope for the underprivileged class that Almereyda's African American Belarius represents.

In line with most *Cymbeline* adapters, Almereyda swerves away from Shakespeare's dénouement – and from any clear resolution. With Imogen seated on a motorcycle and Posthumus riding pillion, the reunited couple ride away from what proves the most temporary of family reunions to an unknown location and an unknown future. The final screen image is of the woodcut love token lying amidst the detritus of the climactic shoot-out. Initially a symbol of an alternative culture, its final appearance marks it out as no more enduring than the digital images it promised to counter.

11

The Winter's Tale

This chapter examines the Victorian fictionalizing of Shakespeare in Mary Cowden Clarke's prequel to *The Winter's Tale* – one of a series of stories that focuses on Shakespeare's heroines as they grow into adulthood. Dramatizing the play in a non-verbal medium is explored through Wheeldon's twenty-first-century ballet, while the RSC's 1999 production is considered as an early experiment in live theatre broadcast.

Mary Cowden Clarke, *The Girlhood of Shakespeare's Heroines in a Series of Tales* (1850–2)

The novelization of Shakespeare in the nineteenth century is not, in itself, a surprising phenomenon, the great age of the novel coinciding with the apotheosis of Shakespeare's reputation as the legendary 'master of the human heart'. Romantic poets and critics had emphasized Shakespeare's 'gift of looking into the inmost recesses of [his characters'] minds' (quoted in Bate, *Romantics* 97), foregrounding the primacy of character in a way that came to dominate nineteenth-century attitudes to Shakespeare. Interiorizing individual response to Shakespeare's plays raised the notion that the best appreciation might be the solitary experience of the reader – Hazlitt was not the only

Romantic critic who asserted that '[we] do not like to see our author's plays acted' (*Selected Writings* 1, 47). At the same time, 'Shakespeare' signified educated taste and culture to aspiring and socially mobile Victorians, among whom female readers and the young child were assuming new significance as independent readers of Shakespeare. Charles and Mary Lamb and their exact contemporaries Thomas and Henrietta Bowdler envisaged their intended reader as the young girl, 'because boys are generally permitted the use of their fathers' libraries at a much earlier age than girls' (Lamb and Lamb 4). The Lambs' synoptic prose reimaginings (1806) established the tone for later, Victorian, appropriation, emphasizing imaginative delight together with moral insight:

> What these Tales have been to you in childhood, that and much more [...] the true Plays of Shakespeare may prove to you in older years – enrichers of the fancy, strengtheners of virtue, a withdrawing from all selfish and mercenary thoughts, a lesson of all sweet and honourable thoughts and actions, to teach you courtesy, benignity, generosity, humanity: for of examples teaching these virtues, his pages are full.
>
> (Lamb and Lamb 5)

The Lambs' proselytizing desire to widen knowledge of Shakespeare through their prose digests can certainly be seen as central to Victorian encounters with the plays. The narrative theoretician Genette raises the question, however, of how far such 'narrative condensation' trivializes:

> [The] passage into the narrative mode brings with it a suppression of the dramatic plurality of voices; it is sacrificed to a univocal narrative that is usually focused by a dominant viewpoint [...] and merges with the moralizing motives to eliminate the ambiguities, indeterminacies, or irrationalities characteristic of the Shakespearean world.
>
> (248)

As Heather Dubrow observes, '[the] choice of one literary genre over another can constitute a ringing affirmation that the genre in question is particularly appropriate for its age' (30), and Genette's reservations over 'moralizing motives' accurately pinpoint Victorian preference for the novel's didactic possibilities. The scrupulous Victorian mother needed to approach Shakespeare cautiously:

> It is scarcely possible to imagine a prudent and judicious mother allowing the unrestrained and private reading of Shakespeare amongst her children [but] it is possible to imagine her reading passages [...] to improve the taste of those around her, and to raise their estimate of what is great and good.
>
> (quoted in Flint 83)

Clearly, judicious reading of expurgated or novelized versions of Shakespeare seemed safer in Victorian households than either the original texts or the experience of theatre itself.

Beyond the world of prose retellings is the stranger phenomenon of the invented prequel or sequel, a fictionalization which moves determinedly outside the source text, elaborating for its protagonists a more fully realized world, the antithesis of the ephemerality of theatre performance or the implied hinterland of the protagonists' lives. Such amplifications could be interpreted as compensating for the lacunae of the original texts – questions which similarly troubled Victorian critic A. C. Bradley at the end of the nineteenth century. The first of his many supplementary 'Notes' addresses 'Events before the opening of the action in *Hamlet*' (Bradley 355–7), blurring boundaries between textual scholarship and fictional invention. If narrative ellipses are troubling for the nineteenth-century reader, Cowden Clarke's fictional worlds are correspondingly dense with prolix adjectival description; equally, there is always an omniscient narrator to point the moral. Cowden Clarke's concern with 'girlhood' locates her chosen heroines in the bildungsroman, the central genre of Victorian fiction, delineating the protagonist's progress towards self-knowledge and self-improvement. Inheriting the Romantics' predilection for interiority, she chooses to foreground the female personae of the plays, focalizing the narrative entirely through their perspectives. In this respect, female writers are operating antithetically to the male Victorian painters of the popular 'Gallery of Shakespeare's Heroines', where a conventionally beautiful, single female figure is arrested in a passive pose, remote from either dramatic performativity or narrative agency. Nina Auerbach, discussing the 'overwhelming popularity' of Cowden Clarke's novelistic inventions, suggests that both Anna Jameson and Cowden Clarke 'employ the format of Carlyle's *On Heroes and Hero Worship*, structuring each chapter upon a biographical exaltation of character' and creating a 'holy medium of perennial vitality beyond the play' (213).

Two female writers of the period cross the border between theatre and fiction: Helena Faucit and Ellen Terry. Faucit, a highly respected actress of major Shakespearean roles, unites her professional understanding of theatre with the impulse to fictionalize: 'I could never part with my characters when the curtain fell and the audience departed. As I had lived with them through their early lives, so I also lived into their futures' (Faucit 39). In epistolary form, addressed variously to Browning, Ruskin or Tennyson, she conjures a world beyond the final curtain calls – Portia, for example, tends the penitent Shylock and reconciles him with Jessica. Ellen Terry, similarly, expresses her debt to Shakespeare for the example of his 'fearless, high-spirited, resolute and intelligent heroines', dismissing as ridiculous the 'masculine dislike of the intellectual woman' (Terry 81, 82). Appropriating Shakespeare's heroines as a means of addressing 'women's exclusion from education' was central to these Victorian female writers (Marshall and Thompson 64): Anna Jameson, writing in 1832, entitled her study of Shakespeare's heroines *Characteristics of Women: Moral, Poetical, and Historical* – the first work 'to treat Shakespeare's female characters with the kind of seriousness which had been accorded to male ones' (Bate, *Shakespearean Constitutions* 155). Among these different types of narrative intervention, Cowden Clarke is unique for fabricating richly complex back-stories for Shakespeare's heroines – characters known to audiences only in the 'meridian blaze of perfection' (Cowden Clarke, *Girlhood*, vol. 1, vii) but who could be seen as 'yearn[ing] for more presence than their plays allow, and hence for more "story"' (A. Poole 89).

Mary Cowden Clarke was born and raised in a cultured musical and literary family: the family friends of her childhood included Leigh Hunt, Keats, Godwin, and Percy and Mary Shelley; Mary Lamb instructed her in Latin. Her autobiography cites her 'boundless joy and interest' in the discovery of Lamb's *Tales*: 'what a vast world of new ideas and delights that opened to me – a world in which I have ever since much dwelt, and always with supreme pleasure

and admiration' (Cowden Clarke, *My Long Life* 8). Cowden
Clarke successfully professionalized female scholarship, making a
significant contribution to Shakespeare studies: she produced the
first complete concordance to the plays (1844–5) and collaborated
with her husband on an annotated edition of the Complete Works
(1865) and on a substantial work entitled the *Shakespeare Key*
(1879). As Marshall and Thompson establish, '[hers] is a body of
work which challenges scholarly categories of the twentieth and
twenty-first centuries [...] was highly regarded in her own time,
and still has powerful insights to offer the modern reader' (60).
From 1850 to 1851 she produced her *Girlhood of Shakespeare's
Heroines*: fifteen stories, each one of novella length, bound in five-
volume sets and republished throughout the late nineteenth century.
Her stated intention in her 'exculpatory' Preface is to 'trace the
probable antecedents [...] to imagine the possible circumstances
and influences [...] to conjecture what might have been' (Cowden
Clarke, *Girlhood*, vol. 1, vii). In short, while leading up to the events
which commence the plays, she allows herself complete imaginative
freedom. Hermione's tale is inspired by a single reference in the
source text: 'The Emperor of Russia was my father' (*WT* 3.2.117).
A highly melodramatic tale of 'Hermione: the Russian Princess'
unfolds, footnoted with an extenuating plea that the play itself is
notoriously anachronistic.

Hermione's story begins with an extended evocation of the
melancholy Russian winter; the 'primeval pine forests' and a 'blank
trackless waste of snow' (Cowden Clarke, *Girlhood*, vol. 5, 7–8)
through which a resolute child – Paulina – journeys alone to her
father, wrongly accused of treason. She encounters the Emperor
himself, lost and disguised as a peasant, and proceeds both to rescue
him and lecture him on the morality of contemporary politics. She
is 'startlingly vehement' (38) but excused on account of her age
and evident sincerity; meanwhile, the child Hermione is already
distinguished by her 'noble character [...] pure beauty [...] high-
minded excellence' (45). Once Hermione is of marriageable age,
foreign embassies send aspirant suitors, and the young princess
is firmly instructed by her father that her duty is to 'promote the
interests of her native land' in making a choice of husband (50).
Her response is dutiful: 'I have no will but yours. Dispose of me as
seems best to you. I have no wish, but to fulfil your desires' (52).
At the same time, Paulina, secretly in love with Camillo, agrees to

marry the much older Antigonus at her own father's request. In the first section of her tale, then, Cowden Clarke has foregrounded the personalities of the two young women, the difficulties of arranged marriage, the absolutism of patriarchal authority in the absence of a mother figure, and the romantic otherness of Russia.

In the second and more imaginatively radical section, a deception is practised upon Hermione: following dynastic negotiations, she accepts, in his absence, the suit of Prince Leontes. Meanwhile a young Sicilian tutor, Leon, has arrived to instruct her in the language and culture of the Mediterranean court. This is, of course, Leontes in disguise, exploiting his anonymity to assess his promised bride. Hermione is aware of his unusually direct gaze – 'a grave, not to say cold, scrutiny' (62) – yet she is also conscious that she finds him physically attractive. Leontes confides by letter to Polixenes that Hermione has first seemed to him, although beautiful, 'too statue-like, too coldly passive' (76). This is just one of several references to Hermione's 'repose of sculptured marble' (76), demonstrating Cowden Clarke's ability to signal to the knowing reader metafictional allusions to the source text. Leontes further reveals that he has discovered beneath Hermione's composure 'profound emotion and generous ardour' (76). However, Leontes' scheme, far from reassuring him, causes him agonies of doubt – a means of anticipating and explaining the inexplicable nature of his jealousy in the play. First, he is passionately suspicious of Hermione's cousin, Alexis; he then further tortures himself with a new impasse, sensing that Hermione might be falling in love with him as Leon. On the one hand, this is evidently good, as she is to be his wife; on the other hand, bad, as she is formally betrothed to his alter ego, the Prince of Sicily. Cowden Clarke's narrative solution is to introduce Gothic motifs into her tale. Hermione is summoned to her father's sickbed and, in a scene worthy of Ann Radcliffe, sets out alone through the Russian winter landscape. Crossing a dangerous river, her carriage is overturned and she is thrown violently onto the cracking ice. Naturally, the faithful Leon is at hand to rescue her. Their sledge passes through a 'wild and desolate' forest (93); they are beset by howling wind, snow and a menacing pack of wolves who close in upon them. The emotional climax to this Gothic scenario is Hermione's impassioned confession of her love for Leon in the belief that she will inevitably die. In another helpful reminder of the source text, Hermione faints into unconsciousness:

Hermione, – like many women who either suppress their feelings, forbidding them the usual vent of tears and sobs; or who, by nature, cannot find relief in such outward demonstrations, – was subject to swoon away, upon a strong overpowering emotion.

(96)

The would-be lovers survive – obviously – and reach the royal court at Kiev. In the concluding coda, Leontes is again tormented with 'perplexing surmises and painful conjectures' (98) until he can privately meet Hermione to confide the truth of his deception. She is initially offended by Leontes' scheming, and becomes 'so cold, so marble still, so statue-like in her lofty quietude' (101). But the climax of their unorthodox courtship is an impassioned scene: Leontes will not claim his bride unless he is certain of her feelings for him: 'my passionate heart cannot starve upon [...] mere compliance, and conformity with duty' (105); Hermione, with equal fervour, assures him that '*I am yours for ever* [...] I could have died with Leon; I would live till death with Leontes' (106). Cowden Clarke leaves her readers in no doubt that this is a marriage of ardent desire, far from the remote formalities of dynastic alliance. To bring the tale towards the opening of the play, the scene is briefly shifted to Sicily; a son is born – Mamillius, 'a sensitive, impressionable child' (111). He is superstitiously drawn to an empty curtained alcove in Paulina's marble chapel, thus signalling the play's tragedy and its dénouement.

As Showalter observes, creating sequels and prequels to Shakespeare has been variously derided or patronised by twentieth-century critics as 'the epitome of naïve criticism' (Showalter 89), although the methodology of invented prehistories is common to psychoanalytic criticism as well as to the practice of theatre rehearsal. But Cowden Clarke's work can now be judged in the light of feminist studies and the rediscovery of female scholarship, as well as the critical exploration of adaptation and genre. In some respects, Cowden Clarke's act of appropriative homage is curiously close to the inventiveness of modern fanfiction, illustrating Lanier's distinction between extrapolated and interpolated narrative (Lanier, *Shakespeare* 83). But above all, there is 'a space for free play'; a 'dynamic and diverse relationship between the daughter story and the parent plot' (A. Poole 94, 95–6).

The Winter's Tale, dir. Gregory Doran, live-screening (1999)

Theatre critic Michael Billington, introducing an online discussion of 'favourite versions' of *The Winter's Tale*, commented that 'we come back to this beautiful play time and again' ('Best Shakespeare Productions'). While this may be true of staged versions, it is not the case with film and TV. Jane Howell directed *The Winter's Tale* for the BBC's complete Shakespeare project (1981); thereafter, the RSC's staged production, directed by Gregory Doran, first appeared on DVD in the form of extracts from the play together with discussion with the principal actors, and it was subsequently filmed live by Robin Lough at the Barbican Theatre (April 1999) for straight-to-video release. Live theatre broadcast has become increasingly popular and high profile: National Theatre Live, the RSC and the Cheek by Jowl theatre company have all promoted live broadcast, often with an interactive space, to promote 'democratisation, innovation, learning, and engagement' (Wardle 136). As Artistic Director of the RSC, Doran has succeeded in his ambition to film every production and permit free access to 'every classroom in the country' (Aebischer et al. 52). As an adaptive process, live broadcast is a new, hybrid medium 'with its own unique ontology' (Hitchman 172). Distinctions between the different methods of digital capture, whether for 'edited theatrical film' or live-screening, are usefully summarized by Aebischer and Greenhalgh in their discussion of this rapidly changing digital environment. Robin Lough's editing of Doran's highly acclaimed production makes for compelling viewing, effectively combining wide shot, to include the Barbican Theatre's audience, and close up to convey the intense emotions of the protagonists. Setting contributed significantly to the Sicilian scenes: the suggested late-nineteenth-century Russian orthodox context emphasized rigid courtly decorum and religious observance; Leontes' state regalia of diamond crown and ermine cape and Hermione's sumptuous dress and elaborate jewellery resembled photographs of pre-First World War European monarchy. Leontes' complete disintegration and Hermione's corresponding degradation thereby appeared all the more extreme – particularly on a stage often crowded with visibly embarrassed courtiers. The Russian theme also intensified religious connotations: the orthodox priests, chanting and incense had the effect of underscoring Leontes' blasphemy in sweeping aside spiritual authority. Mamillius as a frail tsarevich, hunched in a wheelchair, further established the impression of pre-revolutionary Russia (as well as enabling actress Emily Bruni to double the role with Perdita). Robert Jones's design consisted of pairs of sliding panels narrowing in perspective to an upstage ceremonial entrance – panels that closed claustrophobically around Leontes to signify his disturbing descent into madness.

Lough's inclusion of shots of the Barbican audience draws attention to the theatrical atmosphere created by Leontes' feverish delusions: 'Sir Smile' was spoken from the edge of the stage directly to the front row, thereby challenging specific couples to mistrust each other (and causing awkward laughter). Antony Sher interpreted Leontes' 'disease' as a destructive rage overwhelming all 'normal functions of self-censorship':

Inch-thick, knee-deep, o'er head and ears a forked one. (1.2.185) A wonderful image – of flesh, of sewage, of devils and cuckolds – it provided the first clue for me. His subconscious is bubbling up into his wide-awake brain.

(Sher, 'Leontes' 94)

Sher consulted with Professor of Psychiatry Maria Ronn, who diagnosed Leontes as demonstrating classic symptoms of morbid or psychotic jealousy (Sher, 'Leontes' 95), and this underpinned his performance of obsessive paranoia, from the tyrannical shouting at the court to the undignified rummaging in his wife's handbag. Hermione's court dress and the physical limitations of her advanced pregnancy further established Leontes' actions as offensive: when she kneels before him to declare her innocence, it is physically difficult for her to stand up and she stretches out her hand to him for aid – the epitome of a wifely request. But he ignores her, turning away to light a cigarette, and she staggers clumsily to her feet.

The fixed focus of this straight-to-video method – breaking the fourth wall in including the audience as witnesses – creates a notably tense scene for Hermione's trial, perhaps one of the most striking scenes of the production. Leontes appears in full regalia but with little dignity; he stumbles as he ascends the towering throne and appears hesitant when reading the charge against his wife. Hermione's appearance is visually extraordinary, infinitely dishevelled and traumatized. The rough prison shift, stained and bloodied with childbirth, appears shockingly demeaning; a violation of the most basic human rights. Her hair has been hacked off; her face seems unclean; she is in every respect the antithesis of the poised queen of the opening scene. Gilbreath wanted to convey Hermione's fall from grace as a visual shock to the audience: 'I wanted to make her physical traits as vulnerable as possible, thus highlighting her remarkable strength of character and her ability to endure enormous suffering' (Gilbreath 83). In contrast with Leontes' murderous hysteria and Hermione's humiliation, the appearance of the religious procession bearing the oracle's proclamation brings reassurance, the formality of the ritual here suggesting an immutable justice beyond the fallacies of human tyranny.

The acute tension of the first acts seems to demand the carnivalesque reversals of Bohemia and the sheep-shearing festivities – as if gaiety itself could be healing. However, as Patricia Tatspaugh has argued, reviewing major post-war productions of the play, it is difficult to create a convincing Bohemia for a modern audience (138). In Doran's production the adroit mimicry of Autolycus was warmly received by the audience – audible laughter testifies to their relief at escaping the stifling world of Leontes' court. As Gilbreath observes, the 'huge challenge of the play' is Hermione's sixteen-year wait for her daughter; she found an unexpected analogy with American hostages in Iran (1979–81): '[Hermione] was both the hostage held captive and also a member of the family waiting patiently for her loved one to be returned' (88). The return to Sicilia is, initially, bleak: an empty court signifies Leontes' barren state, and the arrival of the fugitive lovers prompts a heart-rending 'What might I have been?' (*WT* 5.1.175) from Leontes. The religious imagery of this production plays a key role in the miraculous quality of the final scene: Hermione is revealed in the characteristic pose of a statue of the Virgin Mary, clad in a silvery gown and veil and standing in a candle-lit shrine – indeed, Perdita kneels before her as if in supplicatory prayer. The enclosed space oddly resembles the prisoner's dock at her trial – a visual leitmotif that symbolizes her changed status: in this numinous atmosphere, it is Hermione herself who can grant forgiveness and redemption. To the reviewer at the *Times Literary Supplement*, she seemed a 'hauntingly beautiful icon of the loss she both represents and redeems' (Cannon 19). Gilbreath felt that the stillness paradoxically gave her the agency of decision:

[The] last time I saw him he was destroying everything around me. Would you trust him? [...] If I stand perfectly still, I can see for myself and it's my choice. I might not want to move; I might just remain where I am. [...] And so the moment when Hermione 'comes to life' was, for me, a moment of choice.

(88)

Antony Sher emphasizes the improbability of the final scene on the page compared with its 'irresistible' power on the stage: 'It works like a dream – literally; a dream come true. Who has never fantasized about a loved one returning? Or about being given a second chance? Everyone is stirred by these thoughts' ('Leontes' 101–2). The emotional intensity of the final moments is evident from the silence that precedes the audience applause; the screen viewer's aural reminder that this is a shared theatre experience.

Christopher Wheeldon, *The Winter's Tale* ballet (2014)

Christopher Wheeldon choreographed *The Winter's Tale* as a full-length classical ballet for London's Royal Ballet in 2014, working alongside composer Joby Talbot. Subsequently performed in Washington and New York as a co-production with the National Ballet of Canada, the ballet was reprised in London (2016 and 2018), broadcast internationally by live relay into cinemas (April 2014) and directed for screen by Ross McGibbon (released on Opus Arte DVD, 2015). Initial reviews acclaimed the work as a significant and original contribution to dance appropriation of Shakespeare, in the tradition of the canonical adaptations of Balanchine and Ashton (*A Midsummer Night's Dream*) and Macmillan's *Romeo and Juliet*. It is certainly the only dance version of the play and the first three-act ballet based on Shakespeare since Macmillan's in 1965. The choice of text was suggested by theatre director Nick Hytner, following Wheeldon's expressed desire to 'choreograph a Shakespeare' (Winship). Research professor in dance Stephanie Jordan explains the complexity of creating a wholly new work: selecting and rejecting from the Shakespearean source, then building a storyboard of individual sections for Talbot to compose in short score. Wheeldon's choreography could then be shaped by the musical score and by practical collaboration with the dancers in the rehearsal studio (Jordan 17–18). The heart of the process is the desire to communicate the emotional intensity of the original; mimed dramatic narrative is not Wheeldon's focus:

> The challenge of creating a Shakespeare ballet is making sure you're still tuned in to the poetry. There are some wonderful images in the text – like the drinking of the spider – and they were tiny clues I would go back and refer to. You have to [...] fuse the imagery of the writing with the choreography.
>
> (Winship)

Robin Wharton suggests that adapting Shakespeare 'permits a choreographer to take advantage of an audience's presumed familiarity with the plot to introduce a previously unavailable level of narrative complexity' (10) – a response to non-verbal performance art which could be seen as perpetuating the primacy of the textual source. In fact, 'presumed familiarity' seems not to be the case with *The Winter's Tale*: Wheeldon found the text initially challenging: '[I] struggled with it, because it's not an easy read' (Winship); further, the reception of the ballet demonstrated a lack of knowledge of Shakespeare's play, very different from theatre reviews. Dance critics tended to be wary, describing it as a complicated story: 'an odd play'; '[not] an obvious choice for a new ballet' (Harss). Dance critic Mark Monahan makes an instructive point: that '[where] Wheeldon's *Alice* (and indeed *Elsinore*) had drawn on source material that enjoys incalculable familiarity and admiration, *The Winter's Tale* is by no means one of Shakespeare's best-known or best-loved plays' (10) – an observation strikingly at odds with theatre audiences. This lack of prior experience of the text seems worth emphasizing at the outset: Wheeldon's dance audience might be encountering the play for the first time, in which case its dénouement could be wholly unexpected.

As Julie Sanders has shown, Shakespeare and dance have long been creative partners: dance has played a significant part in the history of stage productions, and the complex adaptation of Shakespeare into dance forms 'is a tremendous means of studying how one medium encounters and makes sense of another' (Sanders, *Shakespeare* 59). On Shakespeare's Renaissance stage, music signifies celestial harmony as well as visual and aural entertainment; in *A Midsummer Night's Dream*, dance between Oberon and Titania ensures the restoration of cosmic as well as social (and sexual) order, just as the songs and dances of Bohemia play a symbolic role in *The Winter's Tale*. Contrastingly, as a 'highly kinetic discourse' (Sanders, *Shakespeare* 65), dance can communicate extreme emotional states, whether solitary and introspective or the intense erotic discoveries of the *pas de deux*. To the theorist of dance, the mannered artifice of the form and the pure images of beauty that the human body can achieve create a language richer than that of other arts:

> Like music, [dance] constructs rhythms and phrases, but it also gives these elements visible form. It creates colour, line and shape like painting or sculpture, but it moves them around through space and time. It has cinema's freedom to flip between the real and the symbolic, but its performers are living, breathing people. It can achieve the emotional intensity of an opera or play, yet it isn't confined to a single geographical language.
>
> (Mackrell 2)

This combination of psychological intensity and the expressive power of the human body underpins Wheeldon's choreography for *The Winter's Tale*.

The ballet opens with a brief prologue on a bare stage: two small boys are crowned; they become young men deeply attached in friendship. Leontes woos and wins Hermione; a son is born and a precious emerald bestowed upon the young and happy queen. The Sicilian court scene then unfolds ceremoniously: a wintry world is evoked with a large backdrop of Caspar David Friedrich's melancholy *Winter Landscape*, together with white marble statuary. Polixenes and his courtly retinue are about to take their leave; Polixenes summons his own musicians to play the farewell dance and, as composer Joby Talbot explains, the Bohemian players 'create a charged atmosphere of excitement' that leaves Leontes 'marginalised and paranoid'. Hermione fondly places her husband's hand on her swollen belly, followed by the hand of Polixenes, and the scene is frozen: this is Leontes' crucial 'spider' moment. The music is full of panicked glissandi and Leontes writhes in torment, consumed by the delusion that the unborn child is Polixenes'. Courtly decorum disintegrates into chaos, with Leontes viciously rejecting Hermione, the fragmented syntax and abhorrent imagery of Leontes' speech effectively translated into grotesque and contorted physical shapes and movements and jarring orchestration.

Music and dance are effective vehicles for creating an immediate and complete change of tone, and the ensuing nursery scene is a tender antithesis to Leontes' patriarchal world of armed guards and sexual suspicion. The young child's physical closeness to his mother is emphasized as he brings his boat and then his story book to share with her. But this innocent and peaceful idyll is all too short as the musical register shifts to darkly menacing low brass tones – Leontes is seen descending the long staircase, his disturbing gestures violating the tranquillity of Hermione's closeted domesticity. It is painful to watch Leontes and Hermione dance together here: she is physically assaulted by her husband, dragged across the floor, and finally her terrified child is torn from her arms. Flung between the guards, she collapses in childbirth and the stage darkens.

The complete destruction of Leontes' world follows remorselessly from this point; Paulina's hope that the newborn child can effect reconciliation is brutally rejected and banishment follows. As snow falls, Paulina and Antigonus dance an emotional farewell, Paulina drawing attention to the placing of Hermione's totemic emerald in the basket. Wheeldon makes significant changes to Act 3 of the source play, cutting Cleomenes and Dion and the oracle's judgement in order to focus on the domestic and personal tragedy. He interpolates a poignant dance between Paulina and Hermione, the latter frail and diminished in a white penitential shift, before Leontes assumes his vengeful control of the scene. The memory of love is conjured by the lyrical melody and the reciprocal gestures associated with earlier happiness. The presence of Mamillius on the staircase – a poignantly small figure dwarfed by the architectural grandeur of the court – intensifies the darkening mood. The traumatized child attempts to run to his mother but collapses in Paulina's arms. Leontes' desperate attempts to revive him are fruitless; Hermione attempts to rush to her child but is prevented by the guards; she too collapses, seemingly lifeless. As Paulina attacks Leontes, the stage is darkened, leaving the two figures anguished and inconsolable. With highly effective symbolism, Paulina pulls down the silken draperies to reveal stormy skies, the ship that is about to founder and the ominous shape of the bear.

The utopian pastoralism of Act 2 is a powerfully transformative antithesis, visually realized in the immense tree, festooned with brightly coloured charms, that dominates the stage background. A world of exuberant dance emphasizes the collective harmony of Bohemian rural life and the idealized youthful love of Perdita and Florizel. The presence of the on-stage musicians celebrates the role of the joyous ritual that is about to unfold, announced by a lyrical solo on the bansuri flute. Perdita exemplifies the balletic aesthetic of lightness and grace – as she does in the play:

> When you do dance, I wish you
> A wave o' th' sea, that you might ever do
> Nothing but that, move still, still so
> And own no other function.

> (WT 4.4.140–4)

In contrast to the destructive ethos of male power, authority lies with Perdita here. She is crowned as the May Queen, signifying her pre-eminence within Nature; she is also presented with her mother's emerald necklace – she is a royal child. The disguised Polixenes threatens the harmony of this prelapsarian world and, in a disturbing parallel to Act 1, soldiers appear, knives threaten; the love between Perdita and Florizel is denounced. A forceful patriarchy is seen to disrupt and destroy the Edenic pastoralism.

In the final act, Wheeldon subtly reinterprets Shakespeare's redemptive and miraculous conclusion, emphasizing the muted joyousness of tragicomedy in a profoundly moving climax. The act opens to sombre music and the evidently unabated mourning of Leontes and Paulina, both of whom, attired in black, perform a ritual of grief before a shrouded statue of mother and child. The arrival of Perdita into the Sicilian court is thereby heightened; life and colour return. The revelation of Perdita's identity, through the emerald necklace, and the reconciliation between Leontes and Polixenes is a crucial part of the unfolding tension of the dénouement, a significant departure from Shakespeare's off-stage narrative (Act 5, Scene 2). The ensuing betrothal of the young courtly pair is a joyous celebration involving the entire corps de ballet – the traditional climax to romantic ballet. Yet Wheeldon chooses to reject the conventional balletic trope of the big set piece conclusion, moving from the rhapsodic lovers to the quiet melancholy of the statue scene. In a numinous background of drifting white clouds, Leontes is led by Paulina to the white marble statue of his wife and infant son. Gesture here is crucial: it is Leontes who first reaches up longingly towards them and Hermione who separates herself from the stone child and descends, first to Paulina. Leontes kneels, indeed, abases himself at Hermione's feet. Shakespeare's conclusion describes Hermione's gesture but offers no speech for the reunion of man and wife after sixteen years; Hermione's words are only for Perdita. Ballet offers the opportunity for a tentative *pas de deux*: gravely she seems to re-educate him in the language of love they first articulated. Their adagio moves towards reconciliation while conveying intense pain, the antithesis of the ecstatic dance of the young lovers. As Perdita runs on to the stage to embrace her mother, parents and child form a tableau in front of the statue of Mamillius, returning the viewer's gaze to the small, now solitary, figure. And the final steps emphasize the irrecoverable nature of what has been lost: as mother and daughter depart together, Leontes turns back, reaching towards the statue – perhaps a further miracle is possible? But the stone effigy remains forever frozen in time and he must leave, only in part consoled. As the lights fade, Paulina remains alone, the turtle dove who will '[l]ament till I am lost' (*WT* 5.3.134). Wheeldon rejects Shakespeare's brisk matchmaking of Paulina to Camillo in favour of a darker note: as Judith Buchanan argues, the ending of the play offers an 'intricate tapestry of conjured, remembered and rejected narratives' ('*The Winter's Tale*' 110) within which Wheeldon positions his work 'at the most freighted end of tragicomic possibility' ('*The Winter's Tale*' 128). Shakespeare radically reworked Greene's conclusion to the story of Pandosto, where there is no happy reconciliation nor resurrection and the tormented Pandosto kills himself. Wheeldon is consistent with Shakespeare but his modern audience is made acutely aware of darker consequences: the lost years that Hermione and Leontes cannot recover; the much-loved child now memorialized in cold stone.

12

The Tempest

The Tempest is a text which is notably adaptogenic; its strangeness and its narrative lacunae invite reinvention. This chapter examines Dryden and Davenant's exuberant adaptation of *The Tempest* for the Restoration stage, looking at political nuance and performance practice. Auden's 'The Sea and the Mirror', composed in the early years of the Second World War, is explored as a sombre work that decisively rejects the enchantments of illusion. Finally, Derek Jarman's countercultural *Tempest* (1979) is discussed as an experimental and innovative film adaptation.

Dryden and Davenant, *The Tempest or the Enchanted Island* (1667)

[In] this reforming age / We have intents to civilize the Stage.

(*Prologue to* Othello, *1660, quoted in Summers xxii*)

The Restoration stage offers valuable insights into changing views towards Shakespeare, in terms of both textual fidelity and performance practice. The 1660s marks the beginnings of the appropriation, adaptation and rewriting of Shakespeare's Folio texts, arguably 'one of the most subversive acts in literary history' (Marsden, *Re-Imagined Text* 1). Reworking some of Shakespeare's most popular plays initiated concomitant critical analysis where

Dryden, 'the creator of Shakespeare criticism' (H. Love 12), was of central significance in establishing the pre-eminence of Shakespeare at a time when that assumption did not exist. The 1660s also saw the enthusiastic reinvigoration of the stage, with the Shakespearean canon at the heart of theatrical revival. Nearly twenty years had passed since the first Puritan ordinances had shut down London's theatre spaces, bringing to an abrupt end the popular performances of open-air theatres. The long-held view that London's theatres entered a period of complete darkness during the period of the Civil War and ensuing Commonwealth (1642–60) has been the subject of historical and critical interrogation for some time, however, and it is now clear that a more complex, improvisatory situation existed. William Davenant ensured that he was the playwright and theatre manager best placed to take advantage of the new situation at the beginning of the 1660s. In the latter years of the Protectorate, the enterprising Davenant succeeded in producing historical dramas at Rutland House, his London residence. These first performances included Davenant's new sliding screens with perspectival scenery, leading the way to the ambitious stage effects of the new indoor theatres of the Restoration. As Julie Sanders has shown, the prohibitions of the Commonwealth period resulted, ironically, in 'a space of liberation, a site of free play and experimentation' (Sanders, *Shakespeare* 126), and Davenant was key to that process. The triumphant return of Charles II to London in 1660 immediately signalled radical new directions, not a return to the previous freedoms of the Jacobean or Caroline stage, however; culturally, as well as politically, the Restoration was a time of change. Charles identified strongly with the arts, for aesthetic pleasure and as a means of displaying royal power; in both he was undoubtedly influenced by his exilic experiences of the highly cultivated French court. But he had no desire to license uncensored freedom on multiple stages and limited legitimate theatre to two companies: Davenant and Killigrew were authorized to lead, respectively, the Duke's Company and the King's Company. John Dryden, born in 1631, clearly could not boast a direct line of apostolic succession from Shakespeare in the way that Davenant frequently did, but he was adept at reinventing personal loyalties for political expediency. As Secretary of State, Dryden composed a eulogy on Cromwell's death in 1658, while effortlessly embracing Charles II's return with 'Astraea Redux', a poem epitomizing the euphoric mood of the Restoration. Dryden's engagement with Shakespeare was undoubtedly formative. In his Prefaces to individual plays and his important *Essay on Dramatic Poesie*, he constantly evaluates and elevates 'the Divine' Shakespeare. While he accedes to the commonly held late-seventeenth- and eighteenth-century view that Shakespeare needs to be linguistically 'made fit', he invariably moves towards an argument that Shakespeare far surpasses his contemporaries – a radical view at a time when Jonson's satirical writing remained popular and Fletcher was considered to be a superior dramatist. Dryden's reverence for Shakespeare established two premises: first, that Shakespeare is the unequalled god of the theatre; second, that even Shakespeare can be 'improved' to suit sophisticated Restoration tastes.

Davenant's versions of Shakespeare were the first plays to be performed at the Duke's Playhouse, then in Lincoln's Inn Fields: *Hamlet*, *Macbeth* and *The Law Against Lovers* (Davenant's splicing of *Measure for Measure* and *Much Ado About Nothing*) all appeared in the opening seasons. In 1667 Davenant collaborated with Dryden and *The Tempest or The Enchanted Island*, 'A Comedy', was first performed (published 1670). Theatres had been dark for eighteen months during London's plague years, 1665–6, so *The Tempest* signalled a joyous renewal of cultural life in the city. Although lengthy sections of the play correspond with the source text, the incorporation of new characters – in particular new female characters – alters the tone and structure of the drama considerably. Miranda now has a sister, Dorinda; Sycorax is reinvented as Caliban's sister and Ariel has a dancing companion, Milcha, who appears in the play's concluding Sarabande. As a parallel to the device of the young women who have never seen a man (other than Prospero), Davenant introduces Hippolito, rightful heir to the Dukedom of Mantua and 'one that never saw Woman' – he has been sequestered away by Prospero in an island cave. Prospero's magical powers are greatly diminished and, in the scenes involving the courtiers, there is significantly less threatened violence or tragic potential; the role of Sebastian is cut altogether. The comic characters, similarly, are not shipwrecked servants to the court but mariners who, although squabbling for authority over the island, pose no threat to Prospero himself. While music and the supernatural play their part, the new play omits the betrothal masque of Ceres and the aristocratic chess game between Miranda and Ferdinand. For some critics, the tone of the play is substantially altered, the Restoration adaptation lacking 'the atmosphere of wonder so deeply moving in Shakespeare's play' (Auberlen 83). Two distinct areas invite discussion in terms of typifying the new stage and highlighting the key concerns of Davenant and Dryden: the critique of politics, and female actors and the role of gender.

Prospero and the politics of succession

> Perhaps my Art it self is false: on what strange grounds we build our hopes and fears; mans life is all a mist, and in the dark, our fortunes meet us.
>
> (Clark 3.5.154–6)

It is inconceivable that Shakespeare's Prospero would speak these words. As editor David Lindley suggests, Dryden and Davenant find the magic of the play an anachronistic 'embarrassment' (Lindley 43) and diminish the power of the mage accordingly. The introspective renunciation of Prospero's Act 5 soliloquy is cut from the later text, as is the ethereal language of 'We are such stuff as dreams are made on'. Prospero has little bearing on Alonzo and Antonio, who are swift to acknowledge their past guilt; indeed, they have already made an expiatory journey to defend Portugal against Spanish Moors. As a parental figure, his duties are multiplied – two daughters and a male ward need to be kept apart and in a state of primal innocence. Here, too, he is ineffectual: as the play opens, all three swear to obey him and then almost instantly break their promises. More disastrously, Prospero's machinations lead to a fatal duel between Ferdinand and Hippolito – a situation that Prospero neither foresees nor is able to resolve. It is Ariel who has the magical power to seek the necessary antidote, whereas Prospero plans to punish Ferdinand by death, thus jeopardizing both the political restoration he has planned and Miranda's marriage. Clearly, Prospero's role as patriarch of his family unit cannot function as an analogue for benign paternalistic kingship. Yet the later play equally derides and rejects any ideal of Commonwealth democracy: Gonzalo's utopian vision is downgraded to a bunch of comic

sailors drunkenly squabbling over ownership of the island.
When Stephano announces his rulership of this new dominion,
Ventoso rejects the idea: 'I am a free subject in a new Plantation,
and will have no Duke without my voice' (2.3.60–1). The
urgent political issues of the Interregnum have been reduced to
slapstick:

> TRINCALO
> I say this Island shall be under *Trincalo*, or it shall be a
> Common-wealth; and so my Bottle is my Buckler, and so I
> draw my Sword.   [*Draws*]
> [...]
> VENTOSO
> Then Civil-War begins.

> (2.3.131–3, 141)

The play may be 'determinedly about government' (Maus 201)
but, intriguingly, in this Restoration adaptation there are no
kings at all – certainly no suggestion of a graceful compliment to
the restoration of Charles II. Dobson observes that the Prologue
references the only 'King' in the text – Shakespeare himself, whose
'pow'r is sacred as a King's' (Clark 24), suggesting that Shakespeare
is 'being nostalgically promoted to the rank of archaic, Divine Right
monarch' (Dobson 40). While the overall political vision of Dryden
and Davenant's play is essentially conservative, moving towards the
resumption of the status quo, '[the] new play redefines the limits and
uses of sovereignty' (Maus 190). The euphoria of Charles II's return
had diminished by 1667 and a degree of disillusionment marks the
tone of Dryden's reinvention. The new play articulates a warning
against political *hubris* in an interpolated masque of devils:

> *Where does proud* Ambition *dwell?*
> *In the lowest rooms of Hell.*
> *Of the damn'd who leads the Host?*
> *He who did oppress the most.*

> (2.1.47–50)

The language is unspecific but is clearly a warning to any
vainglorious leader. Dryden, the great political satirist of the age,

defined Charles's reign as 'An Age, so sceptical' (Dryden 203), and in this new *Tempest* a Hobbesian acceptance of the necessity of sovereignty has replaced any idea of absolutist divine right.

Sex, gender and *The Enchanted Island*

Perhaps the most radical change from Shakespeare's theatre practice is the immediate appearance on stage of female actors, singers and dancers. The aristocratic women of earlier Stuart courts had participated in allegorical masques and dances – to the outrage of Puritan objectors such as Prynne – but such entertainments were far from the world of the public stage. Montague Summers believes that, as early as December 1660, it was 'not improbable' that Desdemona was publicly performed by Mrs Hughes (Summers xxv) and Mrs Elizabeth Barry was soon to attain 'commodifiable celebrity status' (Sanders, *Shakespeare* 125). *The Tempest* proved an ideal play to exploit this exciting new phenomenon; in Michael Dobson's words, '[no] other Restoration adaptation of Shakespeare makes such extensive or inventive use of the restored theatre's most conspicuous innovation, the professional actress' (38). In Shakespeare's *Tempest* the innocent Miranda is the sole female presence on stage, with passing references to the witchcraft of the 'gross' Sycorax, Caliban's mother, and to Claribel, whose wedding has occasioned the Mediterranean voyage. Miranda, then, is the prelapsarian Eve of the island, yet to discover her own sexual feelings. Dryden's view is that Davenant's symmetry in inventing the 'Man who had never seen a Woman' proved 'an excellent contrivance' (Clark 84). This might be seen as an exercise in baroque patterning, but it also enables a more searching portrayal of unfettered sexuality, with Hippolito's licentiousness contrasting with the idealized perfection of the bond between Miranda and Ferdinand. In fact, the frisson around gender and cross-dressing does not evaporate with the proliferation of female roles but, rather, is intensified: Hippolito was a breeches role, played by a young actress, as was the role of Ariel. Sycorax was played as a pantomime dame – presumably with a large and burly male actor to fully exploit the comedy of the sexual voracity of the character. Dryden's biographer, James Anderson Winn, suggests that drama written and performed after the Plague (1665) shows 'an increasing fascination with sex' (183) and, certainly, in the multiplying of sexual encounters, desire is at the forefront of the play's preoccupations, establishing the play firmly in the tradition of Restoration city comedy.

The sexual politics of the colonial oppressor is parodied in Trincalo, who, when he hears from Caliban of his 'lovely Sister', Sycorax, 'beautiful and bright as the full Moon' (2.3.201), immediately concludes that he can marry her and claim the island by 'Alliance'. Sycorax's unbridled enthusiasm, though, causes Trincalo some anxiety: he needs fortifying alcohol before encountering her eager embraces and fears he might not survive her ardour. With neat comic reversal, it is the swaggering Trincalo who pleads, 'prithee be not too boisterous with me at first' (3.3.96). Both Caliban and Sycorax conform to prevailing European views of the 'natural': the wild man or woman of 'uncivilized' lands, lacking the learned restraints of society. Caliban is considerably marginalized and reduced in Restoration texts, as the Vaughans' cultural history shows: '[his] love of the island, appreciation of natural beauty, poetic language [are] expunged' (Vaughan and Vaughan 96) and he descends to little more than a grotesque. Beneath the farcical verbal comedy, there is a more probing satire of the libertinism that was, by 1667, well established at the court of Charles II. Ariel comments on the 'harsh discord' throughout 'this fatal Isle', observing that '[the] Monsters Sycorax and Caliban / More monstrous grow by passions learn'd from man' (4.3.271–2). Prospero warns Dorinda that Hippolito is 'of such a Salvage race, / That no mild usage can reclaim his wildness' (3.1.89–90) and cautions both his daughters that danger lies with a wild young man 'within Doors, in Chambers, / And in Closets' (2.4.107–8). Miranda and Dorinda swiftly acquire all the manipulative skills of the heroines of Restoration comedy, however, and even the loyal Ferdinand suspects that his adored Miranda is the typical flirtatious tease of the contemporary beau-monde: 'It is too plain: like most of her frail Sex, she's false / But has not learnt the art to hide it' (4.1.105–6). As Elizabeth Howe observes in her study of the female presence on stage: 'society's view of the actress discouraged an idealised presentation of true love [...] fostering instead [...] a harsh, yet subtle appraisal of the complexity of relations between the sexes' (65). The highly sexualized exchanges that typify the drama of Wycherley or Etherege feature significantly in the scenes involving the three ingénues; Hippolito, in particular, fails to understand the concept of sexual continence once he makes the happy discovery that the world offers more than simply Dorinda: 'O, how I rejoyce! More women! [...] I will have all of that kind, if there be a hundred of 'em' (3.6.56, 53). Of course, in order to return to society and his rightful dukedom, Hippolito must be tamed to the extent that he can end the play comprehending a theory of monogamy. Ferdinand, as in the source play, epitomizes courtly love; the outward sign of his devotion is his willingness to endure the humiliation that Prospero imposes upon him. Hippolito's inclination to 'love all women' makes him at once the male equivalent of Sycorax and a comment on the libidinous Charles II. As Catherine Belsey observes, idealized Renaissance humanism does not exist in the Restoration *Tempest*: '[knowledge] is now knowledge of sexual difference, and it is [...] fully empiricist in the sense that it stems from the experience of the individual' (81).

Davenant and Dryden's *Tempest* remained one of the most popular early Restoration dramas, reappearing several times before it was eclipsed by the operatic version produced by Shadwell in 1674. This was a spectacular event mechanically and musically, featuring a troubled sea in continual motion and sailors menaced by flying spirits; a 'shower of fire' formed the climax to the opening. Capitalizing on the play's enduring popularity, Thomas Duffett produced a burlesque version, *The Mock Tempest or the Enchanted Castle* (1675), where the eponymous 'castle' is Bridewell, a prison, with Prospero as the 'Head-keeper'. The opening storm is a raid on a brothel, engineered by Ariel, Prospero's sprightly pickpocket. Sexual double-entendres proliferate and Miranda and Dorinda are far from innocent maidens: Prospero's opening question, 'Miranda, where's your sister?' is answered with 'I left her on the Dust-Cart top' (Summers 121).

The Tempest in these various forms had successfully captured the Restoration imagination – Pepys enjoyed the Davenant and Dryden adaptation so much that he saw it at least seven times, and it remained the version of the play seen by all audiences until 1838, when Macready returned to the Folio text. Early twentieth-century scholars generally approached Restoration adaptations with contempt: Odell employs strikingly moral terms in judging Dryden to be 'despicable' for establishing the fashion for adaptation, with *The Tempest* 'the worst perversion of Shakespeare in the two-century history of such atrocities' (vol. 1, 31). By contrast, Montague Summers, one of the earliest anthologists of Restoration texts, observes that the play was popular for well over a century and 'the reason for such vitality must be seriously pondered' (cvii). Tim Keenan, writing about a modern performance of the Restoration *Tempest*, identifies the later play as a 'a brilliantly crafted adaptation' to be appreciated 'on its own terms' (76).

W. H. Auden, 'The Sea and the Mirror: A Commentary on Shakespeare's *The Tempest*' (written 1942–4)

'The Sea and the Mirror' is Auden's epilogue to *The Tempest*, a verse and prose drama set after the end of the play. The work has two substantial sections, book-ended by short lyric poems: first, poetic reflections from the chief characters; second, a lengthy prose disquisition from Caliban on the nature of Art. Auden punctures the enchantment of *The Tempest*: he regarded the play as a 'disquieting work' (*Dyer's Hand* 128), 'overpessimistic and manichaean' (134), which Shakespeare had 'really left [...] in a mess' (quoted in John Fuller 357). The poem was intended to be his 'Ars Poetica [...] attempting something which, in a way is absurd to show in a work of art, the limitations of art' (quoted in Ford 135). In other words, Auden had chosen to appropriate an iconic work of art to demonstrate that, ultimately, art fails: adaptation as an act of resistance. Auden's disillusionment had much to do with his personal circumstances and the wider context in which he was writing. Throughout the 1940s, Auden was intensely troubled by the fact that Europe's cultural heritage had not prevented the rise of fascism and the barbarism of the Second World War. From January 1939 Auden lived an exiled life in the USA, feeling, in common with many other Europeans in New York, always an outsider, alienated and displaced: 'Thought I heard the thunder rumbling in the sky; / It was Hitler over Europe, saying, "They must die": / O we were in his mind, my dear, O we were in his mind' ('Refugee Blues', Auden, *Collected Shorter Poems* 157–8). He identified strongly with New

York's Jewish refugees; by early 1939, Auden, like Spender and Isherwood, knew of Nazi persecution of the homosexual milieu of Berlin (all three had spent time in 1928–9 discovering the relative freedom of gay life in Berlin). 'The Sea and the Mirror' highlights the anguished survivors' guilt for 'others who are not here' (Auden, 'Sea' 231). Shakespeare was much in Auden's mind during these early years in the USA, not from sentimental nationalism but because he was committed to a lecture course of the entire canon, first at Swarthmore College (1942–5) and later in New York, at the University in Exile. As Neil Corcoran has shown, Auden's lectures forged urgent political connections between the plays and contemporary events, pursuing 'an engaged criticism, prickly with a sense of relevance and contingency, almost a version of what recent critical terminology calls "presentism"' (130).

Auden regarded *The Tempest* as a 'mythopoeic' work, a text that, in its scepticism and unsatisfactory lack of closure, invited adaptation or further elaboration, encouraging writers 'to go on for themselves [...] to make up episodes that [the author], as it were, forgot to tell us' (Auden, *Lectures* 297). The title of Auden's text is itself elusive: the sea, in Shakespeare, invariably destabilizes, often connoting tempestuous change, mutability and instability. Auden was undoubtedly drawing on Freudian readings of the ocean as analogous to the unconscious, 'a vast subterranean place of unexpressed meaning and fecundity' (Mentz 2), adding Christian symbolism in describing the sea as 'the place of purgatorial suffering', the 'death that leads to rebirth' (Auden, *Enchafèd Flood* 20). The mirror, at first sight, is obviously drama itself, 'holding the mirror up to nature' in Hamlet's much-quoted phrase (*Ham* 3.2.21–2), where the theatre as mirror reflects reality back to the audience. In 'The Sea and the Mirror' Prospero calls upon Ariel to hold up the mirror but cautions that 'One peep, though, will be quite enough' ('Sea' 205). *The Tempest* weaves complex variations around ideas of illusion; indeed, it could be seen as 'a play that from first to last presents itself as an illusion of an illusion' (Kirsch, *Sea* xi). In the final revelation of the text, the 'contrived fissures of mirror and proscenium arch' are understood to be no more than symbols and 'we may rejoice in the perfected Work which is not ours' ('Sea' 250): a reality that can only be God.

The Stage Manager's Preface conjures from the outset the magic of illusion – the spectacular, seemingly 'nonchalant couple / Waltzing across the tightrope', the fun of the 'lovely / Lady sawn in half' (201). This is a sorcery that science and authority cannot dispel – 'our wonder, our terror remains'. Echoing the source text, the Stage Manager dismisses 'this world of fact' as 'insubstantial stuff', and he concludes with elegiac Shakespearean echoes: Hamlet's last words, Edgar's consolatory words to Gloucester: 'All the rest is silence / [...] And the silence ripeness, / And the ripeness all' (202). The monologues of individual characters commence, appropriately, with Prospero's farewell to Ariel. Auden saw Shakespeare's Mage as cold and unlikeable, his forgiveness of his enemies as 'more the contemptuous pardon of a man who knows he has his enemies completely at his mercy than a heartfelt reconciliation' (*Dyer's Hand* 129). Auden's Prospero is 'muted, world-weary, vulnerable' (Ford 144), addressing Ariel in a supplicatory rather than imperative manner: 'Stay with me, Ariel while I pack'. He liberates Ariel to 'Ages [...] of song and daring' while knowing his own destiny is 'Briefly Milan, then earth' ('Sea' 203). Crucially, Auden's Prospero understands that he should only gain power when he is indifferent to it: 'I am glad that I did not recover my dukedom till / I do not want it' (203). Further, in confessional tone, he admits that he has broken the two cardinal promises sworn as an apprentice mage, 'To hate nothing and to ask nothing for its love' (206). He does hate, and his 'hot heart' knows jealousy, but his 'impervious disgrace' is Caliban, from whom he wanted 'absolute devotion', a situation that cannot be remedied, so 'I shall go knowing and incompetent into my grave' (207). Prospero's renunciation is extensive; he recalls the temptation of the erotic – the 'green remote Cockayne / Where whiskey rivers run, / And every gorgeous number may / Be laid by anyone' – but is now relieved that youth is over and 'I shall never / Be twenty and have to go through that business again' (207). Rather than an autocratic and magisterial Prospero, Auden creates a persona vividly aware of the inevitable decline that lies ahead, 'an old man / Just like other old men, with eyes that water / [...] and a head that nods in the sunshine, / Forgetful, maladroit, a little grubby' (209). This is a Prospero confronting his mortality and his shortcomings, in particular, his intellectual vanity; he is, finally, a resigned and poignant figure as he bids farewell, 'My dear, here comes Gonzalo [...] O Ariel, Ariel / How I shall miss you' (209).

Section II, 'The Supporting Cast, Sotto Voce', is a bravura display of poetic form: each major character speaks in their own uniquely appropriate verse form as they reveal their 'partial apprehension of their own predicament' (Regan 270). A dark refrain spoken by the unmoved Antonio supplies a mordantly cynical and jarring verse at the end of each separate voice. For Antonio there is clearly no redemptive metamorphosis, and he remains obdurately outside the magic circle, refusing to succumb to Prospero's charms: '[as] I exist so you shall be denied' ('Sea' 212). Auden brilliantly creates mocking tetrameter and trimeter rhythms for Antonio's monologue:

> Your all is partial, Prospero;
>   My will is all my own:
> Your need to love shall never know
>   Me: I am I, Antonio,
> By choice myself alone.

('Sea' 212)

Auden would have known well that the character who famously declares 'I am I' is Shakespeare's Richard III in his haunted final soliloquy (*R3* 5.3.183).

Ferdinand utters a sonnet in perfect alexandrines in the traditional Elizabethan form of two quatrains and a concluding sestet, befitting the lover's adoration of his beloved. Like Donne's love sonnets, his poem is both erotic and spiritual – 'Flesh, fair, unique, and you, warm secret' ('Sea' 212) – and expressive of his awed realization that human love in its highest manifestation reveals the divine – 'my enough, my exaltation'. But as Ferdinand unfolds his epiphany, the malign and discordant voice of Antonio intrudes: 'Hot Ferdinand will never know / The flame with which Antonio / Burns in the dark alone' (213). Auden, like Shakespeare, effectively juxtaposes contrasting moods and speakers, creating a 'schematic dualism' (Kirsch, *Sea* xiii) that undermines any simplistic notion of unity.

Stephano's epicene and Falstaffian world is in comic contrast to Ferdinand's epithalamion, 'Embrace me, belly, like a bride', for his world exists between 'the bottle and the "loo"' ('Sea' 213). His companion, Trinculo, is the sad clown who looks back to the lost days of 'Little Trinculo' while the Master and Boatswain recall drunken visits to brothels. Gonzalo, on the other hand, has fully embraced the wonder of the island, and his verse evokes a spiritual calm: 'Evening, grave, immense, and clear, / Overlook our ship whose wake / Lingers undistorted on / Sea and silence'

(214). His belief in reconciliation is complete: 'All have seen the Commonwealth / There is nothing to forgive' (215). These serene reflections are followed by Alonso's epistle – a letter for Ferdinand to read after his father's death. The fond letter is a sombre warning of the impermanence of princely power – 'The way of Justice is a tightrope / Where no prince is safe for an instant' (218). At the moment of civil perfection, 'griefs and convulsions' can destroy, a reminder that Auden wrote this section of the poem in 1942, by which time America, as well as Europe, was at war. Like Prospero, Alonso is ready to welcome death; unlike Prospero, he has experienced the miraculous: 'Rejoicing in a new love, / A new peace, having heard the solemn / Music strike and seen the statue move / To forgive our illusion' (219). Auden conflates the restorative mood of *The Tempest* with the climax of *The Winter's Tale*.

Sebastian's sestinas proclaim his venality – 'I am Sebastian, wicked still' – but, unlike Antonio, he is pleased that he wakes 'without a crown'. Opportunity tempted him with 'a naked sword', but mercy has decreed that 'nothing has happened', and he finds relief in experiencing only shame. This central section, with its intense and contrasting voices, concludes with Miranda and a villanelle that articulates the 'brave new world' of love. Like Ferdinand, her imagery recalls Donne's world of intense mutuality, lovers who see themselves reflected in the eyes of the beloved. Miranda's refrain – 'My Dear One is mine as mirrors are lonely' – implies that the lovers are captured and mirrored in each other's gaze.

The startling, radical final section of 'The Sea and the Mirror' took Auden some time to plan. Several months of 'fruitless prospecting' (quoted in Carpenter 328) failed to deliver the authentic voice he was seeking; later he claimed that it was one of the best things he had written. The central, astonishing, fact of the concluding prose is that the speaker is Caliban – 'the Prick', as Auden invariably termed him (quoted in Fuller 364) – expressing highly complex views of art in the highly wrought and self-conscious style of late Henry James. In the first section, Caliban speaks as the audience, articulating their indignation that Caliban should have been created at all, straining suburban tolerance and affronting our 'Native Muse' ('Sea' 225). Audiences, it seems, like clear boundaries, 'prohibitive frontiers' without which 'we should never know who we were or what we wanted' (230). The 'savage elsewhere' must be unambiguously banished. Auden satirizes audience squeamishness and timidity, their preference for a theatre of escapism – a brief time of 'craning and gaping at the splendid goings-on' (228). Drama must offer a 'perfectly tidiable case of disorder' that can be resolved 'without so much as a scratch or bruise'. There is no desire to 'expect or even wish at any time to enter, far less to dwell there' (229). The mocking and ironic tone draws attention to Auden's central anxiety: that 'Art', even at its most urbane and sophisticated, is not all-powerful – a preoccupation that emerges in Auden's lectures, 'that art cannot transform men grieves Prospero greatly' (Auden, *Lectures* 306).

The second substantial section of Caliban's address ('Sea' 234–9) is addressed, as if by Shakespeare, directly to any youthful artist, taking him through the initial delights of the imaginative life but inviting him to confront the reality that he is left with: 'the dark thing you could never abide to be with' (239). Stan Smith, interpreting the politics of the text, sees this as the bourgeois artist coming 'face to face [...] with himself as Caliban' (158). Eventually, the artist desires to escape the stranglehold of art, desiring 'ordinary human embraces rather than the Midas touch that transforms everyone into material for your art' (Mendelson 233). There are no ambitious aspirations here, just the suggestion that any hope for the future be kept 'within moderate, very moderate limits' ('Sea' 239). Finally, the audience: their 'transparent globes of enchantment shattered', no longer transfixed by illusion but 'together in the larger, colder, emptier room on this side of the mirror' (240). The audience long for an imagined home, a lost world of prelapsarian perfection 'where the canons run through the water meadows with butterfly nets and the old women keep sweet-shops in the cobbled side streets' (242). But they inhabit a deracinated world where consolation cannot be found – 'Religion and culture seem to be represented by a catholic belief that something is lacking' (246). The essence of Auden's final vision is a startling one: that a profound spiritual truth underpins human uncertainties. His rediscovery of Christian belief at this time was, to Auden, 'the transition from the child's "We believe still" to the adult's "I believe again"' (Kirsch, *Auden* 7–8). As biographer Davenport-Hines observes, however, Auden's views 'left liberal and agnostic readers uncomfortable or aghast' (226). For Auden, the sorcery of art should be resisted and the urgent ethical questions of life addressed directly: 'just here, among the ruins and the bones' can be found the 'great coherences' of the 'perfected Work which is not ours' ('Sea' 250). The 'restored relation' that concludes Caliban's monologue leads to the brief poetic Postscript from Ariel to Caliban, a statement of 'entire devotion' that returns the poem to worldly, imperfect love: 'only / As I am can I / Love you as you are' (251). In Shakespeare, then, Auden finds 'a writer who speaks eloquently and urgently to modern readers in ways that prefigure and illumine their troubled psychological, religious, and political preoccupations' (Regan 274).

The Tempest, dir. Derek Jarman (1979)

When Jarman's filmed version of *The Tempest* was first shown in New York, in September 1980, the film and theatre reviewer of *The New York Times*, Vincent Canby, slated it as 'very nearly unbearable'. The 'drastically cut text' and dialogue that 'might as well be [in Latin]' offended Canby, who dismissed the film's originality as 'impertinent'. Arden editor Frank Kermode 'did not much care' for the film either, finding in it both 'clumsiness and perversity' (553). As Jarman sardonically observed, 'messing with Will Shakespeare is not allowed' (206). Critical discussion of the film's aesthetic has altered radically since those early reviews: '[with] its creative cinematography, innovative set designs and sublime costumes, [Jarman's *Tempest*] is one of the most distinctive and exciting 1970s visual texts' (S. Barber 160). *The Tempest* was conceived as a low-budget art-house film; in Jim Ellis's discussion, a 'liberationist model' that offered 'a space for refuge, resistance or retreat' (Ellis xii, xiii). As a queer artist, Jarman's political resistance is focused on the state's discriminatory policing of sexuality: 'Jarman's homosexuality [...] leads him to concentrate on the repression at the heart of the English state from which all the other repressions follow' (McCabe 12). Jarman was undoubtedly at the forefront of queering the period film, a direction which intensified after his diagnosis of HIV/AIDS in late 1986. At the same time, his profound fascination with and knowledge of the Renaissance underpinned his work, in part because he saw Elizabethan England as an analogous 'terror state' (McCabe 12) and in part because of his 'deep personal identification with [Shakespeare] as a fellow artist with a queer sexuality' (Wymer 71). He was writing the script for *The Tempest* while filming *Jubilee* (1978) – a work in which Elizabeth I is transported into the underworld of late 1970s London. Significantly, he was also beginning to plan *Caravaggio* (1986), a film about an artist whose intense drama and powerful chiaroscuro undoubtedly shaped Jarman's film-making. His training at the Slade in the early 1960s and his first professional commissions as a film and theatre designer underlie the distinctively 'painterly' style of his auteurial vision. He later produced *The Angelic Conversation* (1985), based on fourteen of Shakespeare's sonnets, and adapted Marlowe's *Edward II* (1991) – the latter an avowedly activist work, dedicated to the repealing of all anti-gay laws, particularly Section 28, the 1988 legislation passed by Margaret Thatcher's government which prevented local authorities disseminating positive images of homosexuality in schools. Jarman's absorbed interest in the art and culture of the Renaissance should be clearly distinguished from the world of televised costume drama, a genre he despised as 'excruciating' (Jarman 14). Film offered innovatory possibilities, uniting theatre and painting: '[in] *The Tempest* we paint pictures, frame each static shot and allow the play to unfold in them as within a proscenium arch' (Jarman 194). Jarman's choice of settings was clearly of the greatest importance in terms of his creative adaptation of the source text. His desire was to connote 'an island of the mind, that opened mysteriously like Chinese boxes: an abstract landscape' (Jarman 186). The initial scheme, later discarded, involved conveying the entire action through Prospero's mind – the *donnée* of Greenaway's later *Prospero's Books* (1991).

The 'abstract landscape' was located first at Bamburgh Castle, on the windswept dunes of the Northumberland coast and, for the indoor scenes, at Stoneleigh Abbey in Warwickshire, both sites 'as far from tropical realism as possible' (Jarman 186). The latter, although a grand Georgian mansion, offered interesting ambiguity: filming took place in the partially destroyed west wing of the house, where rooms of neo-classical splendour adjoined empty and fire-damaged parts of the building. The visual impact of the Stoneleigh scenes is intensified by Jarman's lighting: his early experiments with the use of Super 8 film produce dream-like images; similarly, dense use of candlelight and firelight creates shifting and flickering light effects, effectively derealizing the action and establishing an illusory quality. The overall impression of the interior scenes is disorientating: the labyrinthine passages and staircases have a Piranesian quality, seeming to lead nowhere; indeed, the setting suggests the world of gothic fantasy, where medieval architecture has no apparent logic but rather denotes extreme psychological states. Equally, Jarman used blue filters for all the outdoor scenes, 'desperately anxious that the exteriors should not look real' (Jarman 203). The seascape of the waves, the dunes, Bamburgh Castle silhouetted in the background 'could have been anywhere' (Jarman 203). Of course, the most telling difference from conventional stage production is the castle itself, distancing the drama from any concept of an unknown and undiscovered island, home only to Caliban before Prospero and Miranda are shipwrecked on its shores. Yolanda Sonnabend's costume design further removes any historic specificity: Prospero has been variously described as resembling Robespierre, Lord Byron or the then Dr Who (Jon Pertwee); Miranda wears a torn crinoline, her hair braided with shells; neither would have looked out of place in the punk-art world of the time. Indeed, Toyah Willcox, playing Miranda, was strongly identified with the rebellious punk scene of the late 1970s – a choice of casting which creates an independent and characterful Miranda, taunting and mocking Caliban rather than showing any real fear of him. Heathcote Williams as Prospero was, similarly, an unusual choice; he was far younger than, say, Michael Hordern, then recording *The Tempest* for the BBC Time-Life series, or, obviously, the eighty-year-old Gielgud in Greenaway's *Prospero's Books*. Furthermore, Williams was known to be a magician and occultist; Jarman's researches into the world of the Elizabethan John Dee were familiar territory to Williams, as were the arcane alchemical symbols on the walls and floor of his study.

Jarman's Caliban was played by the blind mime actor Jack Birkett, who had already appeared in *Jubilee* and went on to play the Pope in *Caravaggio*. Questions of colonialism were thereby de-emphasized, although, arguably, Jarman had shifted and widened ideas of alterity: '[Birkett] does not conform to any of the familiar and stable categories of otherness and so is able to remain truly "other"' (Wymer 75). His first appearances are marked by his loud laughter and exaggerated physicality – consuming raw eggs with voluptuous delight while obscenely gesturing at Miranda. An interpolated vignette reveals Sycorax as elderly, obese, naked and tenderly suckling her adult child in a scene which, in a Shakespearean context, would certainly have been viewed as transgressive. Ariel, costumed in a white boiler suit or, for the masque, in evening dress, is played with a degree of louche ennui; his appearances are often heralded by non-human manifestations – a spider running across the book, the clicking of skeletal teeth. He speaks from the 'other side' of Prospero's mirror, and, when he vanishes into his newly won freedom at the end of the film, his departure is signalled by the beating of wings. Perhaps the most telling exchange between master and servant – in a text which retained only 20 per cent of Shakespeare's original – is the discussion of pity: 'if you now beheld them, your affections / Would become tender [...] And mine shall' (*Tem* 5.1.18–19). Jarman chose to cut 'Do you love me, master?' (*Tem* 4.1.48), wryly observing that 'with my reputation they'd expect it' (Jarman 196).

Jarman's triumphant finale is a set piece of flamboyant *joie de vivre*, at once a pastiche of the Hollywood lavish production number and an evocation of Jacobean traditions of masque and anti-masque. The entire scene unfolds under Ariel's command and features, first, an irrepressibly camp sailors' hornpipe and, second, the appearance of venerable blues singer Elisabeth Welch singing Harold Arlen's 'Stormy Weather'. Jarman combined the betrothal masque of Act 4 and the play's concluding wonder and reconciliation in a way that is festive and exuberant. The spectacle is greeted with innocent delight by Ferdinand and Miranda, who are arrayed in pantomimic splendour and enthroned in a Spenserian 'bower of bliss'. The high-pitched hysteria of the hornpipe music, together with the film's only vividly bright lighting, builds to a carnivalesque climax. In comparison, Welch's dignified performance sheds a 'redemptive quality' (Chedgzoy 204) upon her entranced audience. 'Stormy Weather' is clearly an ironic choice in this play: the song itself is poignant with haunting lyrics and a melody that drifts into minor keys – an effect not unlike Feste's song at the end of *Twelfth Night*. The choice of singer is important in a film that does not engage directly with post-colonial issues: Welch appears – 'illuminated like a fiery moon' (Jarman 191) – as the presiding goddess, a summation of Iris, Ceres and Juno, so the all-gracious deity is envisioned as the woman of colour. As Wheale argues, '[the] starchy hegemony of white court power is subsumed by the black goddess's charisma' (64).

After the glittering quality of the masque, the drama returns to the solitary Prospero: his final (transferred) text – 'We are such stuff / As dreams are made on, and our little life / Is rounded with a sleep' (*Tem* 4.1.156–8) – harks back to the dream-world of the opening frames. Wymer observes that a 'melancholy awareness of time and death [...] was an undercurrent in all [Jarman's] films', long predating his own diagnosis as HIV positive (13). But, arguably, Prospero's wizardry is not renounced: Jarman cuts the lines where Prospero promises to break his staff and drown his books, 'and this can only give the impression that Prospero's magic continues' (Dillon 90). Jarman believed that 'Shakespeare would have loved the cinema' (Jarman 194), finding a correspondence between film and Prospero's thaumaturgy: a 'wedding of light and matter – an alchemical conjunction' (188).

Afterword

Emma Smith celebrates the 'sheer and permissive gappiness of [Shakespeare's] drama', and it is perhaps this quality that makes the playwright so adaptogenic. There would seem to be no doubt that the refashioning of Shakespeare's texts will continue to increase, seemingly exponentially. An intriguing question emerges: does even the most transgressive and carnivalesque interaction with the Shakespearean source serve to reinforce Shakespeare's unassailable canonicity? What *is* certain is that the intractable belief in the essential 'universality' of Shakespeare will continue to be interrogated, if not dismantled, in the pluralism of adaptive activity.

REFERENCES

Ackroyd, Peter. 'Ran.' *The Spectator*, 15 March 1986, p. 37.

Adelman, Janet. *Suffocating Mothers: Fantasies of Maternal Origin in Shakespeare's Plays, 'Hamlet' to 'The Tempest'*. London, 1992.

Aebischer, Pascale, et al., editors. *Shakespeare and the 'Live' Theatre Broadcast Experience*. London, 2018.

Al-Bassam, Sulayman. *The Al-Hamlet Summit. The Arab Shakespeare Trilogy*, London, 2014.

Al-Bassam, Sulayman. 'Am I Mad? Creating *The Al-Hamlet Summit*.' *Theatre Forum*, vol. 22, 2003, pp. 85–8.

Al-Bassam, Sulayman. 'The Bard of Basra.' *The Guardian*, 22 September 2005. https://www.theguardian.com/stage/2005/sep/22/theatre.classics. Accessed 15 August 2019.

Al-Bassam, Sulayman. 'Shakespeare, Global Debris, and International Political Theatre.' *Doomed by Hope: Essays on Arab Theatre*, edited by Eyad Houssami, London, 2012, pp. 123–37.

Allman, Helen. 'Home-Grown Manga.' *Independent on Sunday*, Arts and Entertainments, 25 February 2007, p. 2.

Appignanesi, Richard and Kate Brown. *Manga Shakespeare: A Midsummer Night's Dream*. London, 2008.

Auberlen, Eckhard. '*The Tempest* and the Concerns of the Restoration Court: A Study of *The Enchanted Island* and the Operatic *Tempest*.' *Restoration Studies in English Literary Culture, 1660–1700*, vol. 15, 1991, pp. 71–88.

Auden, W. H. *Collected Shorter Poems*. London, 1977.

Auden, W. H. *The Dyer's Hand and Other Essays*. London, 1975.

Auden, W. H. *The Enchafèd Flood, or the Romantic Iconography of the Sea*. London, 1985.

Auden, W. H. *Lectures on Shakespeare*. Edited by Arthur C. Kirsch, London, 2000.

Auden, W. H. 'The Sea and the Mirror.' *Collected Longer Poems*, London, 1974.

Auerbach, Nina. *Woman and the Demon: The Life of a Victorian Myth*. Cambridge, MA, 1982.

Aune, M. G. 'The Uses of *Richard III*: From Robert Cecil to Richard Nixon.' *Shakespeare Bulletin*, vol. 24, 2006, pp. 23–47.

Babington, Bruce. 'Shakespeare Meets the Warner Brothers: Reinhardt and Dieterle's *A Midsummer Night's Dream* (1935).' *Shakespearean Continuities: Essays in Honor of E. A. J. Honigmann*, edited by John Batchelor, Tom Cain and Claire Lamont, London, 1997, pp. 259–74.

Bacon, Francis. *The Major Works*. Edited by Brian Vickers, Oxford, 2002.

Ball, Robert Hamilton. *Shakespeare on Silent Film: A Strange Eventful History*. London, 1968.

Barber, John. 'Bond's Sadistic View of Lear.' *The Daily Telegraph*, 1 July 1982, p. 13.

Barber, Sian. *The British Film Industry in the 1970s: Capital, Culture and Creativity*. Basingstoke, 2013.

Barker, Clive and Simon Trussler. 'Towards a Theatre of Dynamic Ambiguities.' *Theatre Quarterly*, vol. 9, 1979, pp. 3–24.

Barthelemy, Anthony Gerard. *Black Face, Maligned Race: The Representation of Blacks in English Drama from Shakespeare to Southerne*. Baton Rouge, 1987.

Bate, Jonathan. 'Parodies of Shakespeare.' *The Journal of Popular Culture*, vol. 19, 1985, pp. 75–89.

Bate, Jonathan, editor. *The Romantics on Shakespeare*. London, 1992.

Bate, Jonathan. *Shakespearean Constitutions: Politics, Theatre, Criticism, 1730–1830*. London, 1989.

Bate, Jonathan, editor. *Titus Andronicus*. 1995. Revised ed., London, Arden Shakespeare, 2018.

Bate, Jonathan, and Sonia Massai. 'Adaptation as Edition.' *The Margins of the Text*, edited by D. C. Greetham, Ann Arbor, 1997, pp. 129–51.

Bates, Robin E. '*Cymbeline* and *Cymbeline Refinished*: G. B. Shaw and the Unresolved Empire.' *Celtic Shakespeare: The Bard and the Borderers*, edited by Willy Maley and Rory Loughnane, Farnham, 2013, pp. 231–43.

BBC. 'Directing and Producing Shakespeare's *The Hollow Crown: War of the Roses*.' *BBC Academy*, 7 September 2016. https://www.bbc.co.uk/academy/en/articles/art20160512135013337. Accessed 19 August 2019.

Belsey, Catherine. *The Subject of Tragedy: Identity and Difference in Renaissance Drama*. London, 1985.

Bennett, Susan. 'Precarious Bodies: *Romeo and Juliet in Baghdad* at the World Shakespeare Festival.' *The Oxford Handbook of Shakespeare and Embodiment: Gender, Sexuality, and Race*, edited by Valerie Traub, Oxford, 2016, pp. 694–708.

Berne, Suzanne. 'Interview with Jane Smiley.' *Contemporary Literary Criticism*, vol. 76, yearbook 1992, pp. 236–8.

Best, Michael. 'Shakespeare on the Internet and in Digital Media.' *The Edinburgh Companion to Shakespeare and the Arts*, edited by Mark Thornton Burnett, Adrian Streete and Ramona Wray, Edinburgh, 2011, pp. 558–76.

Bhardwaj, Vishal, and TRM Editors. 'Decoding Shakespeare: Vishal Bhardwaj in Interview with James Shapiro.' *The Review Monk*, 17 May 2015. http://thereviewmonk.com/article/decoding-shakespeare-vishal-bhardwaj-haider-nyiff/. Accessed 15 August 2019.

Bhardwaj, Vishal, with Basharat Peer. *Haider: The Original Screenplay*. New Delhi, 2014.

Billingham, Peter. *At the Sharp End: Uncovering the Work of Five Leading Dramatists*. London, 2007.

Billington, Michael. 'Best Shakespeare Productions: *The Winter's Tale*.' *The Guardian*, 8 May 2014. https://www.theguardian.com/stage/2014/may/08/best-shakespeare-productions-the-winters-tale. Accessed 15 August 2019.

Billington, Michael. '*Macbett*.' *The Guardian*, 18 June 2007. https://www.theguardian.com/stage/2007/jun/18/theatre. Accessed 13 August 2019.

Billington, Michael. 'Michael Billington on Macbeth: Profile of Greatest Theatrical Poem Ever Written.' *The Guardian*, 29 December 2017. https://www.theguardian.com/culture/2017/dec/29/macbeth-profile-shakespeare-michael-billington. Accessed 13 August 2019.

Billington, Michael. 'Money and Other Demons.' *The Guardian*, 19 June 1999. https://www.theguardian.com/stage/1999/jun/19/theatre.artsfeatures1. Accessed 15 August 2019.

Bond, Edward. 'Drama and the Dialectics of Violence.' *Theatre Quarterly*, vol. 2, 1972, pp. 4–14.

Bond, Edward. 'Interview.' *Gambit*, vol. 5, 1970, pp. 5–38.

Bond, Edward. *Lear*. London, Methuen Drama Student Edition, 1994.

Bond, Edward. *Plays: 2*. London, 1998.

Bonnefoy, Claude, editor. *Conversations with Eugène Ionesco*. Translated by Jan Dawson, London, 1970.

'Bornila Chatterjee Talks The Hungry.' British Council. http://film.britishcouncil.org/comment/192017/the-hungry. Accessed 13 August 2019.

Bottoms, Janet. 'Speech, Image, Action: Animating Tales from Shakespeare.' *Children's Literature in Education*, vol. 32, 2001, pp. 3–15.

Boydell, John. *A Catalogue of the Pictures in the Shakspeare Gallery, Pall-Mall*. London, 1796.

Bradley, A. C. *Shakespearean Tragedy*. 3rd ed., London, 1992.

Bradwell, Mike, editor. *The Bush Theatre Book*. London, 1997.

Bretz, Andrew. 'Prisons Within/Prisons Without: Rehabilitation and Abjection Narratives in *Mickey B*.' *Shakespeare Bulletin*, vol. 34, 2016, pp. 577–99.

Bristol, Michael D. *Big-Time Shakespeare*. London, 1996.

Buchanan, Judith. 'Shakespeare and Silent Film.' *The Edinburgh Companion to Shakespeare and the Arts*, edited by Mark Thornton Burnett, Adrian Streete and Ramona Wray, Edinburgh, 2011, pp. 467–83.

Buchanan, Judith. *Shakespeare on Film*. Harlow, 2005.

Buchanan, Judith. *Shakespeare on Film: An Excellent Dumb Discourse*. Cambridge, 2009.

Buchanan, Judith. '*The Winter's Tale*'s Spectral Endings: Death, Dance and Doubling.' *Shakespeare on Screen: The Tempest and Late Romances*, edited by Sarah Hatchuel and Nathalie Vienne-Guerrin, Cambridge, 2017, pp. 110–32.

Bull, John Stanley. *New British Political Dramatists*. London, 1984.

Bulman, James C. *The Merchant of Venice*. Shakespeare in Performance Series, Manchester, 1991.

Buntin, Mat. 'Shylock.' *Canadian Adaptations of Shakespeare Project*, edited by D. Fischlin, 2004. http://www.canadianshakespeares.ca. Accessed 15 August 2019.

Burnett, Mark Thornton. *Shakespeare and World Cinema*. Cambridge, 2013.

Burrow, Colin. 'Big Rip-Off.' *London Review of Books*, 3 November 2016, pp. 15–16.

Burt, Richard, editor. *Shakespeares After Shakespeare: An Encyclopaedia of the Bard in Mass Media and Popular Culture*. London, 2007. 2 vols.

Butler, Martin, editor. *Cymbeline*. New Cambridge Edition, Cambridge, 2005.

Caines, Michael. *Shakespeare and the Eighteenth Century*. Oxford, 2013.

Calbi, Maurizio. '"Fear No More": Gender Politics and the "Hell" of New Media Technologies in Michael Almereyda's *Cymbeline* (2014).' *Société Française Shakespeare*, vol. 36, 2018. https://journals.openedition.org/shakespeare/4040. Accessed 13 August 2019.

Calderwood, James L. '*A Midsummer Night's Dream*: Anamorphism and Theseus' Dream.' *Shakespeare Quarterly*, vol. 42, 1991, pp. 409–30.

Canby, Vincent. 'Derek Jarman: *The Tempest*.' *The New York Times*, 22 September 1980. https://www.nytimes.com/1980/09/22/arts/the-tempest.html. Accessed 15 August 2019.

Cannon, Christopher. '*The Winter's Tale*.' *The Times Literary Supplement*, 22 January 1999, p. 19.

Cardullo, Bert. *Out of Asia: The Films of Akira Kurosawa, Satyajit Ray, Abbas Kiraostami and Zhang Yimou: Essays and Interviews*. Newcastle, 2008.

Carlson, Ron. 'King Lear in Zebulon County.' *New York Times*, 3 November 1991. https://archive.nytimes.com/www.nytimes.com/books/98/04/05/specials/smiley-acres.html. Accessed 15 August 2019.

Carpenter, Humphrey. *W. H. Auden*. Oxford, 1991.

Carroll, Sydney W. '*A Midsummer Night's Dream*: Reinhardt in Hollywood.' *Sunday Times*, 13 October 1935, pp. 4–5.

Cartelli, Thomas. 'Doing It Slant: Reconceiving Shakespeare in the Shakespeare Aftermath.' *Shakespeare Studies*, vol. 38, 2010, pp. 26–36.

Carter, Angela. *Wise Children*. London, 1992.

Cartmell, Deborah. *Adaptations in the Sound Era: 1927–37*. London, 2015.

Cartmell, Deborah. 'Adapting Children's Literature.' *The Cambridge Companion to Literature on Screen*, edited by Deborah Cartmell and Imelda Whelehan, Cambridge, 2007, pp. 167–80.

Cavendish, Dominic. 'A Tender Thing, RSC Swan, Stratford-upon-Avon, Review.' *The Telegraph*, 8 October 2012. https://www.telegraph.co.uk/culture/theatre/theatre-reviews/9594616/A-Tender-Thing-RSC-Swan-Stratford-upon-Avon-review.html. Accessed 13 August 2019.

Charnes, Linda. *Notorious Identity: Materializing the Subject in Shakespeare*. Cambridge, MA, 1993.

Chaudhuri, Sukanta, editor. *A Midsummer Night's Dream*. London, Arden Shakespeare, 2017.

Chaudhuri, Supriya. '"What Bloody Man Is That?" *Macbeth, Maqbool*, and Shakespeare in India.' *The Shakespearean International Yearbook 12: Shakespeare in India*, edited by Sukanta Chaudhuri, Abingdon, 2016, pp. 97–113.

Chedgzoy, Kate. *Shakespeare's Queer Children: Sexual Politics and Contemporary Culture*. Manchester, 1995.

Chernaik, Warren. *The Merchant of Venice*. London, 2005.

Clark, Sandra, editor. *The Tempest or The Enchanted Island. Shakespeare Made Fit: Restoration Adaptations of Shakespeare*, London, 1997.

Clark, Sandra, and Pamela Mason, editors. *Macbeth*. London, Arden Shakespeare, 2015.

Cohn, Ruby. 'Shakespeare Left.' *Theatre Journal*, vol. 40, 1988, pp. 48–60.

Coleman, Ingrid H. 'Conscious and Unconscious Intent in the Creative Process: A Letter from Eugène Ionesco.' *The French Review*, vol. 54, 1981, pp. 810–15.

Collick, John. *Shakespeare, Cinema and Society*. Manchester, 1989.

Corcoran, Neil. *Shakespeare and the Modern Poet*. Cambridge, 2010.

Cowden Clarke, Mary. *The Girlhood of Shakespeare's Heroines in a Series of Tales*. London, 1892. 5 vols.

Cowden Clarke, Mary. *My Long Life: An Autobiographical Sketch.* London, 1896.

Cunningham, Vanessa. *Shakespeare and Garrick.* Cambridge, 2008.

Davenport-Hines, Richard. *Auden.* London, 2003.

Dent, Shirley. 'Interview with Sulayman Al-Bassam.' *Culture Wars*, 2002. http://www.sabab.org/wp-content/uploads/2012/03/Culture-Wars-Interview-with-Shirley-Dent.pdf. Accessed 15 August 2019.

Desmet, Christy. 'Teaching Shakespeare with YouTube.' *The English Journal*, vol. 99, 2009, pp. 65–70.

Dessen, Alan C. *Rescripting Shakespeare: The Text, the Director, and Modern Productions.* Cambridge, 2002.

Dessen, Alan C. *Shakespeare in Performance: Titus Andronicus.* Manchester, 1989.

Dias, Rosie. *Exhibiting Englishness: John Boydell's Shakespeare Gallery and the Formation of a National Aesthetic.* New Haven, 2013.

Dickson, E. Jane. 'The Romeo and Juliet Strip.' *Sunday Times*, 1 November 1992, pp. 60–1.

Dillon, Steven. *Derek Jarman and Lyric Film: The Mirror and the Sea.* Austin, 2004.

The Discovery of Richard III. University of Leicester. https://www.le.ac.uk/richardiii/. Accessed 15 August 2019.

Dobson, Michael. *The Making of the National Poet: Shakespeare, Adaptation and Authorship, 1660–1769.* Reprint, Oxford, 2001.

Dobson, Michael, and Estelle Rivier-Arnaud. *Rewriting Shakespeare's Plays for and by the Contemporary Stage.* Newcastle upon Tyne, 2017.

Dryden, John. *The Works of John Dryden*, vol. 11. Edited by M. E. Novak and G. R. Guffey, Berkeley, 1978.

Dubrow, Heather. *Genre.* London, 1982.

Dunster, Matthew. *Imogen. Adapted from William Shakespeare's 'Cymbeline'.* London, 2016.

Dustagheer, Sarah, and Gillian Woods, editors. *Stage Directions and Shakespearean Theatre.* London, 2018.

Edelman, Charles. *The Merchant of Venice.* Shakespeare in Production Series, Cambridge, 2002.

Edgar, David. *Dick Deterred.* New York and London, 1974.

Edgar, David. *Plays 2.* London, 1990.

Edwardes, Jane. 'Ben Power: Interview.' *TimeOut*, 14 October 2008. https://www.timeout.com/london/theatre/ben-power-interview. Accessed 13 August 2019.

Eisner, Will. *Comics and Sequential Art.* New York, 2008.

Ellis, Jim. *Derek Jarman's Angelic Conversations.* Minneapolis, 2009.

Erne, Lukas. 'What We Owe to Editors.' *Shakespeare in Our Time: A Shakespeare Association of America Collection*, edited by Dympna Callaghan and Suzanne Gossett, London, 2016, pp. 64–8.

Esslin, Martin. *The Theatre of the Absurd.* Revised updated ed., London, 1974.

Etienne, Anne. 'Interview between Arnold Wesker and Julia Pascal.' *Recherches sur les Arts Dramatiques Anglophones Contemporains* (RADAC), 16 June 2013, pp. 207–30. https://radacblog.files. wordpress.com/2016/04/cdthsshylockinterviewawjp.pdf. Accessed 15 August 2019.

Faucit, Helena, Lady Martin. *On Some of Shakespeare's Female Characters.* London, 1891.

Fernie, Ewan. 'The Last Act: Presentism, Spirituality and the Politics of *Hamlet.' Spiritual Shakespeares,* edited by Ewan Fernie, London, 2005, pp. 186–211.

Fiedler, Lisa. *Dating Hamlet.* New York, 2002. London, 2003.

Fielding, Henry. *A Journey from This World to the Next.* London, 1798.

Fischlin, Daniel, and Mark Fortier, editors. *Adaptations of Shakespeare: A Critical Anthology of Plays from the Seventeenth Century to the Present.* London, 2000.

Fischlin, Daniel, et al. 'Transgression and Transformation: *Mickey B* and the Dramaturgy of Adaptation: An Interview with Tom Magill.' *OuterSpeares: Shakespeare, Intermedia, and the Limits of Adaptation,* edited by Daniel Fischlin, Toronto, 2014.

Flint, Kate. *The Woman Reader, 1837–1914.* Oxford, 1993.

Foakes, R. A., editor. *King Lear.* London, Arden Shakespeare, 1997.

Ford, Mark. 'W. H. Auden's "The Sea and the Mirror".' *A Driftwood Altar: Essays and Reviews,* London, 2005, pp. 135–53.

Freud, Sigmund. 'Some Character-Types Met with in Psycho-Analytic Work.' *The Standard Edition of the Complete Psychological Works,* edited by James Strachey, vol. 14, London, 2001, pp. 309–36.

Friedman, Michael D., with Alan C. Dessen. *Shakespeare in Performance: Titus Andronicus.* Manchester, 2013.

Fuller, Jack. 'King Lear in the Middle West.' *Chicago Tribune,* 3 November 1991, published in *Contemporary Literary Criticism,* vol. 76, yearbook 1992, pp. 230–2.

Fuller, John. *W. H. Auden: A Commentary.* Princeton, 2000.

Fuseli, Henry. *Lectures on Painting: Delivered at the Royal Academy.* London, 1801.

'Gallery of Shakespeare.' *Public Advertiser,* issue 17098, 6 May 1789, p. 3.

Garber, Marjorie. *Shakespeare and Modern Culture.* New York, 2008.

Gardner, Lyn. 'A Tender Thing: Review.' *The Guardian,* 4 October 2012. https://www.theguardian.com/stage/2012/oct/04/a-tender-thing-review. Accessed 13 August 2019.

Garfield, Leon, and Peter Thomas. 'A Present for Mr Patten ...' *Books for Keeps,* vol. 77, November 1992, pp. 36–7.

Garrick, David. *Cymbeline. A Tragedy by Shakespear, with Alterations.* Dublin, 1762.

Garrick, David. *The Letters of David Garrick.* Edited by David M. Little and George M. Kahrl, London, 1963. 3 vols.

Genette, Gerard. *Palimpsests: Literature in the Second Degree.* Translated by Channa Newman and Claude Doubinsky, Lincoln, NE, 1997.

Gentleman, Francis, editor. *Bell's Edition of Shakespeare's Plays As They Are Now Performed at the Theatres Royal in London.* London, 1773–4. 9 vols.

Gilbreath, Alexandra. 'Hermione in *The Winter's Tale.*' *Players of Shakespeare,* edited by Robin Smallwood, vol. 5, Cambridge, 2003, pp. 74–90.

Goodman, Henry. 'Playing Shylock: Interviews with Antony Sher and Henry Goodman.' *The Merchant of Venice,* edited by Jonathan Bate and Eric Rasmussen, Basingstoke, 2010, pp. 156–74.

Grady, Hugh. *Shakespeare and Impure Aesthetics.* Cambridge, 2009.

de Grazia, Margreta. *'Hamlet' without Hamlet.* Cambridge, 2007.

Greene, Graham. '"A Midsummer Night's Dream": At the Adelphi.' *The Spectator,* 18 October 1935, p. 606.

Greig, David. *Dunsinane.* London, 2010.

Greig, David. 'Rough Theatre.' *Cool Britannia? British Political Drama in the 1990s,* edited by Rebecca D'Monté and Graham Saunders, Basingstoke, 2008, pp. 208–21.

Gritzner, Karoline. *Adorno and Modern Theatre: The Drama of the Damaged Self in Bond, Rudkin, Barker and Kane.* Basingstoke, 2015.

Gross, John, editor. *After Shakespeare: An Anthology.* London, 2002.

Gross, John. *Shylock: A Legend and Its Legacy.* New York, 1992.

Guneratne, Anthony R. *Shakespeare, Film Studies, and the Visual Cultures of Modernity.* Basingstoke, 2008.

Guppy, Shusha. 'Eugene Ionesco, the Art of Theater No. 6.' *Paris Review,* vol. 93, 1984, pp. 53–78.

Güvenç, Sila Şenlen. '"[You can't kill me]": Scottish Identity and the Anglo-Scottish Union in David Greig's *Dunsinane.*' *Scottish Literary Review,* vol. 6, 2014, pp. 93–113.

Hanmer, Thomas, editor. *The Works of Shakespeare.* Oxford, 1743–4. 6 vols.

Harris, Frank. *Frank Harris on Bernard Shaw: An Unauthorised Biography Based on Firsthand Information.* London, 1931.

Harss, Marina. 'The Magical Transformations of "The Winter's Tale".' *New York Times,* 27 July 2016. https://www.nytimes.com/2016/07/28/arts/dance/christopher-wheeldon-brings-statues-to-life-in-the-winters-tale-ballet-lincoln-center-festival-national-ballet-of-canada.html. Accessed 15 August 2019.

Hatchuel, Sarah, and Nathalie Vienne-Guerrin, editors. *Shakespeare on Screen: 'Othello'*. Cambridge, 2015.

Hattaway, Michael, editor. *The Second Part of King Henry the Sixth*. Cambridge, 1991.

Hawkins, William. *Cymbeline, A Tragedy, altered from Shakespeare*. London, 1759.

Hay, Malcolm, and Philip Roberts. *Bond: A Study of His Plays*. London, 1980.

Hayley, Emma. 'Manga Shakespeare.' *Manga: An Anthology of Global and Cultural Perspectives*, edited by Toni Johnson-Woods, London, 2010, pp. 267–80.

Hazlitt, William. *Characters of Shakespear's Plays*. London, 1907.

Hazlitt, William. *The Selected Writings of William Hazlitt*. Edited by Duncan Wu, vol. 1, London, 1998.

Henderson, Diana E. 'Othello Redux? Scott's *Kenilworth* and the Trickiness of "Race" on the Nineteenth-Century Stage.' *Victorian Shakespeare, Volume 2: Literature and Culture*, edited by Gail Marshall and Adrian Poole, London, 2003, pp. 14–29.

Hennessey, Katherine. *Shakespeare on the Arabian Peninsula*. Basingstoke, 2018.

Hess, John L. 'Ionesco Talks of His Latest, "Macbett".' *New York Times*, 18 January 1972. https://www.nytimes.com/1972/01/18/archives/ionesco-talks-of-his-latest-macbett.html. Accessed 13 August 2019.

Hickling, Alfred. 'A Tender Thing, Northern Stage, Newcastle.' *The Guardian*, 5 November 2009. https://www.theguardian.com/culture/2009/nov/05/a-tender-thing-review. Accessed 3 August 2019.

Hindle, Maurice. *Studying Shakespeare on Film*. Basingstoke, 2007.

Hirsch, James. *Shakespeare and the History of Soliloquies*. Cranbury, 2003.

Hirst, David L. *Edward Bond*. Basingstoke, 1985.

Hitchman, Lauren. 'From Page to Screen: The Live Theatre Broadcast as a New Medium.' *Adaptation*, vol. 11, 2018, pp. 171–85.

Hobgood, Allison P. 'Teeth Before Eyes: Impairment and Invisibility in Shakespeare's *Richard III*.' *Disability, Health and Happiness in the Shakespearean Body*, edited by Sujata Iyengar, New York, 2015, pp. 23–40.

Hobgood, Allison P., and David Houston Wood. *Recovering Disability in Early Modern England*. Columbus, 2013.

Hodgdon, Barbara. 'Richard III.' *Educational Theatre Journal*, vol. 25, 1973, pp. 374–5.

Hodgdon, Barbara. '(You)Tube Travel: The 9:59 to Dover Beach, Stopping at Fair Verona and Elsinore.' *Shakespeare Bulletin*, vol. 28, 2010, pp. 313–30.

Holderness, Graham. 'From Summit to Tragedy: Sulayman Al-Bassam's *Richard III* and Political Theatre.' *Critical Survey*, vol. 19, 2007, pp. 124–43.

Holderness, Graham. 'Shakespeare and the Novel.' *Shakespeare's Creative Legacies*, edited by Peter Holbrook and Paul Edmondson, London, 2016, pp. 93–106.

Holderness, Graham. *Visual Shakespeare: Essays in Film and Television.* Hatfield, 2002.

Honigmann, E. A. J., editor. *Othello*. 1997. Revised ed., London, Arden Shakespeare, 2016.

Houston Wood, David. 'New Directions: "Some Tardy Cripple": Timing Disability in *Richard III.*' *Richard III: A Critical Reader*, edited by Annaliese Connolly, London, 2013, pp. 129–54.

Howe, Elizabeth. *The First English Actresses: Women and Drama 1660–1700.* Cambridge, 1994.

Huang, Alexa, and Elizabeth Rivlin, editors. *Shakespeare and the Ethics of Appropriation.* New York, 2014.

Hughes, Alan, editor. *Titus Andronicus.* New Cambridge Shakespeare, Cambridge, 2006.

Hulbert, Jennifer. '"Adolescence, Thy Name Is Ophelia!": The Ophelia-ization of the Contemporary Teenage Girl.' *Shakespeare and Youth Culture*, edited by Jennifer Hulbert, Kevin J. Wetmore and Robert L. York, New York, 2006, pp. 199–220.

Hutcheon, Linda, with Siobhan O'Flynn. *A Theory of Adaptation.* London and New York, 2012.

Hutcheon, Linda. *A Theory of Parody: The Teachings of Twentieth-Century Art Forms.* Reprint, Urbana, 2000.

IANS. '"The Hungry" Celebrates Complexity of Women Characters.' *The Week*, 20 October 2017. https://www.theweek.in/news/entertainment/the-hungry-celebrates-complexity-of-women-characters.html. Accessed 9 January 2020.

Ionesco, Eugène. *Exit the King, The Killer, and Macbett.* Translated by Charles Marowitz and Donald Watson, New York, 1973.

Ionesco, Eugène. *Plays, Volume 9: Macbett; The Mire; Learning to Walk.* Translated by Donald Watson, London, 1973.

Ionesco, Eugène. *Théâtre D' Eugène Ionesco.* Edited by Gallimard, vol. 5, Paris, 1974.

Isaacs, J. *Max Reinhardt's Midsummer Night's Dream.* London, 1935.

Iyengar, Sujata, and Christy Desmet. 'Rebooting Ophelia: Social Media and the Rhetorics of Appropriation.' *The Afterlife of Ophelia*, edited by Kaara Peterson and Deanne Williams, Basingstoke, 2012, pp. 59–78.

Jackson, Russell. *Shakespeare and the English-Speaking Cinema.* Oxford, 2014.

Jacobson, Howard. *Shylock Is My Name.* London, 2016.

Jacobson, Howard. 'Villain or Victim, Shakespeare's Shylock is a Character to Celebrate.' *The Guardian*, 5 February 2016. https://www.theguardian.com/books/2016/feb/05/villain-victim-shylock-shakespeare-howard-jacobson. Accessed 25 July 2019.

Jacobson, Howard, and Adrian Poole. 'Shakespeare and the Novel: A Conversation.' *Shakespeare Survey*, vol. 70, 'Creating Shakespeare,' 2016, pp. 19–29.

Jameson, Anna. *Characteristics of Women: Moral, Poetical, and Historical*. London, 1832. 2 vols.

Jarman, Derek. *Dancing Ledge*. London, 1984.

Johnson, Samuel, editor. *The Plays of William Shakespeare*. London, 1765. 8 vols.

Jones, Chris. 'In "Dunsinane", David Greig Offers a Timely Play – Set in 11th Century.' *Los Angeles Times*, 27 March 2015. https://www.latimes.com/entertainment/arts/la-et-cm-ca-dunsinane-20150329-story.html. Accessed 13 August 2019.

Jordan, Stephanie. 'The Timing of Jealousy.' *The Winter's Tale*, Royal Opera House programme, 2017/18, pp. 15–19.

Keenan, Tim. 'Adapting the Adaptors: Staging Davenant and Dryden's Restoration *Tempest*.' *Journal of Adaptation in Film and Performance*, vol. 2, 2009, pp. 65–77.

Kermode, Frank. 'Ideas Strangle Director.' *The Times Literary Supplement*, 16 May 1980, p. 553.

Kern, Edith. 'Ionesco and Shakespeare: *Macbeth* on the Modern Stage.' *South Atlantic Bulletin*, vol. 39, 1974, pp. 3–16.

Kidnie, Margaret Jane. *Shakespeare and the Problem of Adaptation*. London, 2009.

Kiefer, Carol Solomon. *The Myth and Madness of Ophelia*. Amherst, 2001. Exhibition and catalogue.

Kilbourne, Frederick W. *Alterations and Adaptations of Shakespeare*. Boston, MA, 1906.

King, Ros. 'Teaching Shakespeare: Indoctrination or Creativity?' *Shifting the Scene: Shakespeare in European Culture*, edited by Ladina Bezzola Lambert and Balz Engler, Newark, 2004, pp. 205–16.

Kirsch, Arthur. *Auden and Christianity*. New Haven and London, 2005.

Kirsch, Arthur, editor. *The Sea and the Mirror: A Commentary on Shakespeare's 'The Tempest' by W. H. Auden*. Princeton, 2003.

Kirwan, Peter. 'Mis/Quotation in Constrained Writing.' *Shakespeare and Quotation*, edited by Julie Maxwell and Kate Rumbold, Cambridge, 2018, pp. 247–59.

Klein, Lisa. *Ophelia*. London, 2006.

Kostihová, Marcela. 'Richard Recast: Renaissance Disability in a Postcommunist Culture.' *Recovering Disability in Early Modern England*, edited by Allison P. Hobgood and David Houston Wood, Columbus, 2013, pp. 136–49.

Kott, Jan. 'The Edo Lear.' *New York Review of Books*, 24 April 1986. https://www.nybooks.com/articles/1986/04/24/the-edo-lear/. Accessed 15 August 2019.

Kott, Jan. *Shakespeare Our Contemporary*. Translated by Boleslaw Taborski, Bristol, 1983.

Kriegel, Leonard. 'The Cripple in Literature.' *Images of the Disabled, Disabling Images*, edited by Alan Gartner and Tom Joe, New York, 1987, pp. 31–46.

Kristeva, Julia. 'Romeo and Juliet: Love-Hatred in the Couple' ['Le couple amour-haine selon Roméo et Juliette']. *Romeo and Juliet*, edited by R. S. White, Basingstoke, 2001, pp. 68–84.

Kurosawa, Akira. *Ran*, original screenplay and storyboards. Translated by Tadashi Shishido, Boston, MA, 1986.

Lacan, Jacques. 'Desire and the Interpretation of Desire in *Hamlet*.' *Yale French Studies*, no. 55/56, *Literature and Psychoanalysis The Question of Reading: Otherwise*, 1977, pp. 11–52.

Lamb, Charles. *The Letters of Charles Lamb*. Edited by E. V. Lucas, London, 1935. 3 vols.

Lamb, Charles. *The Works of Charles Lamb*. London, 1818. 2 vols.

Lamb, Charles, and Mary Lamb. *Tales from Shakespeare*. 1807. London, 2007.

Lamont, Rosette C. 'From *Macbeth* to *Macbett*.' *Modern Drama*, vol. 15, 1972, pp. 231–53.

Langbaine, Gerard. *An Account of the English Dramatick Poets*. Oxford, 1691.

Lanier, Douglas M. 'Almereyda's *Cymbeline*: The End of Teen Shakespeare.' *Shakespeare on Screen: The Tempest and Late Romances*, edited by Sarah Hatchuel and Nathalie Vienne-Guerrin, Cambridge, 2017, pp. 232–50.

Lanier, Douglas M. '*Hamlet*: Tragedy and Film Adaptation.' *The Oxford Handbook of Shakespearean Tragedy*, edited by Michael Neill and David Schalkwyk, Oxford, 2016, pp. 572–87.

Lanier, Douglas M. 'The Hogarth Shakespeare Series: Redeeming Shakespeare's Literariness.' *Shakespeare and Millennial Fiction*, edited by Andrew James Hartley, Cambridge, 2018, pp. 230–50.

Lanier, Douglas M. 'Post-Textual Shakespeare.' *Shakespeare Survey*, vol. 64, 2011, pp. 145–62.

Lanier, Douglas M. *Shakespeare and Modern Popular Culture*. Oxford, 2002.

Leberg, Dan. 'The Hollow Crown: Quality Television and Colonial Performances.' *Reception: Texts, Readers, Audiences, History*, vol. 10, 2018, pp. 27–49.

Leiren-Young, Mark. *Shylock: A Play*. Vancouver, 1996.

Levenson, Jill. 'Love in a Naughty World: Modern Dramatic Adaptations of *The Merchant of Venice*.' *Shakespeare's Comedies of Love: Essays in Honour of Alexander Leggatt*, edited by Karen Bamford and Ric Knowles, Toronto, 2008, pp. 246–61.

Lindfors, Bernth. *Ira Aldridge: The Vagabond Years, 1833–1852.* Rochester, 2011.

Lindhé, Anna. *Appropriations of Shakespeare's 'King Lear' in Three Modern North American Novels.* Lund, 2013.

Lindley, David, editor. *The Tempest.* Updated edition, Cambridge, 2013.

Litvin, Margaret. 'Tragedy: Interview with Sulayman Al-Bassam.' *PMLA*, vol. 129, 2014, pp. 850–4.

Litvin, Margaret. 'Vanishing Intertexts in the Arab *Hamlet* Tradition.' *Critical Survey*, vol. 19, 2007, pp. 74–94.

Loomba, Ania, and Martin Orkin, editors. *Post-Colonial Shakespeares.* London, 1998.

Love, Genevieve. *Early Modern Theatre and the Figure of Disability.* London, 2018.

Love, Harold. 'John Dryden.' *Great Shakespeareans Vol. 1: Dryden, Pope, Johnson, Malone*, edited by Claude Rawson, London, 2013, pp. 12–65.

MacAlister, Katherine. 'David Greig on His Play Dunsinane.' *Oxford Times*, 12 September 2013. https://www.oxfordtimes.co.uk/leisure/theatre/10667984.david-greig-on-his-play-dunsinane. Accessed 13 August 2019.

'Macbeth Meets Bald Prima Donna.' *The Guardian*, 28 January 1972, p. 11.

Mackrell, Judith. *Reading Dance.* London, 1997.

MacQueen, Scott. 'Midsummer Dream, Midwinter Nightmare: Max Reinhardt and Shakespeare versus the Warner Bros.' *The Moving Image*, vol. 9, 2009, pp. 30–103.

Malone, Edmond, editor. *The Plays and Poems of William Shakespeare.* London, 1790. 10 vols.

Marowitz, Charles. *The Marowitz Shakespeare.* London, 1978.

Marsden, Jean I. 'Improving Shakespeare: From the Restoration to Garrick.' *The Cambridge Companion to Shakespeare on Stage*, edited by Stanley Wells and Sarah Stanton, Cambridge, 2002, pp. 21–36.

Marsden, Jean I. *The Re-Imagined Text: Shakespeare, Adaptation, and Eighteenth-Century Literary Theory.* Lexington, 1995.

Marshall, Gail, and Ann Thompson. 'Mary Cowden Clarke.' *Great Shakespeareans*, edited by Gail Marshall, vol. 7, London, 2011, pp. 58–91.

Marshall, Herbert, and Mildred Stock. *Ira Aldridge: The Negro Tragedian.* London, 1958.

Massai, Sonia. 'What's Next in Editing Shakespeare.' *Shakespeare in Our Time: A Shakespeare Association of America Collection*, edited by Dympna Callaghan and Suzanne Gossett, London, 2016, pp. 68–72.

Mathews, Charles. *Othello, the Moor of Fleet Street*. Edited by Manfred Draudt, Tübingen, Francke, 1993.

Maus, Katharine Eisaman. 'Arcadia Host: Politics and Revision in the Restoration *Tempest*.' *Renaissance Drama*, new series, vol. 13, 1982, pp. 189–209.

Mayer, David. '"Quote the Words to Prompt the Attitudes": The Victorian Performer, the Photographer, and the Photograph.' *Theatre Survey*, vol. 43, 2002, pp. 223–51.

McCabe, Colin. 'A Post-National European Cinema: A Consideration of Derek Jarman's *The Tempest* and *Edward II*.' *Screening Europe: Image and Identity in Contemporary European Cinema*, edited by Duncan Petrie, London, 1992, pp. 9–18.

McCandless, David. 'A Tale of Two Tituses: Julie Taymor's Vision on Stage and Screen.' *Shakespeare Quarterly*, vol. 53, 2002, pp. 487–511.

McKernan, Luke. 'The Bard Is Back.' https://lukemckernan.com/2016/03/20/the-bard-is-back. Accessed 13 August 2019.

Mears, Steven. 'Interview: Michael Almereyda.' *Film Comment*, 13 March 2015. https://www.filmcomment.com/blog/interview-michael-almereyda. Accessed 13 August 2019.

Mendelson, Edward. *Later Auden*. London, 1999.

Mentz, Steve. *At the Bottom of Shakespeare's Ocean*. London, 2009.

Mitchell, David T., and Sharon L. Snyder. *The Body and Physical Difference: Discourses of Disability*. Ann Arbor, 2004.

Mitchell, David T., and Sharon L. Snyder. *Narrative Prosthesis: Disability and the Dependencies of Discourse*. Ann Arbor, 2011.

Monahan, Mark. 'Sheer Madness?' *The Winter's Tale*, Royal Opera House programme, 2017/18, pp. 10–13.

Monsell, Thomas. *Nixon on Stage and Screen: The Thirty-Seventh President as Depicted in Films, Television, Plays and Opera*. Jefferson, 1998.

Morgan, Margot. *Politics and Theatre in Twentieth-Century Europe: Imagination and Resistance*. London, 2013.

Müller, Anja. *Adapting Canonical Texts in Children's Literature*. New York, 2013.

Müller, Beate. 'Hamlet at the Dentist's: Parodies of Shakespeare.' *Parody: Dimensions and Perspectives*, edited by Beate Müller, Amsterdam, 1997, pp. 127–53.

Mullin, Romano. 'Tweeting Television/Broadcasting the Bard: @HollowCrownFans and Digital Shakespeares.' *Broadcast Your Shakespeare: Continuity and Change across Media*, edited by Stephen O'Neill, London, 2018, pp. 207–26.

Murphy, Andrew. 'The Birth of the Editor.' *A Concise Companion to Shakespeare and the Text*, edited by Andrew Murphy, Oxford, 2007, pp. 93–108.

Murray, Barbara A., editor. *Shakespeare Adaptations from the Restoration: Five Plays*. Madison, 2005.

Murray, Melissa. *Ophelia*. Unpublished, 1979.

Nevo, Ruth. *Shakespeare's Other Language*. London, 1987.

Nicoll, Allardyce. *Film and Theatre*. Nicoll, 1936.

Novy, Marianne. *Transforming Shakespeare: Contemporary Women's Re-Visions in Literature and Performance*. Basingstoke, 2000.

O'Connor, John. *Shakespearean Afterlives: Ten Characters with a Life of their Own*. Cambridge, 2005.

Odell, George C. D. *Shakespeare from Betterton to Irving*. London and New York, 1921. 2 vols.

O'Neill, Stephen. 'Theorizing User Agency in YouTube Shakespeare.' *The Shakespeare User: Critical and Creative Appropriations in a Networked Culture*, edited by Valerie M. Fazel and Louise Geddes, Cham, 2017, pp. 129–47.

Orgel, Stephen. 'Shakespeare Illustrated.' *The Cambridge Companion to Shakespeare and Popular Culture*, edited by Robert Shaughnessy, Cambridge, 2007, pp. 67–92.

Osborne, Laurie E. 'Poetry in Motion: Animating Shakespeare.' *Shakespeare, the Movie: Popularizing the Plays on Film, TV, and Video*, edited by Lynda E. Boose and Richard Burt, London, 1997, pp. 103–20.

Page, Malcolm, and Simon Trussler. *File on Edgar*. London, 1991.

Painter, Susan. *Edgar the Playwright*. London, 1996.

Pascal, Julia. *The Shylock Play: An Adaptation of William Shakespeare's 'The Merchant of Venice'*. London, 2008.

Pask, Kevin. *The Fairy Way of Writing: Shakespeare to Tolkien*. Baltimore, 2013.

Patricia, Anthony Guy. *Queering the Shakespeare Film: Gender Trouble, Gay Spectatorship and Male Homoeroticism*. London, 2017.

Pensalfini, Rob. *Prison Shakespeare: For These Deep Shames and Great Indignities*. Basingstoke, 2016.

Peterson, Kaara L., and Deanne Williams, editors. *The Afterlife of Ophelia*. Basingstoke, 2012.

Pipher, Mary. *Reviving Ophelia: Saving the Selves of Adolescent Girls*. New York, 1994.

Poole, Adrian. *Shakespeare and the Victorians*. London, 2004.

Poole, John. *Hamlet Travestie: In Three Acts, with Burlesque Annotations*. London, 1810.

Pope, Alexander, editor. *The Works of Shakespear*. London, 1723–5. 6 vols.

Potter, Lois. *Othello*. Manchester, 2002.

Power, Ben. *A Tender Thing*. London, 2009.

Price, Victoria E. '"Two Kingdoms … Compassed with One Sea": Reconstructing Kingdoms and Reclaiming Histories in David Greig's

Dunsinane.' *International Journal of Scottish Theatre and Screen*, vol. 5, 2012, pp. 19–32.

Purkiss, Diane. 'Uncaring Iowa: *A Thousand Acres*.' *The Times Literary Supplement*, 30 October 1992, p. 20.

Rabinowitz, Peter J. '"What's Hecuba to Us?"': The Audience's Experience of Literary Borrowing.' *The Reader in the Text: Essays on Audience and Interpretation*, edited by Susan R. Suleiman and Inge Crosman, Princeton, 1980, pp. 241–63.

Radin, Victoria. 'Tricky Dicky and the Puppets.' *The Observer*, 3 March 1974, p. 38.

Raman, Shankar. *Framing 'India': The Colonial Imaginary in Early Modern Culture*. Stanford, 2002.

Ravenscroft, Edward. *Titus Andronicus, or The Rape of Lavinia. Acted at the Theatre Royall, A Tragedy. Alter'd from Mr. Shakespears Works*. London, 1687.

Ray, Michelle. *Falling for Hamlet*. New York, 2011.

Regan, Stephen. 'Auden and Shakespeare.' *W. H. Auden in Context*, edited by Tony Sharpe, Cambridge, 2013, pp. 266–75.

Reisert, Rebecca. *Ophelia's Revenge*. London, 2003.

Ritchie, Fiona, and Peter Sabor, editors. *Shakespeare in the Eighteenth Century*. Cambridge, 2012.

Rivlin, Elizabeth. 'Adaptation Revoked: Knowledge, Ethics, and Trauma in Jane Smiley's *A Thousand Acres*.' *Shakespeare and the Ethics of Appropriation*, edited by Alexa Huang and Elizabeth Rivlin, New York, 2014, pp. 73–87.

Roberts, Philip. *Bond on File*. London, 1985.

Rodgers, Amy. 'Vishal Bhardwaj.' *Shakespeare Bulletin*, vol. 34, 2016, pp. 500–4.

Rodosthenous, George. '"I Let the Language Lead the Dance": Politics, Musicality, and Voyeurism: David Greig in Conversation with George Rodosthenous.' *New Theatre Quarterly*, vol. 27, 2011, pp. 3–13.

Rokison, Abigail. *Shakespeare for Young People: Productions, Versions and Adaptations*. London, 2013.

Rome, Emily. 'Interview: "Cymbeline" Director Michael Almereyda on Reuniting with Ethan Hawke.' *Hitfix*, 13 March 2015. https://uproxx.com/hitfix/interview-cymbeline-director-michael-almereyda-on-reuniting-with-shakespeare-and-ethan-hawke. Accessed 13 August 2019.

Rooney, David. 'Cymbeline: Venice Review.' *Hollywood Reporter*, 9 March 2014. https://www.hollywoodreporter.com/review/cymbeline-venice-review-729713. Accessed 13 August 2019.

Rosenthal, Daniel. *100 Shakespeare Films*. London, 2007.

Rothwell, Kenneth S. *A History of Shakespeare on Screen: A Century of Film and Television*. 1999. Cambridge, 2004.

Rothwell, Kenneth S. 'Trevor Nunn's *The Merchant of Venice*: Portia's House of Mystery, Magic, and Menace.' *Acts of Criticism: Performance Matters in Shakespeare and His Contemporaries*, edited by Paul Nelsen and June Schlueter, Cranbury, 2006, pp. 204–16.

Rowe, Nicholas, editor. *The Works of Mr William Shakespear*. London, 1709. 6 vols.

Royal Shakespeare Company. 'Interview with A Tender Thing Writer Ben Power.' YouTube, 7 September 2012. https://www.youtube.com/watch?v=3_Mu50R36c4. Accessed 13 August 2019.

Rozett, Martha Tuck. *Talking Back to Shakespeare*. Cranbury, 1994.

Ryan, Kiernan. '*King Lear*: A Retrospect, 1980–2000.' *Shakespeare Survey*, vol. 55, 2002, pp. 1–12.

Ryan, Kiernan. *Shakespeare's Universality: Here's Fine Revolution*. London, 2015.

Rymer, Thomas. *A Short View of Tragedy*. London, 1693.

SABAB (Sulayman Al-Bassam Theatre). *The Al Hamlet Summit*. http://www.sabab.org/the-al-hamlet-summit. Accessed 15 August 2019.

Sanders, Julie. *Adaptation and Appropriation*. 2nd ed., London, 2016.

Sanders, Julie. *Novel Shakespeares: Twentieth-Century Women Novelists and Appropriation*. Manchester, 2001.

Sanders, Julie. *Shakespeare and Music: Afterlives and Borrowings*. Cambridge, 2007.

Saunders, Graham. *Elizabethan and Jacobean Reappropriation in Contemporary British Drama: 'Upstart Crows'*. London, 2017.

Schaap Williams, Katherine. 'Enabling Richard: The Rhetoric of Disability in *Richard III*.' *Disability Studies Quarterly*, vol. 29, 2009. http://dsq-sds.org/article/view/997. Accessed 15 August 2019.

Schoch, Richard W. *Not Shakespeare: Bardolatry and Burlesque in the Nineteenth Century*. Cambridge, 2002.

Semenza, Gregory Colón. 'The Globalist Dimensions of Silent Shakespeare Cinema.' *Journal of Narrative Theory*, vol. 41, 2011, pp. 320–42.

Semenza, Gregory Colón. 'Teens, Shakespeare, and the Dumbing Down Cliché: The Case of "The Animated Tales".' *Shakespeare Bulletin*, vol. 26, 2008, pp. 37–68.

'Shakespeare Gallery.' *Gazetteer and New Daily Advertiser*, issue 21 035, 12 May 1789, p. 3.

'Shakespeare Gallery.' *The Times*, issue 1148, 7 May 1789, p. 2.

'Shakespeare and Mr Shaw: *Cymbeline* at the Embassy.' *The Times*, issue 47844, 17 November 1937, p. 14.

Shapiro, James. *Shakespeare and the Jews*. New edition, New York, 2016.

Shaw, Bernard. *Collected Letters*. Edited by Dan H. Laurence, London, 1965–88. 4 vols.

Shaw, Bernard. *Cymbeline Refinished: A Variation by Bernard Shaw*. Privately printed, Edinburgh, 1937.

Shaw, Bernard. *Geneva, Cymbeline Refinished, & Good King Charles: By Bernard Shaw*. London, 1946.

Shaw, Bernard. *Shaw on Shakespeare*. Edited by Edwin Wilson, Harmondsworth, 1969.

Shepard, Richard. 'Dick Deterred: A Watergate Musical.' *New York Times*, 24 January 1983, p. 14.

Sher, Antony. 'Leontes in *The Winter's Tale*.' *Players of Shakespeare* vol. 5, edited by Robin Smallwood, Cambridge, 2003, pp. 91–102.

Sher, Antony. *Year of the King*. London, 1985.

Sher, Antony, and Gregory Doran. *Woza Shakespeare! Titus Andronicus in South Africa*. London, 1996.

Showalter, Elaine. 'Representing Ophelia: Women, Madness, and the Responsibilities of Feminist Criticism.' *Shakespeare and the Question of Theory*, edited by Patricia Parker and Geoffrey Hartmann, London, 1985, pp. 77–94.

Siebers, Tobin. 'Shakespeare Differently Disabled.' *The Oxford Handbook of Shakespeare and Embodiment: Gender, Sexuality, and Race*, edited by Valerie Traub, Oxford, 2016, pp. 435–54.

Sillars, Stuart. *Painting Shakespeare: The Artist as Critic, 1720–1820*. Cambridge, 2006.

Singh, Harneet. '"Kashmir Is the Hamlet of My Film": Interview with Vishal Bhardwaj.' *The Indian Express*, 5 October 2014. https://indianexpress.com/article/entertainment/bollywood/kashmir-is-the-hamlet-of-my-film. Accessed 15 August 2019.

Smiley, Jane. 'Shakespeare in Iceland.' *Transforming Shakespeare: Contemporary Women's Re-Visions in Literature and Performance*, edited by Marianne Novy, Basingstoke, 2000, pp. 159–79.

Smiley, Jane. *Thirteen Ways of Looking at the Novel*. London, 2006.

Smiley, Jane. *A Thousand Acres*. London, 1992.

Smith, Bruce R. *Shakespeare | Cut: Rethinking Cutwork in an Age of Distraction*. Oxford, 2016.

Smith, Emma. 'Reading Shakespeare's Stage Directions.' *Stage Directions and Shakespearean Theatre*, edited by Sarah Dustagheer and Gillian Woods, London, 2018, pp. 93–114.

Smith, Leslie. 'Edward Bond's Lear.' *Comparative Drama*, vol. 13, 1979, pp. 65–85.

Smith, Peter J. '"Under Western Eyes": Sulayman Al-Bassam's *The Al-Hamlet Summit* in an Age of Terrorism.' *Shakespeare Bulletin*, vol. 22, 2004, pp. 65–77.

Smith, Stan. *W. H. Auden*. Oxford, 1985.

Spurgeon, Caroline F. E. *Shakespeare's Imagery and What It Tells Us*. Cambridge, 1935.

Stafford-Mills, Yvonne. '"Blood Draws Flies": Arab-Western Entanglement in Sulayman Al-Bassam's Cross-Cultural *Hamlet*.'

Language, Literature, and Interdisciplinary Studies, vol. 2, 2018. http://
ellids.com/archives/2018/12/2.2-Mills.pdf. Accessed 15 August 2019.

Stam, Robert. 'Beyond Fidelity: The Dialogics of Adaptation.' *Film
Adaptation*, edited by James Naremore, London, 2000, pp. 54–76.

Stern, Tiffany. 'Shakespeare in Drama.' *Shakespeare in the Eighteenth
Century*. edited by Fiona Ritchie and Peter Sabor, Cambridge, 2012,
pp. 141–60.

Stone, George Winchester Jr. 'A Century of *Cymbeline*; or Garrick's Magic
Touch.' *Philological Quarterly*, vol. 54, 1975, pp. 310–22.

Strehle, Susan. 'The Daughters' Subversion in Jane Smiley's *A Thousand
Acres*.' *Critique: Studies in Contemporary Fiction*, vol. 41, 2000,
pp. 211–25.

Summers, Montague. *Shakespeare Adaptations*. London, 1922.

Swain, Elizabeth. *David Edgar, Playwright and Politician*. New York,
1986.

Talbot, Joby. 'Joby Talbot Talks about His Ground-Breaking Ballet
Score for The Winter's Tale.' *The Gramophone*, 20 January 2015.
https://www.gramophone.co.uk/feature/joby-talbot-talks-about-his-
groundbreaking-ballet-score-for-the-winters-tale. Accessed 15 August
2019.

Tatspaugh, Patricia E. *Shakespeare at Stratford: The Winter's Tale*.
London, 2002.

Taylor, Gary, et al., editors. *The New Oxford Shakespeare: Critical
Reference Edition*. Oxford, 2017. 2 vols.

Taylor, Marianne. 'Playwright David Greig on William Shakespeare and
the Unmatched Brilliance of Macbeth.' *The Herald*, 4 June 2016.
https://www.heraldscotland.com/arts_ents/14535495.playwright-
david-greig-on-william-shakespeare-and-the-unmatched-brilliance-of-
macbeth. Accessed 13 August 2019.

Tennyson, Hallam. *Alfred Lord Tennyson: A Memoir by His Son*. London,
1897. 2 vols.

Terry, Ellen. *Four Lectures on Shakespeare*. London, 1932.

Thompson, Ann. '*Cymbeline*'s Other Endings.' *The Appropriation of
Shakespeare: Post-Renaissance Reconstruction of the Works and the
Myth*, edited by Jean I. Marsden, New York, 1991, pp. 203–20.

Thompson, Ayanna. *Performing Race and Torture on the Early Modern
Stage*. London, 2008.

Thompson, Ayanna. 'Unmooring the Moor: Researching and Teaching on
YouTube.' *Shakespeare Quarterly*, vol. 61, 2010, pp. 337–56.

Tripney, Natasha. 'A Tender Thing Review at Swan Stratford-upon-Avon.'
The Stage, 4 October 2012. https://www.thestage.co.uk/reviews/2012/
a-tender-thing-review-at-swan-stratford-upon-avon. Accessed 13
August 2019.

Trivedi, Poonam. 'Shakespearean Tragedy in India: Politics of Genre – Or
    How Newness Entered Indian Literary Culture.' *The Oxford Handbook
    of Shakespearean Tragedy*, edited by Michael Neill and David
    Schalkwyk, Oxford, 2016, pp. 881–95.
Vaughan, Alden T., and Virginia Mason Vaughan. *Shakespeare's Caliban:
    A Cultural History*. Cambridge, 1996.
Vaughan, Virginia Mason. *Othello: A Contextual History*. Cambridge,
    1994.
Vaughan, Virginia Mason. *Performing Blackness on English Stages,
    1500–1800*. Cambridge, 2005.
Wainewright, Thomas Griffiths (Cornelius van Vinkbooms). 'Exhibition of
    the Royal Academy.' *London Magazine*, 4 July 1821, pp. 66–76.
Wallace, Clare. *The Theatre of David Greig*. London, 2013.
Walsh, Marcus. 'Editing and Publishing Shakespeare.' *Shakespeare in
    the Eighteenth Century*, edited by Fiona Ritchie and Peter Sabor,
    Cambridge, 2012, pp. 21–40.
Wardle, Janice. '"Outside Broadcast": Looking Backwards and Forwards,
    Live Theatre in the Cinema – NT Live and RSC Live.' *Adaptation*, vol. 7,
    2014, pp. 134–53.
Wayne, Valerie. '*Cymbeline*: Patriotism and Performance.' *A Companion
    to Shakespeare's Works*, edited by Richard Dutton and Jean E. Howard,
    Oxford, 2003, pp. 389–407. 4 vols.
Wayne, Valerie, editor. *Cymbeline*. London, Arden Shakespeare, 2017.
Welsh, James M. 'What IS a "Shakespeare Film", Anyway?' *Journal of the
    Wooden O*, vol. 5, 2005, pp. 145–54.
Wesker, Arnold. *Shylock and Other Plays*. London, 1990.
West, Shearer. 'Shakespeare and the Visual Arts.' *Shakespeare in the
    Eighteenth Century*, edited by Fiona Ritchie and Peter Sabor,
    Cambridge, 2012, pp. 227–53.
Wetmore, Kevin J., Jr. '"The Amazing Adventures of Superbard":
    Shakespeare in Comics and Graphic Novels.' *Shakespeare and Youth
    Culture*, edited by Jennifer Hulbert, Kevin J. Wetmore Jr. and Robert
    L. York, London, 2006, pp. 171–98.
Wharton, Robin. 'There Are No Mothers-In-Law in Ballet: "Doing"
    Shakespeare in Dance.' *Shakespeare Bulletin*, vol. 23, 2005, pp. 7–22.
Wheale, Nigel. 'Screen/Play: Derek Jarman's *Tempest* as Critical
    Interpretation.' *Ideas and Production*, vol. 8, 1988, pp. 51–65.
White, R. S. *Shakespeare's Cinema of Love: A Study in Genre and
    Influence*. Oxford, 2016.
Williams, W. E. 'Film and Literature.' *Sight and Sound*, vol. 4, 1935,
    pp. 163–5.
Willson, Robert F., Jr. *Shakespeare in Hollywood, 1929–1956*. Madison,
    2000.

Winn, James Anderson. *John Dryden and His World*. London, 1987.

Winship, Lyndsey. 'Jeté, Pursued by a Bear: Dancing *The Winter's Tale*.' Interview with Christopher Wheeldon, *The Guardian*, 7 March 2016. https://www.theguardian.com/stage/2016/mar/07/the-winters-tale-christopher-wheeldon-shakespeare. Accessed 15 August 2019.

Winston, Joe, and Miles Tandy. *Beginning Shakespeare 4–11*. London, 2012.

Woolf, Virginia. *Congenial Spirits: The Selected Letters of Virginia Woolf*. Edited by Joanne Trautmann Banks, London, 2003.

Worth, Katharine. *Revolutions in Modern English Drama*. London, 1973.

Wray, Ramona. 'The Morals of *Macbeth* and Peace as Process: Adapting Shakespeare in Northern Ireland's Maximum Security Prison.' *Shakespeare Quarterly*, vol. 62, 2011, pp. 340–63.

Wrench, Nigel. 'Writing Macbeth after Shakespeare.' *BBC News*, 10 February 2010. http://news.bbc.co.uk/1/hi/entertainment/arts_and_culture/8508803.stm. Accessed 13 August 2019.

Wymer, Rowland. *Derek Jarman*. Manchester, 2005.

Yost, Michelle K. 'Stratford-upon-Web: Shakespeare in Twenty-First Century Fanfiction.' *Shakespeare and Millennial Fiction*, edited by Andrew James Hartley, Cambridge, 2018, pp. 193–212.

INDEX